Edward. G. Hay

History of the English Lutheran Church of Pottsville, PA.

From its origin, May 16th, 1847, to September 1st, 1888

Edward. G. Hay

History of the English Lutheran Church of Pottsville, PA.
From its origin, May 16th, 1847, to September 1st, 1888

ISBN/EAN: 9783337038120

Printed in Europe, USA, Canada, Australia, Japan

Cover: Foto ©Lupo / pixelio.de

More available books at **www.hansebooks.com**

HISTORY

OF

THE ENGLISH LUTHERAN CHURCH

OF

POTTSVILLE, PA.,

From its Origin, May 16th, 1847,

TO

September 1st, 1888.

By the Present Pastor,

E. G. HAY.

POTTSVILLE, PA.:
ROBT. D. COLBORN, PRINTER.
1888.

DEDICATION.

—:✳:—

. TO MY ESTEEMED FRIEND, MRS. SUSAN M. STECK,
THE FAITHFUL COMPANION, IN LABOR, OF HIM WHO LAID SO
WELL THE FOUNDATIONS OF OUR BELOVED LUTHERAN
ZION IN THIS CITY, THIS VOLUME IS MOST
RESPECTFULLY DEDICATED.

THAT SHE MAY HAVE GREAT DELIGHT, AS SHE READS THESE
PAGES, IN LEARNING HOW MANY HAVE BEEN LED UNTO
THE LORD THROUGH THE AGENCY FIRST ESTAB-
LISHED HERE BY THE EFFORTS OF HER
NOW SAINTED HUSBAND, IS THE SIN-
CERE WISH AND PRAYER OF
THE AUTHOR.

ENGLISH LUTHERAN CHURCH AND PARSONAGE, POTTSVILLE, PA.

CLERICAL CALENDAR.

Rev. Daniel Steck, D. D. was the First Pastor of this Church. He took charge May 16, 1847. His resignation took effect November 26, 1857.

The Second Pastor was Rev. W. H. Luckenbach. He was elected November 26, 1857. He resigned August 20, 1859.

The Third Pastor was Rev. S. A. Holman, D. D. He was elected August 23, 1859. He resigned September 1, 1861.

Rev. Philip Willard of Schuylkill Haven, supplied the congregation from January 1, 1862, to October 1, 1862.

The Fourth Pastor was Rev. L. M. Koons. He was elected October 12, 1863. He resigned October 11, 1865.

The Fifth Pastor was Rev. Uriel Graves. He was elected November 9, 1865. He resigned July 6, 1868.

The Sixth Pastor was again the Rev. Daniel Steck, D. D. He was elected September 22, 1868. He resigned July 17, 1870.

The Seventh Pastor was Rev. J. Q McAtee. He accepted the pastorate February 22, 1871. He resigned November 8, 1877.

The Eighth Pastor was Rev. John McCron, D. D. He was elected January 20, 1878. He resigned August 1, 1880.

The Ninth Pastor of this Church is its present one, who was elected November 6, 1880.

PREFACE.

NO HISTORY is perfect. And he who reads what is contained in this volume will do well to remember this. It is not the design of the writer to note every particular fact he can glean concerning the Church's past and present state. It will serve his purpose best, and interest the reader more, if he can succeed in presenting, in a readable form, the leading events in the career of this Congregation. Nor even here can he hope to be free from all error. The records themselves are imperfect, and so at times may the interpretation of them be. He asks only the reader's belief that an honest effort has been made to present a history substantially correct, and as complete as is consistent with his purpose.

The publication of a small congregational paper, styled THE ENGLISH LUTHERAN, in which certain fragments of our Church's history have been already given, has suggested to the writer the thought of preparing this volume, while his own interest in a Church with which he has been so closely identified for a considerable period, an interest in which he knows that many share, has ripened that thought into a purpose, and that purpose into action.

To gather fragments, already published, into *one volume*, to arrange them in chronological order, correcting, so far as possible, any errors they may have contained, and to add to them a narrative of other leading events in our Church's life, is a task in which the author feels he must have the approbation of all the intelligent people who are, or have been, members of the congregation.

The reader will please bear also in mind that the author is naturally better acquainted with the facts of the present pastorate than he ever could be with those of others, and has therefore given in many respects, a fuller narrative. The varied notices of the press are worthy of the prominence that he has given them, both as presenting to the reader a fair idea of the standing of the Church in the community, and one of the important means by which her prosperity has been attained.

These pages have been printed form after form, as the author amid the constant press of pastoral duties, could find time to prepare them. His original design was to have terminated the History with the record of Whitsuntide, and the figures given in the Introduction are accordingly based upon the state of the Congregation at that time : but, as other interesting events were continually transpiring while the later pages were in course of preparation, he could not pass them by in silence and has described them as they have occurred.

In the preparation of copy, he has designedly made a more liberal use of capitals, for the purpose of emphasis, than the strictest rules would allow.

Desiring that these pages should appear as a pleasant surprise to as many of our people as possible, we have pursued our self-imposed task in comparative silence, but return our heartfelt thanks to all who have responded to inquiries it was found needful to make.

Hoping that this little volume will be welcomed and cherished by many, that it may be helpful to the memory of the aged as they ponder the path of their feet in Zion, and that the evidence it brings to all of God's goodness to us in the past may stir us all up to a more ardent gratitude and active endeavor, we send it forth upon its mission of love.

E. G. HAY.

POTTSVILLE, PA., September 1, 1888.

CONTENTS

INTRODUCTION.

OUR readers will doubtless be glad to learn, before entering upon the past history of the English Lutheran Church of Pottsville, the present standing of the Congregation in the Community and in the Synod of East Pennsylvania with which it has, from the beginning, been organically connected.

There are Sixteen Protestant Churches in the city of Pottsville.

There are three Welsh Churches. Their Calvanistic and Baptist congregations have each a Membership of 6 and are without Sunday Schools altogether. The Welsh Congregational Church has a Membership of 20 and a Sabbath-School of 50; the African Methodist Church, a Membership of 20 and School of 35; the Primitive Methodist Church, a Membership of 30 and School of 35; the Olivet Baptist Church, a Membership of 50 and School of 70; the First Baptist Church, a Membership of 110 and School of 125; the Second Presbyterians, a Membership of 124 and School of 135; the Evangelicals, a Membership of 208 and School of 277; the German Reformed, a Membership of 225 and School of 200; the First Presbyterian, a Membership of 290 and a School of 300; the Trinity Reformed, a Membership of 320 and School of 260; the Methodists, a Membership of 450 and School of 400; the German Lutherans, a Membership of 463 and School of 283; the Episcopalians, a Membership of 558 and School of from 450 to 500 in the congregation proper, and 150 in the suburbs; and our own, the English Lutheran a Membership of 490 and School of 600.

These figures are derived from reliable, and with one exception, from official sources and represent the actual membership of the Churches and the enrolled membership of the Schools, and give the reader a just idea of the standing of our Church and School in the Community.

The position of our Congregation and its Sabbath-School in the Synod of East Pennsylvania, as apparent from the minutes of the latter's Forty-Sixth Annual Convention in September, 1887, is as follows :

Of the One Hundred and One congregations comprised within its limits, there are but Three that have attained a larger membership and but Seventeen that give larger amounts to the Missionary Cause.

Of the One Hundred and Twenty Four Sabbath-Schools (Sixty-Nine Lutheran and Fifty-Five Union) contained in these various charges, there are but Three more numerously attended, and Ten whose contributions are higher.

It shall now be our pleasant task to lay before our reader the varied and alternating experiences of prosperity and trial through which our present standing as a Congregation has been attained.

HISTORY.

CHAPTER I.

THE ORIGIN of our English Lutheran Church must be traced back to the German Lutheran Congregation, which gave it birth. A general knowledge of that Church's history is essential also to a proper understanding of our own.

There were both Lutheran and Reformed Church-going people in this place prior to 1834. They spoke the German language and occasionally were ministered to by visiting pastors of their own denomination, but until June 29, 1834, there was no attempt among either, so far as known, at anything like the organization of a congregation. At that time Rev. Wm. G. Mennig began preaching to people of both denominations in a block-house, used during the week as a school-house and occupying the site of the present Grammar School Building, on the corner of Centre and High Streets.

On June 18th, 1837, all united in laying the corner-stone of a new frame structure, upon Third Street, as their common place of worship. Rev. Thomas Leinbach of the Reformed, and Revs. George and William Mennig of the Lutheran Church officiated upon that occasion. On the 8th and 9th of October of the same year the Church was dedicated under the name of Emanuel's Church. Revs. Thomas Leinbach and David Hassinger of the Reformed, Revs. Daniel Ulrich Jonathan Ruthrauff, Gottlieb Yeager and William Mennig, of the Lutheran Church, officiated. By this time the Reformed portion of the people had elected Rev. David Hassinger as their pastor, and the two congregations worshipped henceforth in this edifice upon alternate Sabbaths. Prior to 1850 the Reformed Congregation withdrew and located on West Market Street, leaving the Church Property in the hands of the Lutherans. On the 16th of May, 1847 some members left the pastoral care of Rev. Wm. G. Mennig and formed our English Lutheran Congregation under the Rev. Daniel Steck.

OUR FIRST PASTOR.

Rev. Daniel Steck, D. D., was born near Hughesville, Lycoming County, Pa., November 18th, 1819. He was next to the eldest of six brothers, two of whom—Jacob and Charles—also entered the ministry of the Lutheran Church. He was sent to a common school in his youth, and the progress he made in his studies gave promise of future usefulness. He received a Christian training, confirmed, in due time, his baptismal vows, and became a full member of the Lutheran Church. Regarding himself called to the ministry, he went to Gettysburg, pursuing a partial course in the College, and the prescribed course in the Seminary.

The circumstances that led him to Pottsville, and those which attended his coming and the origination of our English Lutheran Congregation, are thus graphically described by his own pen.

ORGANIZATION OF THE CONGREGATION.

"After completing my studies in the "Theological Seminary" of the Lutheran Church at Gettysburg, Penna., in the autumn of 1846, I made application to the Synod of East Penna., for a license to preach the Gospel. The brethren admitted me to an examination and judging me to be possessed of the requisite qualifications, they voted me the license for which I applied. This occurred on the 28th of September, in Milton, Pennsylvania.

After spending several months in assisting various members of the Susquehanna Conference, in special or protracted meetings, my attention was directed by the Rev. R. Weiser and others to Pottsville as a suitable place in which to commence efforts for the organization and establishment of an English Lutheran Church. Accordingly on the 27th of March 1847. I made my first visit to the place. As soon as I arrived I called on the Rev. W. G. Mennig, who was then pastor of the German Lutheran Church of Pottsville. He received me very cordially, and on stating the object of my visit, he expressed himself well pleased with it, and gave it his most hearty sanction, assuring me that the Lutheran interest in this place, to be well sustained, must have preaching in the English language. Brother Mennig accordingly made an appointment for me to preach in his Church on Sunday evening, March 28th, 1847. The time arrived and the sermon was preached. At the close of the service a statement was made to the congregation, setting forth the design of my visit, and asking the judgment of the people in regard to the matter thus brought before them. A second service was held in the Church occupied by Brother Mennig in two weeks from the previous date, viz: on the 4th of April at 3 o'clock p. m. By this time it appeared that there was a general anxiety on the part of the Church for the introduction of regular English services.

Application was accordingly made by a number of persons favorable to the admission of English, to the vestry of the German Church, for permission to hold English services in their house of worship. Permission was granted to this extent, viz : that the present English service might be held in the Church, provided said service did not interfere in any respect with the regular service. As the house was built by the Germans and was designed for their exclusive use, this offer was considered by the English members to be quite as liberal as any which the Germans in justice to themselves could be expected to make. The offer was accordingly accepted and efforts were at once made to secure my services as pastor of the English portion of the congregation. Whereupon, after due and prayerful consideration, I agreed to accede to the urgent request of the friends of Engglish preaching, and took them under my pastoral charge on the 16th of May, 1847. This then is the date of my regular entrance upon the pastoral office in Pottsville."

RESIDENCES OF THE PASTOR.

It may be interesting to our local readers to know something of the domestic arrangements of our successive pastors before the parsonage was built. Doctor Steck boarded during the first six months of his pastorate at the residence of Mr. Nathan Haas, on Schuylkill Avenue above Third Street, afterwards for a season at Mr. David Heisler's on the North-West corner of Arch and Centre Streets. On the 18th of April 1848 he was married to Miss Susan M. Edwards of Muncy, Pa., and took up his residence at 613 West Market Street, and afterwards successively at 706, and 909 Mahantongo Street, the North-West Corner of Norwegian and Sixth Streets, and finally at 803 West Market Street.

From one who was present from the beginning and is still living we learn what follows concerning

THE SEPARATION FROM THE GERMAN CHURCH.

Dr. Steck preached regularly, at intervals, in the German Lutheran Church on Sunday-Afternoons after Sabbath-School. He also frequently assisted Rev. Mennig in his evening services, when there would be some English singing permitted, but no English speaking. He also went occasionally with a little company of workers to Port Carbon, where he founded the congregation still in existence.

On Sunday Evenings the Doctor would often conduct regular services at the houses of the members. Rev. Reuben Weiser, who first called Rev. Steck's attention to this field, would occasionally visit and assist him at these services, being entertained by members of the congregation. During the winter of 1847, Revs. Steck and Mennig held jointly a protracted meeting in the German Lutheran Church, mingling the German and English promiscuously in their effort to save souls. For a while all moved smoothly enough until, just as might have been expected, the vigor of the English participation awakened the fears of the German pastor, who rose in the midst of a hymn started in the English tongue, exclaiming with considerable asperity, "Sing it Deutsch, nicht English!"

The harmony was henceforth broken, although the English services continued for a season in that place. With greater frequency Port Carbon was now visited. On the way thither on one occasion, in the little band of those who accompanied the Doctor, the suggestion was made "Now let us strike out for ourselves!" It was determined to worship no longer in the German Church, but to try to rent one of their own; until they should succeed in in this, meeting only at the houses. Very soon their efforts were crowned with success, and they rented

THE TWO-STORY FRAME STRUCTURE

midway between West Market and West Norwegian Street in Second Street, previously used by the Second Presbyterian congregation and owned by Mr. D. H. Leib — a building not eventually removed until under the present Pastorate. Eleven persons are recalled by the giver of the above information, of whom she herself is one, as having been identified with this movement from the start. Mrs. Mary Bock, Mr. Samuel Born, Mrs. Annie Born, Mr. Daniel

Heil, Mr. (now Rev.) Washington L. Heisler, Mrs. Sarah H. Heisler, Miss Barbara A. Heisler, Mr. Henry G. Kurtz, Mrs. Sarah A. Kurtz, Mr. John Henry Kurtz, and Mr. Wm. Zern.

OUR PRESENT EDIFICE.

In April 1851, ground was broken for the erection of the present Church building. The corner-stone was soon laid with impressive ceremonies, Rev. E. Breidenbaugh, and Rev. John E. Graeff assisting in the services. The building was so far completed as to admit of worship in the lecture-room during the Winter. In the following Spring (of 1852) it was solemnly dedicated to the service of the triune God, the Pastor enjoying the presence and assistance of Rev. B. Kurtz, D. D., who preached in the morning the Dedicatory sermon, Rev. A. C. Wedekind, D. D., who preached in the afternoon and Rev. E. W. Hutter who addressed the congregation in the evening.

THE MAN FOR THE FIELD.

Dr. F. W. Conrad, Editor of the Lutheran Observer, remarks of this pastoral relationship : "Mr. Steck proved to be the right man in the right place. He entered upon his work with all the ardor of youth, prosecuted it with fidelity and energy, and is justly recognized as the founder of the English Lutheran congregation in the emporium of the Schuylkill coal region. He continued his labors at Pottsville ten years, and there laid the foundation of his reputation as a preacher and pastor. Although he received a number of invitations to leave, he usually consulted us, and we uniformly advised him to decline them, and go on with his work. As the anglicised Lutherans multiplied in Port Carbon, Schuylkill Haven and Minersville, Rev. Steck took the oversight of them, and preached to them occasionally, and sometimes regularly, frequently going on foot, and walking eight miles on the Sabbath. By these missionary efforts he contributed largely to the organization and growth of English Lutheran Churches in these important towns. He may therefore be properly styled the pioneer of English Lutheranism in the Pottsville region."

But, to proceed with the history of the congregation itself.

At the earliest congregational meeting of which minutes have been preserved, January 1, 1853, a Church Discipline was adopted, harmonizing in all essential particulars with that contained in the Hymn-Book of the General Synod published in 1852.

Resolutions were adopted in favor of the continuance with greater energy, of the efforts toward the liquidation of debt incurred in the erection of the Church, and a Sinking Fund Society already in existence, was urged to renewed activity.

On the 24th of January, 1853, the salary of the Doctor was raised to $500. The reader must remember, however, in his reflections upon this fact, that the congregation at this juncture numbered only Seventy-Seven and that a proportionate expectation from our membership to day would obligate them to the extent of more than $3,000 per year. All honor to the self-sacrificing band of moral heroes from which, beloved, ye are come!

But the congregation then realized that they had other duties than financial ones. They wanted to keep the standard of membership high and pure, and encouraged and sustained their representatives the Council, in actions such as these.

"Whereas, Mrs.—— having recently attended the Ball given for the benefit of the Pottsville Brass Band, and having attended similar places of worldly amusement repeatedly against the remonstrances of the Church Council, therefore

Resolved, That she be hereby suspended from the communion of this Church, until she give satisfactory evidence of sincere repentance."

We are glad to know that a little kind severity was not hurtful to the soul, and that this sister, restored, is a faithful communicant to this day.

Our worthy sisters then appear, however, to have been slower to attempt any effort in the line of a Church fair than those of the present time (perhaps because having less experience) for while, as early as June 21st, 1853, they talked of such an effort, and made application to Council for permission to conduct it, and while such consent was granted, provided it be for the benefit of the Church and under the supervision of the Church Council, it was not until upon May 30th, 1854, the Council urged them to carry out their purpose as early as possible, and earnestly requested them meanwhile to organize themselves into Sewing Societies to prepare articles therefor, that they were spurred into the necessary activity and decided to hold it in *October*.

On the other hand, when they did commence it, they would have smiled at the idea of the modern two-evening affair, deciding that nothing less than four whole days would satisfy them, and the 17th, 18th, 19th and 20th of October, 1854, were hard days upon the pocket-books of such as visited the " Town Hall."

On the Sixth of February, 1855, the Doctor received an invitation from the Lutheran Church at Norristown to visit them with a view of becoming pastor at that place ; and the Council of our congregation being aware of the fact, and deeming a severance of his relation here unwise and undesirable, advised him not to visit that congregation, and raised his salary to Six Hundred Dollars. The congregation at this time numbered 125, or more correctly this is the number that the Doctor had already admitted, up to January, 1855.

The records preserved of the Doctor's work are comparatively meagre. The persons he received into membership are as follows:

In 1848.

Mrs. Mary Bock, Samuel Born, Mrs. Amelia Born, Mrs. Cook, Mrs. D. L. Esterly, Mrs. Mary Geanslen, Mrs. Lovina Grim, Miss Sarah Hadesty, Daniel Heil, Washington L. Heisler, Mrs. Sarah H. Heisler, Miss Barbara A. Heisler, Miss Hower, John Junk, Henry G. Kurtz, Mrs. Sarah Kurtz, John Henry Kurtz, Mrs. Maria Kurtz, Wm. B. Kurtz, John Marsden, William Reifsnyder, Mrs. Sarah Reifsnyder, Mrs. A. P. Smith, Mrs. Susan Steck, Mr. William Zern, Mrs. E. C. Zern.

In 1849.

Mr. Henry Auman, Mrs. Henry Auman, Miss Amelia Auman, Miss Mary Auman, Mr. Geo. Beyerle, Conrad Bower, Samuel Bower, Benjamin Evert, Mrs. B. Evert, Mrs. Elizabeth German, Miss Mary German, Mrs. Margaret Junk, John Reifsnyder, Mrs. Seiler.

In 1850.

Mrs. Martha A. Bower, Mrs. Brown, Jared Daniel, Peter Haas, Mrs. Haas, Adam Hoffman, Mrs. Mary Hummel, Mrs. Mantz, Joseph Yost, Miss Zuegler.

In 1851.

Miss Sarah Auman, Miss C. Auman, Mrs. Hannah Beck, Matilda Bright, Mrs. Daniel, Miss Hannah Good, John Hehr, Wm. A. Heisler, Mrs. Mary Hoffman, Abraham Osman, Mrs. Osman.

In 1852.

Mrs. Allison, Mrs. Mary Artley, Wm. A. Beidleman, Mrs. Sarah Bell, Mrs. Eliza Bennet, Mrs. C. J. Fry, Mrs. Harriet Haas, D. N. Heisler, Mrs. Hill, Mrs. C. Moore, Mrs. J. Oren, Jacob D. Rice, Miss Annie Rice, Lewis Reeser, Mrs. Lewis Reeser, Mrs. Wogonseller.

In 1853.

Solomon Adams, Mrs. Emma Adams, Miss Mary Allison, Mrs. Anthony Dengler, Miss Rebecca Dengler, Miss C. Fisher, Miss Louisa Geanslen, William Haas, Mrs. Phoebe Heil, Mrs. Mary James, Miss Louisa Matz, Mrs. Mary Reppard, Miss Phoebe Rumble, Mrs. Mary Seitz, Mrs. Martha Wolfinger, George Wagner, E. McMurray.

In 1854.

A. M. Allen, Kate Allen, Miss Elizabeth Auman, J. G. Beyerle, Miss Diana Bock, Edward H. Boehmy, Mrs. E. H. Boehmy, Adam Eiler, Mrs. Esther Eiler, Miss Margaret Eiler, Miss Amelia Eiler, Annetta Evert, William Fernel, Miss Charlotte Frish, James German, James Matter Mrs. C. Matter, Mrs. Hannah Nagle, Mrs. Sarah Norton, Mrs. Henrietta Reeser, Miss Annie Eliza Reed, Miss C. R. Rice, Miss Mary Riland, Geo. N. Shultz, Mrs. Barbara Ann Snyder, Mrs. Mary Strauch, Geo. W. Wagner, Mrs. Isaac Ward, Mrs. Margaret Wardly, Mrs. Mary Weaver, Mrs. Mahlon Wolf, Mrs. Mary Wolfinger.

In 1855.

John L. Batz, Mrs. Sarah Batz, Mrs. E. Bell, Isabella Beyerle, Miss Amelia Boehmy, Miss Rosalie Boehmy, Miss Mary Born, Miss Mary Brown, John Dannahower,

Chas. H. Dengler, Mrs. Mary Ann Derr, Mrs. C. Dimmick, Mrs. Sarah Doebley, Irwin Gallagher, Mrs. I. Gallagher, Miss Hannah Garret, Louisa German, Cordelia Griesemer, Leonard Greishund, Miss Annie Griffith, Henry Grossman, Mrs. Wm. Haas, Mary A. Hill, Luther R. Kieffer, Jeremiah A. Kurtz, Louisa Kurtz, Mrs. Mary Mann, Henry Marson, Miss Sarah McCurdy, Mrs. Sarah Rice, Adelia Seitzinger, Abraham K. Whitner.

In 1856.

Mrs. J. B. Chichester, Mrs. Malburn, Elizabeth Mines, Charles Mines, Ellen Murphy, Edward Haas, Mary E. Reed, Mrs. Edward Rishel, Miss Anna M. Strauch, Geo. M. H. Wagner, Miss Sallie Whitner.

In 1857.

Mrs. Elizabeth Bell, Miss Esther Beck, Daniel H. Bickel, Miss Ellen Hoffman, Daniel S. Kline, Mary Kline, Mrs. Louisa Kline, Miss C. Klineginny, Miss Mary Klineginny, Geo. Saylor, Mrs. Sarah Stout, John Strauch, Mrs. John Strauch.

Upon the 26th of November, 1857, at a congregational meeting at which his successor was elected, we have the first recorded intimation of Rev. Steck's resignation. It is at that time referred to as having recently transpired, and is therefore recorded in our Clerical Calendar as having *taken effect* upon that date.

At this meeting the following was unanimously adopted : Whereas, our beloved Pastor, the Rev. Daniel Steck, is about to remove from our midst to another field of labor; and whereas, he has endeared himself to the Church and community by his arduous, zealous and successful labors and consistent deportment among us for the last ten years: therefore,

Resolved, That it is with feelings of unmingled regret that we consent to the severance of the endearing tie which has so long bound us together.

Resolved, That we hereby express our entire confidence in his character as a Christian and as a man, as well as our admiration of him as an able speaker and expounder of the Gospel of Christ.

Resolved, That when he finally leaves our midst our best feelings, prayers and sympathies, shall follow him to his new and very important field of labor, and when there may he be abundantly successful in building up the Kingdom of the Saviour !

Upon leaving Pottsville, Rev. Steck became pastor of St. John's Lutheran Church at Lancaster. Five years later, in the Fall of 1862, he took charge of the Main Street Lutheran Congregation at Dayton, Ohio; whence, in September, 1868, he was again called to this field of labor, in the midst of which it will be our pleasure to view him when this point in our historical narrative shall be reached.

By permission, we are happy to present to our readers a sermon of Doctor Steck, which we were not privileged to hear, but have often heard highly spoken of by others. It is our comfort to know that, though we here mourn his departure, he himself has now entered upon the joy and glory which his words describe.

. The theme of this discourse is

THE VOYAGE OF LIFE.

PSALM CVII: 30. "So he bringeth them unto their desired haven."

The grand excellency of the Bible lies in the fact, that in it we have the revelation of God's will to man. Fallen, alienated, ruined, it makes known the way of his recovery, his reconciliation, his salvation. It is the rule of his duty to God, himself, and the world. It is the perfect rule: "The law of the Lord is perfect, converting the soul." As a moral agent, accountable to God, and destined to an immortal existence beyond the grave, it leaves him in ignorance of nothing which he needs to know. "Having God for its Author, Truth without any mixture of error for its matter, and Salvation for its end," it is a gift whose value to the race, no language is adequate to set forth. It is the *Book of Life*; and this fact alone invests it with a priceless worth.

But though the Bible derives its crowning glory from the fact that it teaches lost sinners the way to heaven; still, we claim that, in addition to this paramount consideration, it possesses other *subordinate* excellencies which entitle it to the highest place in our esteem. It is a book abounding, in all its parts, with literature of such exquisite beauty that one may traverse all the seas of human learning, and shall find none to equal them. As a mere composition it is the most sublime and beautiful of books.

Said Sir William Jones, a man rendered famous by his vast attainments in the world of letters, and well understanding the force of his words: "This volume, independently of its divine origin, contains more true sublimity, more exquisite beauty, more pure morality, more important history, and finer strains of poetry and eloquence, than can be collected from all other books, in whatever age or language they may have been written."

Does any one call for a passage in proof or illustration of this high claim? If so, here it is, in the Psalm which contains the text, and the text is part of it. We read: "They that go down to the sea in ships, that do business in great waters: these see the works of the Lord, and his wonders in the deep. For he commandeth and raiseth the stormy wind, which lifteth up the waves thereof. They mount up to the heavens, they go down again to the depths: their soul is melted because of trouble. They reel to and fro, and stagger like a drunken man, and are at their wit's end. Then they cry unto the Lord in their trouble and he bringeth them out of their distresses. He maketh the storm a calm, so that the waves thereof are still. Then are they glad because they be quiet; *so he bringeth them unto their desired haven.*"

How beautiful, how grand this description! And where else, in so brief a compass, can you find anything like it, so real, so true to nature?

The text admits of an easy adaptation to a spiritual purpose. It is proposed, accordingly, to make such an application of it on this occasion. The subject it suggests is that of THE HEAVENLY VOYAGE. There are, in a voyage, three principal things: The *Embarkation;* the *Passage;* and the *Landing.*

I. The EMBARKATION.

When a person takes ship, intent on visiting some place beyond the seas, he is said to *embark.* At some pains and cost he has put himself in readiness for the voyage. He has taken leave of friends and kindred; and with his heart up-lifted to God for his blessing on them and himself, has passed from the solid shore, entered the waiting ship, and committed himself to the mercy of the deep. The bells have ceased to ring; the last moment has expired; the sails are spread; and he is afloat upon the waters. He has *embarked* for the voyage.

Now, there is something analagous to this in the commencement of the Christian course. When one starts for the heavenly country, that good land beyond the ocean of time, there is a sense in which he must leave the world behind him. Its spirit, and maxims, and aims, all of which are carnal, are hostile to those of the true child of God. To this import is the teaching of Christ, when to the disciples he said: " Ye are not of the world, even as I am not of the world."

Nor is it easy for man, with his strong, in-born attachment to that which is seen and temporal, to yield to the high demand which this teaching involves. To separate one's self thus, in spirit, from the world, is not to be done without a struggle. The achievement is not to be won without an effort. Ah, no! In the bloodless conflict which here takes place many a mere earthly hero has fallen. It requires a courage other than that which is earth-born, to raise a man to the lofty plain on which this battle is fought. It is a battle against all the carnal impulses and sinful passions of our nature. It is a warfare against the world, the flesh, and the devil; and to get all these under one's feet, and behind one's back, as both the failure and success of thousands have proved, is no easy achievement.

We repeat it: to embark for the heavenly country involves the necessity of a mighty inward struggle, a conflict with self, and sin, and the world. These, dear to us, by nature, as they are; powerful in their hold upon us, as they are; inwrapt with all the cords and fibres of our being as they are; must be sacrificed, and left to wither and die on the shores from which we propose to embark.

Nor is this all: there must, in many cases, be a separation, in spirit, from the friends we love. Their hearts are not with us; their sympathies are not with us. They have no spiritual tastes and aim in common with ours. In this respect there must be a separation, a world-wide space, between us and them. In this respect they have nothing in common with us. They are of the earth, earthy; and we must leave them.

But O, the natural ties which still bind us to them, and them to us, how strong, how tender they are; would that we could induce them to break away from the earthly considerations which keep them back, and prevail on them to join us in the heavenly voyage! But many of them will not. Though we plead with them, pray for them, and weep over them; though the Father calls, and the Son invites, and the Spirit strives; yet to all they turn a deaf ear, and maintain their stand on the bleak and barren shore, in the face of certain death, and in spite of the proffered rescue of the glorious ship which rides at anchor in the harbor, and waits to bear them with all its happy crew to an immortal and cloudless home beyond the world's dark sea.

But the believer has counted the cost, and is ready to venture. Obedient to the voice of the Great Captain who stands on the deck of the mighty ship, and bids him come, he tarries not, but bows his farewell to weeping friends, turns his back on the shore, and takes his place within the ship.

And what a ship it is! Salvation its name! Its timbers were gathered from the hills of heaven. Its keel was laid in the beginning of time. Its Builder and Maker is God. Its attendants are innumerable hosts of angels. Its Captain is the Lord Jesus Christ. Its passengers are sinners of the human race. And the first soul it landed on the shores of immortality was that of the martyred Abel. It has plowed the waves of time's broad sea for nearly six thousand years, and to day there is no worm in its timbers, nor any signs of decay. It has come down through the ages to our day. It has touched upon our shore. With sails expanded, and waiting for passengers, it rides at anchor right before you; and this sanctuary, and every sanctuary in the land, has been erected in the interest of its Captain as a depot from which sinners may embark for the heavenly land.

II. The Passage

When a man has chosen to visit some place beyond the seas, has attended to the leave-taking on the shore, has entered the ship, enrolled his name, and met all the conditions necessary to the embarkation, *then* comes the voyage proper. The anchors are weighed, the sails are given to the breeze, the vessel recedes from the shore. and moves out upon the surface of the deep. The voyage is begun.

All now wish for fair skies, favorable winds and a prosperous journey across the watery waste. But what the incidents of that journey will turn out to be, not a passenger on board can tell. If there should be bright skies, and sunny days, and prosperous gales; it were not strange if there should, in turn, be the exact reverse of all this, causing the heart of the voyager, at one time, to swell with emotions of delight, and at another to tremble with the most fearful apprehensions of coming disaster. Thus it often is with "Those who go down to the sea in ships, that do buisness in the great waters. These see the works of the Lord, and his wonders in the deep. For he commandeth and raiseth the stormy wind, which lifteth up the waves thereof. They mount up to the heaven, they go down again to the depths : their soul is melted because of trouble. They reel to and fro, and stagger like a drunken man, and are at their wit's end. "

And, to such vicissitudes of calm and of storm, there is a correspondence in the *heavenly* voyage. It is not all smooth sailing when the Christian has weighed anchor and left port for the heaven beyond. When he first launches on the deep, all is fair and bright. He is in a happy state of mind. How could he be otherwise? His long and painful struggle with his sinful nature, before he could get his own consent to leave the world behind, has terminated in a condition of internal repose the most serene and blessed he has ever known. He has " Peace with God through our Lord Jesus Christ."

With his eye of faith uplifted to the lofty sky, he hails God as his Father, and feels his love ; and, the happy captive of this new and blissful experience, he is, for the time, oblivious to the possibility of any adverse feeling or circumstance. His inmost soul sings for joy. And everything that meets his eye has a voice to sing in harmony with the strains of that inner anthem. The twinkling stars that look down from the ethereal fields above, sing his Maker's praise ; the surging sea that rolls its billows beneath and around him, joins in the strain. Meanwhile the glorious ship, its sails expanded and filled with the gentle gales of the Spirit, glides smoothly and happily onward in the straight line of the destined port.

Thus far all is well. But a change will take place ere long. New scenes will occur, and new feelings will be awakened. For if, as already suggested, there is, in a literal voyage, liability to storms, so there are *moral* storms to be encountered by the Christian in the spiritual voyage. Here, as in the former case, the sun does not always shine; the sky is not always clear; the sea is not always calm; the winds are not always propitious. There are times when the spiritual sun hides his face; when the sky is overspread with clouds; and when the sea, made furious by the raging winds, fills the soul with alarm and dread.

Thus it is when afflictions come, whether they assail us in our own persons or in the person of those who by reason of kindred ties are as dear to us as our own life. Often under their influence the heart which before was exultant with joy, now pulsates with emotions of sorrow too deep for utterance, and the afflicted soul can only sigh up its complaint to God and say: "Thou hast laid me in the lowest pit, in darkness, in the deeps. Thy wrath lieth hard on me, and thou hast afflicted me with all thy waves. * * Lover and friend hast thou put far from me and mine acquaintance into darkness." Ah, yes! the afflictions of life often sweep like storms athwart our sea, and make rough sailing for many a day.

But especially do the treachery of professed friends and the persecution of open enemies, deserve to be regarded in the light of storms and tempests in the way of the heavenly voyager. These, having their origin in the machinations of "the prince of the power of the air, the spirit that now worketh in the children of disobedience," often come down with such fury as to appal the stoutest heart.

They have their fitting type in the storms which St. Luke describes in the 27th Chapter of the Acts of the Apostles, and which Paul and his companions encountered, when on their voyage to Rome. When the South wind blew softly, and sailors and captain were all hopeful of a safe and happy passage, they weighed anchor, and launched upon the deep. But not long after, there arose against them a tempestuous wind called Euroclydon. In a moment it lashed the sea in fury. It caught the ship in its arms and tossed it hither and thither at will. Every sparable article had to be thrown overboard. And the historian adds that, "When neither sun nor stars in many days appeared, and no small tempest lay on us, all hope that we should be saved was then taken away." But great Paul was on board that rocking, labouring, sinking ship; and in that night, a night made doubly dark by reason of the extinguishment of all hope of safety in each man's soul, it is revealed to Paul by an angel of God, for the comfort of all on board, that though the vessel should be wrecked, not a single life would be lost.

And thus when, as sometimes happens, we are tossed to and fro by moral tempests, the spiritual Euroclydons that lash the sea of time, and roll the waves on high, and toss the ship in air, and sink it in the deep; it is not in the ordination of God that the tremendous emergency should result in the loss of a single soul on board. Our ship, as already remarked, built of God, built of immortal timbers gathered from the hills of heaven, is strong enough to weather the storms of every sea. It has plowed the billows for nearly six thousand years; and yet every beam and piece of timber is as firm and entire as when first laid; nor has a single shred or fibre been torn from its sails.

Besides, it is under the command of a Captain who knows whence all tempests arise, and can, at will, bid them back to their chambers. Yea, and often, in the course of our voyage through life, he does for us spiritually what he did for the disciples literally, in the period of their distress on the sea of Galilee:

> " Fear was within the tossing bark,
>   The angry winds grew loud,
> And waves came rolling high and dark,
>   And the tall mast was bowed ;
> And men stood speechless in their dread,
>   And baffled in their skill,
> But one was there who rose and said
>   Peace, be still—peace, be still !
>
> And the wind ceased ; it ceased.
>   That word passed through the stormy sky.
> The troubled billows knew their Lord,
>   And sank beneath his eye.
> And slumber settled on the deep,
>   And silence on the blast,
> As when the righteous fall asleep,
>   Peaceful sleep—peaceful sleep."

And because the Lord is with his people in all their afflictions, to control every storm and temper every trial, and make all things work together for their good, they can say with the Apostle, even in their darkest moments : " We are troubled on every side, yet not distressed; we are perplexed but not in despair; persecuted, but not forsaken ; cast down but not destroyed ; always bearing about in the body the dying of the Lord Jesus, that the life also of Jesus might be made manifest in our body."

But if the voyager is sometimes obliged to make head against the storm, or what is worse, submit to be driven back upon his course ; so there is a state of things scarcely less to be dreaded in consequence of the distressing *calms* which often take place. The winds are asleep in their caverns. For days together the air is motionless. The sails drop. The waves sink. Not a ripple appears on the surface of the deep. And under the influence of this dead calm the ship stands motionless in the midst of the sea. And now time hangs heavily on the hands of all on board. The hours seem like months, the days like years. Distress is pictured on every face, and each soul sighs : "Awake ye sleeping winds, and bear us hence from this scene of death!"

And have we not the moral of this state of things in that condition of spiritual torpor which at times afflicts the soul of the Christian? All his powers of spiritual motion are for the time paralyzed ; so at least they seem. He would go forward, but he cannot. He is on the deep, but he is in the midst of a dead calm. There is not a breath of the Spirit in his sails. O that from the presence of God the moving power would descend and bear him hence, he cries. He is distressed on account of the spiritual stagnation, and would be redeemed from its death-like influence.

But he must wait and pray, and pray and wait, until the suspended breath of the Spirit shall return, and waft him onward in the direction of his destined port. He does thus wait and pray, and pray and wait, and God in due time grants him the longed-for deliverance.

And now again all is well. The sails are filled with the Spirit's breath, and sweetly, beautifully, gloriously, onward glides the ship. All is bright sunshine, all is fair weather now. The soul of each passenger is exultant. The whole company break forth in songs of thanksgiving to the Great Ruler of wind and wave, until the echoes thereof roll out upon the broad bosom of the deep, and die away at last amid the sublime music of the surging billows.

And now while thus hopeful, and happy, and joyful in God, they begin to discover evidences of a near approach to the shores of the happy continent they seek. And their exultation rises to an intense height. Some clap their hands, some shout aloud for joy. In a little while they will see the land !

When Columbus made the immortal voyage which resulted in the discovery of the American continent, he had to pass through great trials before success rewarded his pains. But O, with what rapture did he, and his adventurous companions, hail the first signs of approaching land ! When they saw sea-weeds and small pieces of timber floating on the waves ; and saw birds, such as they had never seen before, flying through the air, and performing their gyrations among the rigging of the ships, they *knew* they were pressing hard upon the shores of the land of their search. An undiscovered continent was before them; and we wonder not that we are told they were extatic with joy, and that on bended knees and with loud voice they returned thanks to the great God who was "bringing them to the desired haven."

And so when the Christian voyager is almost home, when he discovers, in the blessed intimations which the God of grace is pleased to grant him, that he is pressing hard upon the shores of the glorious world which he seeks, who shall blame him if, in the blissful moment of that triumphant discovery, he should give expression to the jubilant emotions which pervade his soul? Who should think it strange, if, when about to land in the heavenly harbor, and looking out from the deck of the God-made ship which has borne him in safety through so many storms, and concentrating his intense spiritual gaze upon the "ever-green shore" that reaches down to the waters of the harbor, he should exclaim, in the transports of the moment,

"O the transporting, rapturous scene
    That rises to my sight!
Sweet fields arrayed in living green
    And rivers of delight!

There generous fruits that never fail,
    On trees immortal grow;
There rocks, and hills, and brooks, and vales
    With milk and honey flow.

All o'er those wide extended plains
    Shines one eternal day;
There God the Son forever reigns
    And scatters night away."

III. BUT THE LANDING.

Every voyager to lands across the sea looks forward with the deepest interest to the day when he will reach the coast beyond; and safe from the perils of the deep, will find himself in happy communion with the people of a foreign clime. The same is true of the Christian voyager. Him we have now followed from the day, when with tearful eyes, but hopeful heart, he took his leave of weeping friends, and obedient to the call of his heavenly Captain, embarked for the land of the blest. We have pursued his journey across the sea of time. Amid sunshine and storm, beneath clear skies and starless heavens, today exultant with joy, and tomorrow oppressed with fear, we have steadily watched his course until he passed within the haven whose waters lave the heavenly shore, where, in joyous exultation, he looked out from the deck of the gallant ship, on the hills, and plains, and temples, and towers of heaven: and from this point we are to follow him now.

The ship is in the harbor. Slowly and solemnly it approaches the shore. And there in the harbor, close by the shore, and in full view of the eternal city, he lays aside this robe of mortality, this corruptible body, that in the character and habilaments of a pure spirit, redeemed by the blood of Christ, and sanctified by the Holy Ghost, he may be fitted to mingle with the celestial throng. And while this process is going on, the angels, on swift wing, come flying over from the heavenly city to mingle in the scene, to array the parting soul in garments of white, and, when the ship touches the shore, conduct the ransomed spirit home.

Hark! the bells of the heavenly city are ringing! There is joy among the angels of God, and among the spirits of just men made perfect. They come to greet their brother, and bid him welcome home. See! forth from the golden streets and broad avenues of the city of God they come! Through the gates of pearl they come! Down the verdant slopes and embowered lawns they come! Multitudes on multitudes, they come! They come to hail their brother, and bid him welcome home.

And now, led by ministering angels, he comes down from the vessel to meet the waiting host, and receive their salutations. His feet have touched the immortal strand! He is safely landed on the heavenly shore! He is at *home*, at home in heaven, at home forever — a monument of the mercy of God, a trophy of redeeming grace, he is at home!

And now, standing on the shining shore of the heavenly land, the witness for the first time of its transcendent glories, what must his *emotions* be! He had learned of those scenes before, but had learned of them as scenes of "glory to be revealed." Now he is in the midst of them! Now they lie open to his view! Now he beholds them with eyes undimmed by mortality, without a veil between, without a cloud to obscure his perfect vision! O the raptures of this moment! They are too great for mortal utterance, too high for human conception, in this infantine state of our being!

And then how happy must the newly arrived voyager be in the privilege of meeting and greeting loved ones who had gone to glory before him! He had known them in the world of time. He had met them in the sanctuary of God. He had bowed the knee with them at the throne of grace. He had communed with them at the table of the Lord. Now he meets them beneath the dome of the grand temple above. Now he joins them in the seraphic worship of the redeemed host before the throne of God and of the Lamb. Happy meetings, joyful greetings, in the renewed fellowship of loved ones in heaven!

And our fathers, and mothers, and brothers, and sisters, and husbands, and wives, who have died in the faith — and children, sweet babes that in the early morning of their being, at the bidding of the blessed Jesus, took wing and fled to his bosom — will we not find them there ; and finding will we not embrace them, and rejoice with them forevermore?

And will we not meet and know others whom we have never met and known on earth — Abraham and Isaac, and Jacob, and Moses, and Samuel, and David, and Isaiah, and Daniel, and Peter, and Paul, and John, and a host of others whose names are embalmed in the book of God ; and Justin Martyr, and Polycarp, and Chrysostom, and Huss, and Wickliffe, and Luther, and Calvin, and Knox, and Wesley, and Edwards, and Dwight, and a thousand more whose names are enshrined in the hearts of the good; and meeting and knowing them, will we not enjoy their fellowship, and blend our voices with theirs in everlasting ascriptions of praise to the common Savior of us all? Yea doubtless ; for to say nothing about the distinct intimations of the word of God in favor of this view, such is one of the deep intuitions and longings of our spiritual being. This desire, this unavoidable aspiration to know and to enjoy, will be gratified in heaven. The Maker of the soul did not implant it, and grace does not foster it, to be disappointed.

Come then, brethren, throw open your souls to the quickening influence of this inspiring theme! Endeavor to rise to the height of this great argument! Each one of you has an interest in the subject: and can it be that the subject has no interest for you? Can you look over the narrow sea of time, and feel no interest in the question of your destination on reaching the opposite coast? Is it no matter to you where you land, or what your end shall be?

You that are aground amid rocks and shoals, and you that have been stayed in your progress by appalling spiritual calms, cry up to God for help to bear you hence! And you who are under bright skies, and are wafted on in your heavenward course by happy gales of the Spirit, lift up your eyes and rejoice, for the day of your redemption draweth nigh! You may have rough sailing for yet a little while ; but the last storm will ere long have spent its fury ; and so will the Captain of your salvation *"bring you unto the desired haven."*

CHAPTER II.

OUR SECOND PASTOR.

Rev. W. H. Luckenbach was born at Doylestown, Bucks County, Pa., on the 13th of April, 1828. In his infancy his parents moved to Easton, Pa., where they united with St. John's Lutheran Church, Rev. John Hecht, pastor. In 1845, he accompanied his parents in their removal to Philadelphia, where, several years later, he united with St. Matthew's Lutheran Church, Rev. E. W. Hutter, pastor. He pursued a classical course of three years at Dickinson College, Carlisle, and privately read Theology. On the recommendation of Rev. Drs. T. Stork, C. A. Smith, and E. W. Hutter, he applied for, and received, in Lebanon, Pa., in March, 1855, Ad Interim Licensure, from the Rev. Dr. J. A. Brown, President of the East Pennsylvania Synod. Having meanwhile accepted a call to the English Lutheran Church of Lockport, Niagara County, New York, he entered upon this field of labor on the 7th of October, 1855, and was there, on the 13th of April, 1857, united in marriage with Miss Mary Jane Compton. On the 15th of September, in the same year, he was ordained by the Hartwick Synod. Called to the pastorate of our Pottsville English Lutheran Church upon the 26th of November, 1857, he accepted, and preached his first sermon here on the Third of January, 1858. He was called upon a salary of $700., and lived at Number 211, West Arch Street.

In October, 1858, he delivered a lecture for the benefit of the Church. Although the net proceeds are not afterwards mentioned, they must have been encouragingly large, as there is evidence of the payment, out of them, of $290.

Rev. Luckenbach, we are glad to state, kept a private record of ministerial acts, and although he left no record *here* of aught besides his reception of members, has, in answer to inquiry, supplied all deficiencies, giving the subjoined statement as to Baptisms administered, Weddings solemnized and Funerals conducted.

HE RECEIVED.
In 1858.

Mrs. Bodefeld, Mrs. Sarah Beyerle, Mrs. Elizabeth Bennet, Mrs. Denions, Miss Denions, Mrs. C. Dunkelberger, Charles A. Gundaker, Mrs. Sarah German, David German, Mrs. Edward Haas, Mrs. Wm. Heffner, Mrs. Chas. Heffner, Miss Sarah Haller, Mrs. Jane Herner, Mrs. Wm. Hoffman, John Klineginny, C. L. Kurtz, Mrs. Phoebe McQuade, Miss Mary Mill, T. Montgomery, Mrs. T. Montgomery, Miss Maria Mooney, James Nagle, Mrs. James Nagle, Edward Nagle, Ellen Nagle, Emma Nagle, J. L. Reed, Miss Elizabeth Riland, William Rippard, Mrs. Maria Saylor, Mrs. Eliza Shearer, James Shoup, Mrs. Shoup John E. Small, Mrs. J. E. Small, Henry Strauch, Adam Yost, Mrs. Yost.

In 1859.

Mrs. Dreher, Daniel DeFrehn, William Wirtz, Mrs. Mary Ann Wirtz.

HE BAPTIZED.
In 1858.

Samuel Dimmick, Ellen Dimmick, Catharine Dimmick, John Jacob Kienzle, William Okem, John Wents Fesler, Emily Henrietta Conrad, Lorena Catharine Matter, Frank Walter Nagle, Catharine Erdman, Sarah Lizzie Reeser, Mary Ada Mahar, George Edgar Nagle, Catharine Amelia Kern.

In 1859.

Mary Laura Nagle, Eve Elizabeth Bobbs, Sarah Matilda Calhown, Helen Mar Calhown, George Henry Kienzle, Clara Sophia Kepner, Thomas Reed M'Quade, Charles Edward Haas, Kate Arlington Reichard, Alfred Riland, Fanny Elizabeth Kienzle, Mary Melissa Kienzle, Ida Kalbach, Elwood Kalbach, Ida Priscilla Wertz, Ellen Louisa Hutchinson, Clara Gallaher.

HE MARRIED.
In 1858.

Edward Haas and Louisa A. German; William F. Hofman and Sarah Depley; Charles Brown and Mary Jane Miller; Samuel E. Ritter and Sophia E. Oran; Harrison Riland and Martha Jane Hutchinson; R. C. Russel and Mary A. DeSilva; Harry Depken and Mary Ann Riland.

IN 1859.

Jacob B. Hoffman and Mary Ann Fink; John Mieucas and Catharine Auman; Thomas L. Holt and Mrs. Emma R. Sorber; Martin Hutchinson and Sophia Barlett; Benjamin Kershner and Sarah Jane Rupert; Herman Rabenau and Ellen Hoffman; George Reed and Louisa Kline; Jacob Wees and Sarah Koons; Charles Minds and Anna Catharine Klineginney.

HE BURIED.

IN 1858.

Daniel Lindemuth, Mrs. Elizabeth Place, James C. Nagle, Charles Reichly, Harriet Drehr, Lora Wire, Mrs. Mary Mann, Charles Edwin Bock, Bloomfield Butler, John Wilson, Harvard Thomas, Adeline Trayer, William Carter, Frank Walter Nagle, Lorena Catharine Matter, Ida Callista Whitner, Walter Morris Schlaseman, Child of John Marsden, Mary Ada Mahar, Catharine Erdman.

IN 1859.

—— DeFrehn, Mrs. Kuhns, Emanuel Hause, Benjamin Jackson, Mrs. Hasler Heck, Sarah M. Calhoun.

On the 8th of July, 1859, Rev. Luckenbach announced his intention to be absent for a season upon a visit, and that he expected, upon his return, to resign. He requested Council in his absence to supply the pulpit with a view to his successor. This seems to have been done, as a motion was made, but not carried, at a special meeting of the congregation, on the 20th of July, "That the Secretary be instructed not to write for any more pastors until after Rev. Luckenbach's return and the handing in of his resignation." The Secretary was thereupon instructed to write Rev. S. A. Holman, that as soon as Rev. Luckenbach handed in his resignation, an election would be held for him.

On Sunday morning, August 20th, 1859, Rev. Luckenbach announced his resignation, to take effect October 1st, or sooner, should it please the congregation. He remained eventually until the 1st of September.

On the 25th of September, 1859, Rev. Luckenbach entered upon the pastorate of St. Luke's Mission Church in Philadelphia. He was called afterwards successively to the Lutheran pulpits of Rhinebeck, Canajoharie and Red Hook, New York, beginning his ministrations respectively on the 20th of August, 1861, the 9th of December, 1866, and the 10th of January, 1869.

He entered afterwards upon the pastorates of Hagerstown, Maryland, May 5th, 1872, Taneytown, Maryland, April 11th, 1875, and Germantown, Columbia County, New York, January 20th, 1878. Here he is still laboring with pleasure and success in the great harvest field of the Lord.

Rev. Luckenbach is a lover of poetry, and has frequently been called upon to publish poems of his own composition. He is a regular contributor to the Homiletic Review, and a number of articles from his pen have appeared in our own Quarterly Review. He is author of a valued book upon The Folly of Profanity, the only exhaustive treatise in the English Language, so far as known, upon that vice. He is still engaged in literary pursuits, and is on the eve of publishing another useful volume.

CHAPTER III.

OUR THIRD PASTOR.

Rev. S. A. Holman, D. D., was born at Harrisburg, Pennsylvania, on the Sixth of October, 1831. He was prepared for College in the Schools of Harrisburg and at Norwich, Vermont. He entered the Freshman Class of Pennsylvania College in 1851, became a member of the Philomathæan Society, and was appointed Valedictorian of his class.

He was a Druggist in Harrisburg from 1855 to 1857, began a Theological course under Rev. C. A. Hay, D. D., pastor of Zion Lutheran Church in that city, and completed it in the Seminary of the General Synod at Gettysburg, Pa. In September, 1859, at the Convention of the East Pennsylvania Synod at Harrisburg, he was licensed to preach the Gospel.

He had already been called, on the 23rd of August, 1859, by a more than two-thirds ballot, immediately made unanimous, and entered upon his duties here on the 14th of October, 1859.

He made his home at the residence of Mrs. Levi Huber, Second Street, and afterwards, during the last year of his pastorate, at the Exchange Hotel, Centre Street.

On the 19th of April, 1860, it was resolved to undertake certain repairs upon the Church, and to hold a festival to meet the outlay anticipated. The repairs cost $163.63 and the festival netted $439.16, the surplus being at once devoted to the payment of outstanding debts.

In December 13th, 1860, all claims against the Church were summed up and tabulated upon the Minutes. The total was $989.10. Toward this the sum of $613.74 was paid upon the 27th of the same month. The record of other work accomplished under Rev. Holman's pastorate is as follows :

HE RECEIVED.

IN 1859.

Mrs. Hannah Dawson, George Hofferkamp, Edward Reichart.

IN 1860.

Samuel Born, Jr., Salome Beyerle, Mrs. H. L. Cake, Celestine Glassmire, Mrs. U. Glassmire, Mrs. Annie Heisler, John Kirkpatrick, Miss Kate Ohnmacht, Mrs. Eliza Ann Pugh, Sarah Jane Palmer, Miss Mary Rosengarten, Miss Emma Rosengarten, Mrs. Elizabeth Riffert, Mrs. Riland, Mrs. Sarah Stichter, Alice Shearer, Agustus Seiler, Mrs. Mary Vaughn.

IN 1861.

Wm. Auman, Miss Ellen Derr, Mrs. Mary M. Fessler, Miss Isabella Fasolt, Mrs. Levi Huber, Mrs. Jacob Haas, Mrs. Henry Huntzinger, Mrs. Catharine Hart, Miss Fannie Hazen, Miss Lucetta Harlan, Mrs. William Heffner, Miss Mary Olewine, Mrs. Geo. Rahn, Franklin Snyder, Emma Zern.

HE BAPTIZED.

IN 1860.

Emanuel De S. Russel, Sarah E. Russel, Child of Chas. Heffner, Child of Daniel Nagle, Sarah Jane Palmer, Chas. Conrad Matter, Florence L. Reichert, Mary Emily Whitner, Oscar Peter Whitman, Anna Elizabeth Brown, Frank Steck Bock, Child of Andrew Miller, Hannah Catharine Haas, Emma R. Jenkins, Child of Mr. Kirkpatrick, Eli Lewis Heisler, Georgiana H. Heisler, Mary Haas, Frederick Haas, John Bell Haas, Magaret Dimmick.

IN 1861.

Benjamin A. Shum, Daniel Lewis Esterly, Frank Lincoln Nagle, Elizabeth Huntzinger, Bertha E. Huntzinger, Benj. F. Rhinehart, Wm. Alfred Rhinehart, Arabella Rhinehart, Savannah Rhinehart, Child of Mr. Heffner, Child of Mr. Spohn, Clara Spohn Stichter, Reuben L. Reeser, Child of Mr. Hofferkamp, Child of Mr. Garret, Child of Mr. Rabenau, Son of Mr. Yost, Ellen Boyd Reed.

HE MARRIED.

IN 1859.

George W. Ernst and Miss Sarah J. Scott.

IN 1860.

Rev. Eli Huber and Miss Ellen Deibert; John K. Dennehower and Miss Catharine Ann Souser; Richard Holman and Miss Mary Leonard; Thomas Reed and Miss Sallie Russel.

IN 1861.

Joseph H. Heisler and Miss Sarah Garland; Samuel Auman and Mrs. Elizabeth Hollenbach.

On Sunday evening, Sept. 1, 1861, Rev. Holman announced to the congregation his appointment as Chaplain in Colonel James Nagle's 48th Regiment of Pennsylvania Volunteers, and his own consequent desire for the severance of his relations with the Church. His resignation was, on the 12th of the same month, regretfully accepted.

He served in the important position to which he had been called, while the regiment was at Fortress Monroe, Va., Hatteras, N. C., and took part in the battles of Roanoke Island and Newberne, N. C., Chantilly, Va., Second Bull Run, Va., South Mountain, Antietam, Md., and Fredericksburg, Va.

On the 17th of March, 1863, he was married to Frances, daughter of J. A. Hazen, Esq., of Pottsville, and upon May 1st, of the same year, again entered the pastoral relation, accepting the call of the First Lutheran Congregation at Altoona, Pa.

In 1865, he founded the Lectureship on the Augsburg Confession in the Theological Seminary at Gettysburg, Pa., thus eliciting from the pen of the ablest of our ministers articles of great and permanent value to our Church. The series has been as follows:

ART. I. The Trinity; by J. A. Brown, D. D., LL. D. ART. II. Original Sin; by S. Sprecher, D. D., LL. D. ART. III. The Person of Christ; by S. S. Schmucker, D. D. ART. IV. Justification by Faith; by M. Valentine, D. D., LL. D. ART. V. The Office of the Ministry; by C. A. Hay, D. D. ART. VI. New Obedience; by C. A. Stork, D. D. ART. VII. The Church; by J. G. Morris, D. D., LL. D. ART. VIII. The Church as it is; by H. Zeigler, D. D. ART. IX. Baptism; by F. W. Conrad, D. D. ART. X. The Lord's Supper; by G. Diehl, D. D. ART. XI. Confession; by A. C. Wedekind, D. D. ART. XII. Repentence; by S. W. Harkey, D. D. ART. XIII. Use of the Sacraments; by W. M. Baum, D. D. ART. XIV. The Call to the Ministry; by L. A. Gotwald, D. D. ART. XV. Human Ordinances in the Church; by S. A. Holman, D. D. ART. XVI. Civil Polity and Government; by L. E. Albert, D. D.

Art. XVII. The Future of the Church; by E. J. Wolf, D. D. Art. XVIII. Free Will; by H. L. Baugher, D. D. Art. XIX. The Cause of Sin; by S. A. Repass, D. D. Art. XX. The Relation of Faith and Good Works; by E. Huber, D. D. Art. XXI. The Invocation of Saints; by J. C. Koller, D. D.

In 1868 he founded Grace Lutheran Church, West Philadelphia, Corner of 35th and Spring Garden Streets, and was pastor until 1873.

In 1874, he organized Calvary Church, Corner of Forty-Third and Aspen Streets, West Philadelphia, of which he is to the present time the esteemed and honored pastor. His residence is 433 North 65th Street.

He received his title of Doctor of Divinity from Pennsylvania College, Gettysburg, September 24th, 1884. Among the publications that have issued from his fertile pen we note the following: "Laborers are few," — Evangelical Review, Vol. XVI; "The Conflict in the Church," an address before the Alumni of the Theological Seminary, Gettysburg, — Evangelical Review, Vol. XX; "The Providence of God in the History of the Church," — Lutheran Quarterly, Vol. IV; Lecture upon Article XVth of the Augsburg Confession, "Human Ordinances in the Church," — Lutheran Quarterly Vol. X.

CHAPTER IV.

REV. PHILIP WILLARD.

After Rev. Holman's resignation, it was a question among many whether it would be most expedient to secure a regular pastor at once, or to attempt to sustain the congregation for a season by temporary supplies. From the 12th of September, 1861, when his resignation was accepted, to the 11th of December, no definite action appears to have been taken. But upon the latter date it was agreed, at a congregational meeting, that Rev. Philip Willard, then of Schuylkill Haven, be invited to supply this congregation for the term of six months, to preach once a Sabbath, morning and evening alternately, during this time, for a compensation of $150.00. He accepted the invitation, and although never regularly *installed* as pastor, performed all pastoral duties well within this period, and eventually three months longer.

Rev. Philip Willard was born at Jefferson, Frederick County, Maryland, September 29th, 1809. He became a tanner and farmer. He was confirmed by Rev. David F. Schaeffer, D. D., of Frederick, Maryland, at the age of seventeen. At the age of twenty-five he entered the Preparatory Department of Pennsylvania College, and one year later the College itself. He was for four years the room-mate of Rev. C. A. Hay, and was graduated in the fall of 1839. He entered the Seminary at Gettysburg immediately, and the ministry in the fall of 1841, his first charge being Manchester, Maryland. There were seven Churches in this charge, which one year later was divided, Rev. Willard removing to Westminster, and still ministering to four of them. He organized St. John's Church in Westminster, and the Lutheran congregations at Finksburg and Reisterstown. In the fall of 1845, he was called to Lovettsville, Va., where, after a three years pastorate, he became disabled by bronchitis. Returning to Gettysburg, in December, 1848, he travelled thence for about a year gathering funds for the endowment of the Alumni Professorship in the Theological Seminary there.

Called in January, 1850, to the Churches in Danville and Reed's Station, he served them for over six years, organizing meanwhile the Lutheran Church in Shamokin, and the German Lutheran Church in Danville, and resigned to take charge at Loysville.

In the fall of 1858 he became pastor at Mifflintown, serving them until the spring of 1861, during which time the field was amicably divided into two charges, when, upon the urgent persuasion of Doctor H. L. Baugher, he resigned, to become Financial Agent of Pennsylvania College, Gettysburg. When about to enter upon this work the Civil War broke out, and, abandoning a forlorn hope, Rev. Willard again assumed pastoral relations, taking charge of Schuylkill Haven. He remained nearly three years. The congregation was but in its infancy, and, being composed largely of the younger part of the community, became so much decimated by drafts from the government and volunteer service, that the pastor suffered from want of support. He organized at this time the Lutheran congregation at Mahanoy City.

It was at this juncture, as we have seen, that he was called to supply the pulpit of our Church. His ministry was as fruitful of good results as could be expected under the circumstances, and among those received into the congregation are several who are with us to this day.

HE RECEIVED.

IN 1862.

Nicholas Brownmiller, Mrs. N. Brownmiller, Mrs. Catharine Eisenhuth, Margaret Mines, Maria Reed, Henry Strauch, Edward Westly.

IN 1863.

William Alexander, Mrs. Alexander, Daniel Krebs, Mrs. Daniel Krebs, Ellen Krebs.

As this period of our Church's history has more largely to do with the contact of congregations than the labor of the pastor, we will conclude at this point our sketch of Rev. Willard's life, and return again to events that transpired under his ministry. Completing his services here on the First of October, 1862, in the spring of 1863, he accepted the Superintendency of the Lutheran Publication House in Philadelphia, where he remained five years.

Many of our ministers at this time believing that there should be an Orphans' Home supported by our Church, Rev. Willard presented the matter at four of the Synods, the East Pennsylvania, the West Pennsylvania, the Central Pennsylvania, and the Allegheny. Each of these assumed one fourth of the needed purchase money, and authorized Rev. Willard to buy the property at Loysville, and take charge of the School. Before doing so, he secured from the Department at Harrisburg the promise of the guardianship of as many *soldiers'* orphans as he could accomodate in connection with the orphans of the Church, as long as they should be well provided for. Rev. Willard has stood faithfully at this post for nineteen years, and though verging upon his eightieth year, is still ardent in the work. He has had under his care 325 Soldiers' Orphans and 209 Orphans of the Church, and in the support of these and impovements put upon and around the Home has expended about $100,000. or more than the Church ever invested in it. He has baptized 1500 children and 200 adults, received over 2200 persons into the Church, organized 8 congregations, and writes that he hopes to be able to "labor on, till the Master says 'It is enough, come to thy rest.'"

The reading of such a record of usefulness is calculated to do anyone good, and though it has led the reader for a moment aside from the history of our own Zion, we feel that the digression has been profitable and instructive.

But to return to the thread of our narrative. We must now consider the

CORRESPONDENCE BETWEEN OUR LUTHERAN CHURCHES.

We have described, up to this point, the history of our congregation from the time of its separation from Emanuel's Church. During this time the two congregations held on their way in independence of each other, and a third Lutheran congregation had an existence.

It was in the year 1847, under the pastorate of Rev. Wm. G. Mennig, that our congregation was organized. Under the same pastorate, on the Twenty-ninth of December, 1850, another exodus took place and a number of persons formed a third Lutheran congregation under the charge of Rev. C. F. Nance, Ph. D. His successor, the Rev. Frederic Walz, who became pastor in July, 1851, first properly organized this congregation, which received the name of Zion's Lutheran Church. They soon afterwards secured, as their place of worship, the building on Second Street, from which the English Lutherans had meanwhile gone out.

Rev. Walz was succeeded, in the early part of the year 1854, by Rev. Julius Erhart, who continued as its pastor until 1864, when the wanderers returned under him to their old home on Third Street, with which they have since remained. Rev. Erhart remained with this united family until October 1865, after which time the congregation was without a minister until June 1866, when the present efficient pastor was called, the Rev. Doctor G. A. Hinterleitner, through whose kindness the preceding facts have been gleaned.

We have thus shown, in general, the attitude of the two children towards the mother Church. The English Lutheran Child wanted English Services only, and has never returned. The German Lutheran Child who departed because dissatisfied with some *new measures* introduced into the household, returned when these had been set aside.

But it is particularly now of the events of the year 1862 that we would speak, for the better understanding of which the above facts have been recounted. In this year there were three Lutheran congregations in Pottsville.

The original one, on Third Street, organized already in 1834, and known as Emanuel's Congregation, and accustomed usually to German services only.

One on Second Street, Zion's Lutheran, a colony of the former, which left it prior to 1851, and returned in 1864. Its services were conducted only in the German language.

One on West Market Street, our own, in which, from the time of its organization to the present, services have been conducted in the

English language only, justifying our charter title, The English Lutheran Church.

At the time of which we speak, Rev. T. C. H. Lampe was pastor of Emanuel's Congregation, but had departed from the customary observance in conducting occasional English services there — in order, we presume, to retain such as desired English preaching ; Rev. Julius Erhart was pastor of the Zion's Congregation, preaching in the German language only ; and the English Lutherans were without a regular pastor altogether, but were supplied as we have seen by the ministrations of Rev. P. Willard, who on January 1, 1862, had agreed to serve the congregation once a Sabbath, morning and evening alternately, for the term of six months.

On the Eleventh of May, 1862, a congregational meeting was held by our people "for the purpose of taking into consideration the importance of procuring the services of a pastor for this congregation after the expiration of Bro. Willard's Term, which would occur upon the First of July." After some exchange of opinion, action thereon was deferred, and considerable discussion followed upon another matter then broached, culminating in the following :

"Whereas, it has been brought to the notice of the English Lutheran Congregation that considerable conversation has been had in reference to the expediency of

MERGING THE THREE LUTHERAN CONGREGATIONS OF POTTSVILLE INTO TWO,

"Resolved, That, in the opinion of this meeting, it would be much to the advantage of all concerned to have one exclusively English and one exclusively German Congregation ; and that this congregation entertain propositions from the German congregations looking to that end."

On motion, a committee consisting of Bros. George Hofferkamp, George Beyerle and William Zern, was appointed to confer with the respective Councils of the German Congregations and ascertain their views in reference to the matter.

REPORT OF COMMITTEE.

On the Second of June, 1862, the English Lutherans assembled in a Congregational Meeting. The Chairman of the Committee recently appointed, made a verbal report concerning the

ZION LUTHERAN CONGREGATION,

Second Street, Rev. J. Erhart, pastor. "They would be willing to unite with the other German congregation, Emanuel's, Rev. F. C. H. Lampe, pastor, as soon as it would agree to become an entirely German congregation, permitting those who wish to have English preaching to connect themselves with the English Lutheran congregation, thus leaving but two Lutheran Congregations instead of three.

From this it appears that, while the question of language had nothing to do with the original separation of Zion's Lutheran Church from Emanuel's, inasmuch as nothing but German was used in Emanuel's at that time, that it *did* prove a barrier at this time to their *return*, Rev. Lampe, as we have seen, occasionally preaching in English.

As the Zion's Congregation was accustomed to German service only, it is not strange that they should demand, as a condition of again worshipping in Emanuel's Church, the abolition of English services there. Nor did they eventually return until such services were discontinued.

The proposition of

EMANUEL'S CONGREGATION

was also presented at this meeting. It is from the pen of the pastor, but had first been submitted to, and endorsed by, the members of his congregation. It is as follows:

"DEAR BRETHREN,

The proposition made by the English Lutheran Church of Pottsville, for a union of all the Lutheran Congregations of this place into two Churches, viz: one English and one German, has been received and presented to the members of the Church. We are well satisfied that there ought to be but two Lutheran congregations in this place to make things work rightly. We might then dispose of one of the Church buildings, pay the debt of the other, and pay our pastor, whoever he may be, with ease. Our Church would be filled with our own Lutheran people, and it would give us greater pleasure to attend our religious meetings than if the Church in order to be filled had to be filled up with strangers.

But there seems to be a difficulty in the way to form one entirely English and one wholly German congregation — inasmuch as it would separate in nearly all cases our families. The parents would have to go to the German Church and the children to the English Church. This, as must be plain to all, would be exceedingly unpleasant and unsatisfactory. We all know how desirable it is to let our children accompany us to the same house of worship which we are attending, for then only can we have them under our own care and supervision.

Now, brethren, allow us to suggest a plan by which our Church and yours could be successfully and beneficially united, viz; if you would agree to have the preaching one half English and the other half in the German language, we believe our congregation would be unanimous in accepting such a proposition. Our congregation might sell our Church edifice, go in a body to the Market Street Church, which is larger and more convenient, and would accomodate us all. We could then take the proceeds of the sale of our Church-building and pay both the small debt still resting on our Church and the heavier debt still resting upon yours; and money to build an addition to your edifice, to make it larger could be easily obtained. We could then select a preacher to preach to us in both languages, and pay him without being worried and annoyed in getting the amount of the salary collected together, because we should then have a membership of at least 350. We could then keep our families together, bring them up by our side and under our supervision in the Lutheran Church, all which, you will readily admit, ought to be done. And instead of the German preaching and the German teaching in the Sabbath-School being injurious, it would be a great blessing and advantage to us all, and especially to our children. Nearly all the parents of both Churches can speak the German language, and most of the children can understand it, and by this means the German language can be retained, a language which is so necessary, beneficial and desirable that even entirely English people send their children, if they can afford it, to German school, so that they may be able to converse with all persons in everyday life, business transactions, &c.

But some may say that our congregation is mostly made up of Germans, who might rule in the management of the affairs of the Church and in the selection of a pastor. To this only imaginary objection we reply that we have quite a number of old citizens of American birth, who are members of our congregation and who are not at all apprehensive of any such difficulty. And why should there be any such feeling; surely whether German or English we all profess to be Evangelical Lutherans! But if, nevertheless, you should deem the German element too strong, we would inform you that, if the congregations were united, the English portion would be quite as strong, if not stronger or more numerous than the German. Brethren, we all aim at the same Heaven, where party feeling will be forever excluded. Feelings of disunion ought therefore not to influence Christians belonging to the same Church. In Heaven all party feelings are forever excluded, and what must be thought of our party here, who hope to meet in Heaven, if such feelings keep us a parton earth. Must not our religion be in a state of declination, instead of in a progressive and onward march?

Hoping that we may be able, under the providence of God, and with prayerful hearts, yet to bring a solid union between these two Lutheran congregations, we leave the matter with you.

Yours in the bonds of Christian love and union,

EMANUEL'S CONGREGATION.

Here then was a plain and serious proposition upon the part of the mother Church to make her home with her child. It was not the mere hint of her then pastor, but the deliberate proffer of the entire congregation.

THEY WERE WILLING TO SELL THEIR OWN CHURCH, and come in a body to ours, and even assume the payment of our debt, if we would but consent to admit the use of the German language at half of our services. They were willing to endure one half English. Surely the times had changed since 1847, when the vigor of the English service, and preponderance of English hymns in the united protracted services of Revs. Steck and Mennig within their walls, led directly to the birth of our English congregation.

It is hardly necessary to add that this proposition received no serious consideration. It was respectfully received and filed and ordered to be recorded upon the minutes, but there is no accompanying evidence that it was even discussed. The rank and file of our membership had emerged from the walls of Emanuel's Church, not only because they wanted *some* English, but *all* English. They knew the value of the German language, as described at such length in the above communication, but proposed that their children should acquire it, if at all, somewhere else than in Sunday School and Church. What they aimed at, in this whole movement, if we do not misinterpret their action, was not a re-alliance with Emanuel's congregation, but to effect a consolidation of *Emanuel's and Zion's.* They deplored the division of Lutheran forces in the community, as then represented by a German and English, an English, and a German congregation. And they believed that a mutual comparison of views upon the situation would lead, as it eventually did, to the "merging of the three Lutheran congregations into two," by the healing of the breach between *Emanuel's and Zion's.*

Nor was this, as might at first sight appear, a selfish or unreasonable purpose to cherish.

Our people wanted, and had organized, for the purpose of having English, *only* English. Zion's people wanted German, and could find it at Emanuel's, should they return. They had severed their connection with the parent church because of measures adopted by *one* pastor, who has now been succeeded by *another.*

Our people had already erected a costly building in a magnificent situation, and numbered nearly two hundred members (according to the calculations in Rev. Lampe's letter)—Zion's people were not strong numerically, and were but indifferently situated in a rented structure.

It was therefore most natural that any merging anticipated on our part should be that of Zion's Church into Emanuel's and not Emanuel's into ours, as suggested in the proposition of the latter. Although the communication of Emanuel's congregation did not meet with the approval of our people so far as the proposed consolidation was concerned, they certainly could not fail to appreciate the fraternal spirit expressed by this congregation.

"Surely, whether German or English, we all profess to be Evangelical Lutherans."

Brethren of Emanuel's congregation, who may read these pages, this is a good sentiment to cherish *today!*

OUR OWN CONDITION.

The conference of the committee appointed by our Church in June, 1862, with the Councils of the two German Lutheran Congregations, not having resulted in any overtures, upon the part of either, upon which we felt disposed to act, the attention of our congregation was turned for a season exclusively upon its own condition.

Leaving the question as to the unwise multiplication of Lutheran congregations to be eventually settled as it might, our people decided to call a regular pastor as soon as possible, and with this in view notified, upon the 10th of June, the Rev. P. Willard not to depend upon their continued need of his services after the expiration of the term for which he had been engaged. This term (of six months) expired upon the First of July. He was requested, however, to continue his services until a regular pastor should be elected, which it appears he eventually did until the First of October. An effort was then made to select a pastor, and replies, from two of our ministers, to overtures upon the part of the congregation, were presented at a congregational meeting held on the Ninth of October, 1862.

One replied he "thought he could not keep his family in our place for less than about $600., and house-rent free."

Another, that "if the congregation would give him a call, he wanted

1st. His moving expenses paid by the congregation.

2nd. A good house sufficiently large.

3rd. Five Hundred Dollars promptly paid, quarterly.

4th. A general donation by the congregation between Christmas and New Year's."

To the latter we know not whether any reply was made. To the former it was replied that "the congregation could not pay more than five or six hundred dollars at the highest for pastor's salary.

A NEW MOVEMENT.

On the Fifth of December, 1862, at a congregational meeting, our people were informed that a petition had been presented to the Church Council, signed by a large number of the members and supporters of the Church, asking them to make arrangements with the members of Emanuel's congregation (Third Street) for their pastor, Rev. F. C. H. Lampe to hold his English service every Sabbath evening in our Church. The Council had been equally divided upon the wisdom of this step, and now asked the congregation for direction. Action thereon was deferred until another congregational meeting appointed for the Twenty-Second of December.

Pending its assemblage, brothers George Beyerle and James Matter were chosen Delegates to the Lebanon Conference which convened December Seventh, at Lebanon. They were to state the condition of the congregation and ask the advice of the brethren. In case they should be hindered from going, they were instructed to write. They wrote as follows:

POTTSVILLE, December 8th, 1882.

To the President and Members of the Lebanon Conference:

DEAR BRETHREN:

We would hereby inform you that we were entirely unable at this time to represent our congregation at the meeting of Conference today. We are exceedingly sorry for it, but we are all so circumstanced at present that none of us could go. We are the more sorry for this, because of this, the time of perhaps our greatest difficulty since we are a congregation. We had no preaching since the First of October last, the people are scattering very fast, the Prayer-Meeting and Sunday School are neglected to a very great extent. Religion is, of consequence, at a low ebb amongst us. There are measures on foot to have Rev. Lampe to hold his English services every Sunday evening in our Church. Your immediate advice under the circumstances might be of some benefit to us.

Two days later, December 10th, the

REPLY OF CONFERENCE

was given.

It is an interesting fact to me, and should be to our people, that the writer's father, Rev. C. A. Hay, D. D., then pastor of the First Lutheran Church of Harrisburg, was chairman of the committee of Conference to which the letter from our Church was referred, and author of the reply which Conference saw fit to make. The action of the Committee, adopted by Conference, is as follows:—

The document referred to the undersigned is a letter from the Council of the English Lutheran Church at Pottsville, in which they state that they have had no preaching since the First of October; that the people are scattering very fast; that the Prayer Meeting and the Sunday-School are neglected to a very great extent, and that religion is at a low ebb amongst them. Further, that measures are on foot to have Rev. Mr. Lampe hold his English services every Sabbath evening in their Church, and that they desire immediate advice in the premises.

In view of all the circumstances in the case, your committee respectfully propose that the Conference advise the brethren in Pottsville, instead of making the arrangements spoken of in their letter, to secure *immediately* the services of some energetic, faithful minister, this being, in the opinion of the Committee, the only means of saving their Church from dissolution. Also that, as a Conference we will exert ourselves to secure an appropriation for them from the Mission Committee of our Synod, in case, after having made every possible effort, they still find themselves unable to make up a competent support for a minister.

C. A. HAY, E. A. AULD, G. H. HUMMEL, *Committee.*

THE REPLY WITHHELD.

The Congregational Meeting of December 22nd, appointed at that of December 5th, was conducted, to all appearances, without the peoples' knowledge of this communication of Council with Conference and the reply of that body, no reference whatever to this correspondence being found on the minutes of that meeting, and the question being considered and acted upon as though no further light had been thrown upon it since the 5th of December, when its discussion was postponed.

One can scarcely now conceive why so kind an offer as Conference made should not have been thoroughly considered and gladly accepted at this meeting. We believe it would have been, had it been generally known. It seems, however, not to have been brought forward at all, save at a Council meeting the following day, December 23rd. The only reason for this silence which the writer can imagine is, that they who originated this correspondence had views of their own that differed from those of Conference. That they really wished to try the experiment of Rev. Lampe's preaching at our evening services (two of them being known to have originally favored it.) In other words, that while they were curious, and not a little anxious, to know what Conference would advise, they were by no means clear, when that advice was given, that it was for the best. The sequel shows that the wisdom, in this instance, was on the side of Conference, and that time and trouble would have been saved had this advice been taken at the beginning, as it was eventually.

The congregation, convened December 22nd, decided, after discussion, to grant the petition before it, and try to effect the arrangement asked for with Emanuel's Congregation. In accordance with this action, the Council upon the following day, after hearing of the action of their delegates to Conference, and the reply of that body, at once made the

PROPOSITION TO EMANUEL'S CONGREGATION,

asking and securing their consent to the proposed arrangement, which was to take effect on the First Sabbath in January 1863, and to continue until some better plan could be adopted by our people.

It was but little more than three months, however, on the 16th of March, 1863, that

ANOTHER CONGREGATIONAL MEETING

was called to "consider the feasibility of securing a pastor."

Another meeting of Conference had intervened, at which brother J. D. Rice had been our delegate, and he at this time reported to the congregation the great interest that Conference took in its welfare, and read the following action they had taken :

Resolved, That we, as a Conference, deeply sympathize with the English Evangelical Lutheran Church of Pottsville, and that we recommend them to do that which they deem best in their case, with a view however to the interest of the English language.

The Rev. C. A. Hay, D. D., of Harrisburg was also present on this occasion as a committee of Conference and informed the people of action taken after brother Rice's return, namely, the passage of a resolution appropriating $200. for one year to aid the congregation in securing a pastor, *if they would make one more earnest effort to sustain their Church.*

This advice and proffer was accepted with thanks, and efforts were at once made to secure a pastor. But although this was in March, it was not until October that success attended them.

CHAPTER V

OUR FOURTH PASTOR.

Rev. L. M. Koons was elected, upon the 12th of October, 1863, to the pastorate of our congregation, upon a salary of $700.00. The vote was unanimous. He was a married man, and took up his residence at 710 West Market Street.

He applied himself with energy to the work, and upon the Fourth of April, 1864, less than six months after his arrival, reported having raised by subscription the sum of $1193.50, toward the liquidation of the debt, which was thought to be sufficient to cover the whole amount. The present bell, and, for aught we can learn to the contrary, the only one we have ever owned, was purchased at this time at a cost of $350. Notwithstanding the extent of these efforts, the salary of the pastor was paid in full at the end of the first year.

A Ladies' Fair held in the following January, 1865, yielded $796.40. On the 17th of March a shingle roof was ordered for the Church in place of the slate one, which was no longer serviceable, and the re-papering and repairing of the interior was determined upon. The internal alterations cost $425.27, and the outside $426.-

45, a total of $851.72. Upon the 29th of June, 1865, Rev. Koons reported collections (by himself) since March, 1864, of $1490.08, only $83.00 of which was yet unpaid; and upon the First of July acknowledges payment of salary in full to date. No record of Baptisms, Marriages or Funerals was left by this pastor.

HE RECEIVED.

In 1864.

Louis Biltz, Mrs. Bowe, Mrs. Bensinger, Susannah Dindorf, Mrs. Dillman, Miss Cassie Faus, Elias Faust, Sarah Faust, Mrs. Margaret Garrett, Jacob Huntzinger, Mrs. Elizabeth Huntzinger, Henry Hart, D. N. Heisler, Mrs. Anna E. Heisler, Mrs. Lydia Houser, Mrs. Jenkins, Nicholas Kemp, Mrs. N. Kemp, Daniel Kershner, Miss Caroline Pitts, George Rishel, Mrs. George Rishel, Mrs. Elizabeth Russel, Mrs. Caroline Saylor, Albert Smith, Mrs. Louisa Smith, Daniel Whitman, Mrs. Mary Whitman, Dr. Whitner, Lavinia Wittenmoyer.

In 1865.

Anna Alexander, Sarah Bruns, Mrs. Bowman, Mary Burkey, John Donnehower, Catharine Donnehower, Daniel DeFrehn, Mary DeFrehn, Alice Eisenhuth, Mary Hewes, Clara Heisler, Anna Hill, Miss Isabella Haas, John Cable, Henry Kurtz, Barbara Kurtz, George Kurtz, Louisa Kurtz, Mrs. Eliza Miller, Mrs. Mary Parton, Sarah Shaffer, Sarah Stichter, Mrs. Amelia M. Stichter, Mrs. Mary Shum, William Sterner, Mrs. Esther Sterner, Mrs. Wilkinson, Anna Maria Westley, Mrs. Mary Williams.

Upon the 11th of October, 1865, Rev. Koons notified the Council that the East Pennsylvania Synod had elected him as missionary to Denver City, Colorado Territory, and in consequence he desired to resign the pastorate of the Church. With a vote of thanks for past services, his resignation was accepted.

CHAPTER VI.

OUR FIFTH PASTOR.

Rev. Uriel Graves was born at Minden, Montgomery County, New York. He received his primary education in the schools near his home, afterwards entering the Academy at Ames, and the institution at Fort Plain, New York. He entered the ministry of the Evangelical Association in his native state. While identified with this denomination he preached successively in Canada West, near Toronto, at Dansville, Livingston County, New York, and again in Canada.

He then entered the Lutheran ministry, taking charge at Orleans Four Corners, Jefferson County, New York, serving also, at the time, congregations at Perch Lake Chapel, Stone Mills and Perch River. His next field of labor was the Womelsdorf Charge, Berks County, Pa., embracing within its limits, at that time, congregations also at Stroudsburg and Schaefferstown. Here two-thirds of his preaching was in the German language.

On the 9th of November, 1865, while yet at Womelsdorf, he was unanimously elected pastor of this congregation, upon a salary of $1000.00. He appeared at a meeting of the Church Council on the 7th of December, and declared his acceptance of the call he had received, and his intention to enter upon the work upon the 1st of April, 1866. He was installed by Rev. Drs. M. Valentine, and E. Huber.

He resided at first upon Coal Street between East Norwegian and East Arch, in a house then owned by Mrs. E. Nagle, but since removed. He afterwards lived on the North-East corner of Sixth and West Market Streets.

PURCHASE OF A LOT FOR A PARSONAGE.

On the 27th of July, 1866, a Committee was appointed to secure, if possible, from the Court, a change in the Charter, qualifying *"all members,"* instead of simply *"all male members,"* as hitherto, to vote at all congregational elections. On the 1st of January 1867, the Committee reported the petition of the congregation granted, and the change effected.

At a congregational meeting held January 9, 1867, the following action was taken :

"Whereas, we have great difficulty in renting a suitable house for our pastor,

Resolved, That immediate measures be taken to build or buy a house for that purpose.

Resolved, That it is the sense of this meeting that the lot adjoining the Church, owned by brother James Matter, is the proper and most suitable location for the purpose, and that a committee, therefore, of three be appointed, of which the pastor shall be Chairman, to see Mr. Matter and ascertain from him definitely upon what terms, if at all, the lot can be bought, and report to the congregation next Thursday evening."

This Committee, consisting of Rev. U. Graves, Nicholas Kemp, and Daniel Kershner, made a report in due season, when the matter was indefinitely postponed.

On the 4th of March, 1867, it was again taken up, and a Committee consisting of brothers J. H. Kurtz, H. H. Huntzinger and Benjamin Wagner, was authorized to purchase the lot for the congregation upon the best possible terms they could secure.

On the following day it was agreed to purchase the lot at the figure asked, namely, $1700. The sum of $500. out of the purchase money received, was, on the 11th of May, refunded to the congregation, as a gift, by brother Matter.

ENLARGEMENT OF THE CHURCH.

On the 29th of April, 1867, the congregation decided upon the Enlargement of the Church. It was designed to lengthen the building twenty-eight feet, toward the South, said addition to be six feet wider than the rest of the building, and to have a vestibule of six feet on the West side. The estimated cost of this structure was $6000.

It was decided to erect this addition as soon as sufficient funds could be secured. A different conclusion concerning funds must have been reached, as the structure was erected at once, though not fully paid for until 1883.

The Building Committee consisted of Bros. Benjamin Evert, John Parton, Nicholas Kemp, Peter Fasolt, and Samuel Auman. The Finance Committee comprised Rev. U. Graves, H. H. Huntzinger, C. H. Dengler, Daniel Kershner, and J. H. Kurtz.

It was hoped that these alterations could be completed before the meeting, on the 25th of September, 1867, of the East Pennsylvania Synod, which had been invited to convene in our Church. This could not, however, be accomplished, and its sittings were held, by the courtesy and kindness of our Second Presbyterian friends, in their cosy edifice on the corner of Fifth and Market Streets.

The enlargement of the Church was completed in November, and Rev. Doctor F. W. Conrad officiated at the services of Rededication.

The Record preserved of Rev. Graves' pastoral work is as follows:

HE RECEIVED.
In 1866.

Miss Mary Bonawitz, Miss Mary A. Bock, Annie M. Clark, Ellen Dimmick, Mrs. Annie H. Heisler.

In 1867.

Caroline Auer, Mrs. Esther Britton, William Bobb, John H. Boyer, John Bedford, Margaret Bramin, Nicholas Brownmiller, Isaac Bobst, Annie Cruikshanks, Sarah Crossland, Henrietta C. Conrad, Mrs. C. H. Dengler, Sophia Dewald, Charles Dentzer, Henry C. Dentzer, Matilda Dentzer, Mrs. Sarah Ecker, Miss Elenora C. Evert, William Frederic, Mrs. William Frederic, Peter Fasolt. Mrs. Maria Fredericks, Miss Joanna Fasolt, Miss Louisa Faus, William Faust, Mrs. Joanna E. Grim, Mary Glover, Emma Gallagher, Mrs. Catharine Hart, William Haring, Mrs. William Haring, Annetta Heisler, H. H. Huntzinger, Mrs. Rosa Huntzinger, Ann Hardy, Hannah Hill, Miss Martha Lindenmuth, Ellen J. Lindenmuth, Mrs. Rebecca Loose, Mrs. Emma C. Mortimer, Adaline Matter, Julia A. Matter, Washington Mortimer, Clara Mortimer, Clementine J. Mortimer, Mary Miller, M. A. E. Morgan, Daniel W. Nagle, James W. Nagle, John Rath, Mrs. Mary Rath, John A. Rath, Benjamin Rath, Solomon Shantz, John Shantz, Tillie Shantz, William P. Scharf, Lydia A. Super, Mary S. Sterner, Lydia StClair, Henry Shelly, Catharine Shelly, Peter G. Tonkinson, Benjamin Wagner, William J. Wells, Annie E. Weisner, Henrietta Weaver, Agustus Wise, Julia Zern, Emma Zern.

In 1868.

Mary Beyerle, J. W. Bock, Samuel Beyerle, Wm. Becker, Annie Betz, Sallie Betz, Regina Bobb, Olympia D. Burnette, J. W. Clarke, Geo. H. Drehr, Joseph A. Dunkleberger, Geo. Dentzer, Mary Dentzer, Susan Dentzer, Elmira F. Ebert, Miss Eckert, Samuel East, Joseph R. Ebert, Margaret Ebert, Elizabeth Fasolt, Hannah R. Fertig, Wm. Fertig, John Glover, Nathan Houser, Geo. Haring, Wm. Haring, Cecelia Hoffer, Theodore Kershner, Ruella Loyd, Albert H. Levy, Lewis Lee, Benjamin Mattis, Maria Morgan, Mary Ann Mattis, E. C. Neidt, Clara J. Neidt, Anna M. Nagle, Rosanna Robertson, Leah C. Shellenberger, Wm. H. Shertel, Jennie Scott, Henry Trough, Esther Thomas, Geo. W. Womer, Rachel A. Weir.

HE BAPTIZED.

In 1865.

Sallie Grant Heffner.

In 1866.

Ann E. Williams, Catharine Quinn, Lillie Fox, Charles Fox, Katie Nagle, Elwood Grant Moyer, Annie L. Dannehower, Edwin A. Sterrett, David Christopher Bow, Laura May Brown, William H. Dentzer, Emma Elenora Reeser, Libbie N. Mortimer, Harry W. Mortimer, John Herman Rabenau, George W. Shum, Clara R. A. Neidt, William S. Sheetz, George Geary Nagle, Florence E. Dengler, Alice R. Fredericks, Amelia Salina Snyder, Ida Francis Snyder.

In 1867.

George W. Smith, Jacob Geary Rath, Caroline R. Tonkinson, Clara Maggie Cake, Anna E. Stichter, Oscar Daniel St. Clair, Lamie William Bocam, Anna G. Fredericks, Mary M. Moser, Francis Paul Heller, Clara E. Whitman, Laura May Houser, Clinton Daniel Rishel, Martha Wirtz, Frank Wirtz, Wallace Wirtz, Katie Lugan Hannetley.

In 1868.

Charles T. Huntzinger, Catharine C. Reeser, John G. Dannehower, Bessie Alice Boyer, John Andrew Snyder, James Geary Nagle, Robert P. Lindemuth, Harry M. Phillips, Catharine Pamilla Dindorf, Mary Adelia Morgan, Catharine L. Tonkinson, Katie E. Memmorank, Wm. Francis Jennings, Arthur H. Rosengarten, Laura Dentzer, Preston W. Christian, John Geary Haring, Harry Luther Kurtz, Emma Savilla Cake, Winnifred Jones Cake, Mary Adolphus Cake, Susannah Dimmick, Franklin M. Christian.

HE MARRIED.

In 1866.

William Auman, Emma E. Rosengarten; Samuel Houser, Mary Bonawitz; Geo. B. F. Kitchen, Carrie M. Dust; James A. Bowen Emma E. Nagle.

HE BURIED.

In 1865.

Harriet Ursula Matter.

On the 18th of March, 1868, Rev. Graves presented the following communication to Council:

To the Council of the English Evangelical Lutheran Church of Pottsville, Pa.

GENTLEMEN AND BRETHREN:

A duty I owe to myself, my family, as well as—I believe—my God, impells me to lay before you my resignation as pastor of the Church.

I have tried to overlook things and to feel it my duty to remain as your minister and spiritual adviser ; and yet, despite every effort, I am not only convinced, but more than ever persuaded, and that too from reasons most potent, that it is my religious duty to ask you to relieve me, and, I pray, bid me God-speed in my work.

It is not my intention to take any other charge, but to engage in a work which will enable me to meet my current expenses, and at the same time do the will of the Master. What I shall do in the way of earning my living, as yet I have not fully settled ; but it will be something honorable, and, I believe, for the good of men and the glory of God. I can, at this time, more easily resign, from the fact that you can, with ease, supply yourselves with one in every way fitted to become your pastor, and whose family will make it possible for him to live comfortably on what you cheerfully offer me, the Rev. C. H. Shindle of Minersville, Secretary of East Pennsylvania Synod, a scholar, a gentleman and a Christian, and one whom you all have heard.

Hoping that my prayer will be heard and answered with your blessing and prayers, I am

Yours in Christ,

URIEL GRAVES.

This resignation was accepted upon the day it was tendered. The day afterwards, some rumors having gotten afloat that Rev. Graves would remain with the congregation could he succeed in getting his finances into better shape, he was asked to make a statement in relation thereto. Whereupon he offered the following proposition—That he would remain upon condition that the Church pay $1200. salary and assist him in effecting a loan of $700. for him at two years, with the understanding that, if possible, he would pay it before that time. The proposition was accepted on condition that the loan could be effected, Rev. Graves giving his individual notes for the amount.

On the 13th of April the loan had been effected, and the acceptance of Rev. Graves resignation was rescinded. Upon the 6th of July the pastor again offered his resignation, which was accepted.

The following action was passed :

" Resolved, That the Church Council part with their pastor in the best feeling of brotherly love, and with the earnest wish that, in any charge he may accept, he may be able to accomplish much good in the cause of Christ."

Upon leaving Pottsville, Rev. Graves removed to Milton, Pa., thence to Danville, Montour County, and Scranton, Lackawanna County, Pa., and afterwards to Baltimore, Maryland. His death occurred July 13th, 1884. He was laid to rest in Baltimore, after suitable funeral services had been conducted in Hoy's Tabernacle, on the 15th of July, by the Rev. S. Domer. D. D., pastor of St. Paul's English Lutheran Church, Washington, D. C.

CHAPTER VII.

OUR SIXTH PASTOR.

The Rev. Daniel Steck, after an absence of eleven years, was a second time called to the pastorate of our congregation. He was located, at the time of his call, at Dayton, Ohio. As his correspondence with those who addressed him in relation to this matter will serve to acquaint the reader more fully with the worthy character of the man, we present it in full.

CORRESPONDENCE RELATIVE TO HIS CALL.

DAYTON, September 28, 1868.

To Peter Fasolt and Daniel Kershner, Officers E. E. Lutheran Church, Pottsville, Pa.

DEAR BRETHREN:

Yours of the 25th has just come to hand. It informs me that, at a general congregational meeting of your Church, held on Tuesday evening last, I was elected as pastor by a more than two-thirds vote. The salary fixed upon, I am informed, is twelve hundred dollars a year. You desire me, at the earliest moment, to inform you whether or not I accept the call thus extended. Before I can see my way clear to a final answer, there are several particulars about which it is important that inquiry should be made, and information given.

1. In case I accept, is it understood that the congregation agrees to pay the expenses of my removal? These will not be less, perhaps, than $150.00.

2. What would it cost for house-rent, and is it understood that the preacher should pay his house rent out of the $1,200.00 offered?

3. There are appended to the call but two names instead of four. Why are the other members of the council missing? Is it because they were unwilling to sign it, or were they not accessible at the time? If the latter, it makes no difference, but the real state of the case should be known.

4. Is it likely that my coming would cause any of those who did not vote for me to leave the Church? And, if they should not leave, would they, in your judgment, be an element of discontent and trouble?

My reasons for putting these questions before I give my final answer will occur to you at once. If I should have to pay moving expenses, to begin with, and my house rent afterwards, all out of the $1200., you see I would be financially crippled from the start. But if my passage should be paid by the Church and, possibly, my rent also, it would make a great difference on the favorable side of the question. Aside from the matter thus brought to your notice, I am prepared to say I am ready to accept your call. But I must hold the matter of my final answer under advisement until I hear from you or from others whom you may authorize to speak in your name. If I come, I can be with you by the middle of November, I think. In the mean time, may God make plain to us all the way of duty.

Your Brother,
D. STECK.

To the reply given to this letter, Dr. Steck responds as follows:

DAYTON, October 7, 1868.

J. D. Rice, Sec. of Council E. E. L. Church, Pottsville, Pa.

Dear Sir and Bro.:

Your letter was received yesterday. It contains satisfactory answers to the several questions I proposed, so I am no more in doubt how the matters adverted to were understood. You wished to have my answer by the end of this week. I should like to gratify you in this, but the question to be decided is so grave a one, that I must ask you, and the Council for whom you speak, to allow me till the first of next week for further deliberation. The matter is too important, in my view, to justify even the appearance of haste. My inclination is to accept, all that remains for me to do, is to determine the question whether duty and inclination are on the same side. For this I need the time I ask. for further prayer and reflection. Besides, I am looking for a private letter from one or more of the brethren who will perhaps be able to give me a little additional light on the subject. Your letter encourages me, and, if the word I am daily expecting should have the same effect, my final acceptance is more than probable. You will be able to announce my final answer by next Sunday a week. Should I accept; my aim will be to be with you by the middle of November at the furthest. This would be but a short time for the Church to be without a pastor.

Yours Truly
D. STECK.

One week later, came the announcement of the Doctor's acceptance, as follows:

DAYTON, Oct. 14, 1868.

J. D. Rice, Secretary of Church Council E. E. L. Church, Pottsville, Pa.

DEAR BROTHER :

Permit me now, according to promise, to make my final answer to your call extended to me, some two weeks ago, to become pastor of your Church. After due and prayerful consideration, I hereby accept the position, hoping that the blessing of the great Head of the Church will rest upon the decision at which I have arrived. The salary offered is less than I could have desired, but by faithfulness on my part as well as on that of the Church a suitable compensation will, no doubt, be assured. It will be my aim to be with you about the middle of November, as we desire to move before the weather gets very cold. I will notify you hereafter of the exact time when we will be ready to start. Answer this at your earliest opportunity, that I may be assured in good season of its safe arrival.

Hoping that the Great Shepherd may keep watch over the Church until I am settled among you, and that you may all be of good cheer,

I Remain, Yours in Christ
D. STECK.

Rev. Steck arrived in due time, according to his expectation, and entered again upon the work he had so well begun; residing at 410 Minersville Street, and afterwards at 416 Mahantongo Street. He presided at Council Meeting, December 10th, 1868. The work completed, but not fully paid for, under the preceding pastorate, called for the first attention. An effort was made to borrow the amount needed ($1,000.) and pay all outstanding claims arising from this source. On the 19th of February, 1869, it was reported that a Mrs.

Caroline Lins, of Schuylkill Haven, was willing to loan $1000. for five years, with interest, payable semi-annually on the First day of April and First day of October of each year, on the following conditions : That the Church give a Bond and Mortgage, executed by the Church Council, with seal of corporation attached : that a writing be given her by individual members of the Church, pledging themselves to see her paid, and standing thus between her and the Church. Her offer was accepted, the money received, and on the 25th of March, 1869, the treasurer of the Building Committee was instructed to pay $987.30 of the then claims against the Church. We shall meet with this Mortgage again. In September, 1869, in-inside shutters were purchased at a cost of $176,92.

Rental Of Pews.

On the 16th of January, 1870, the question as to the adoption of a system of pew rents was presented to the congregation. It was determined that one week be given for reflection upon the subject, and that, in the mean time, printed slips be circulated among the people, on which they should indicate what each subscriber would pay in case the seats were free, and what in case they were rented, the understanding being that, in case more money was subscribed for the free seats, then the seats were to be declared free for the year : but if more were subscribed on condition that the pews were rented, then it was to be understood that the pews were to be rented for the year. A report to Council four days later revealed a total subscription of $1360. secured. Of this amount, $800. was pledged by such as were in favor of either system, $320. by those who wanted the pew system, and that only, and $240. by those in favor of free pews. The system of Pew-Rent was therefore adopted, February, 4th, 1870. It has since been abandoned.

At the date just given the salary of Doctor Steck was raised from $1200. to $1400. for the year 1870, to take effect from the first of April, and it was further agreed to pay him, if possible, $1500.

On May 13th, 1870, the following action was taken against a certain member who had been received the year before. We record it here for the benefit of whomsoever it may concern.

The complaint made against this brother, and resulting finally in his excommunication, three days later, consisted of the following particulars :

1. The habit, long persisted in, of finding fault with almost everybody and everything pertaining to the Church, thus injuring its good name, and standing in the way of the Gospel.

2. The habit of speaking uncharitably of the pastor, and thereby impairing his usefulness, and that, too, after he had given his

solemn promise to the pastor that he would lay aside all ill feeling and be at peace with him.

3. Neglect of the services of the Church willfully and under circumstances which render his example one of most injurious tendency.

We were unable, under the first pastorate of Doctor Steck, and are equally unable here, under his second administration, to record the names of persons Baptized, or Married, or Buried by him. Whether no record of these things was ever made, or having been made, was afterwards lost or destroyed, does not, with certainty, appear. We are glad that a record of Receptions has been preserved.

HE RECEIVED.
In 1869.

Mary Jane Brown, Mrs. Uri Conrad, Joseph DeFrehn, Mrs. J. DeFrehn, Miss Clara DeFrehn, Morris E. Done, Samuel East, Joseph R. Ebert, Margaret Ebert, P. F. Eisenbrown, Sarah S. Eisenbrown, Charles Fasolt, Mrs. Maria Feather, George Fey, Mrs. Anna Gallagher, Albert Hoeller, Mrs. Rebecca Hower, Levi Huppert, John M. Kienzle, Sarah E. Kienzle, Levi Laubenstine, Lydia Laubenstine, Charles Lord, Mrs. Charles Lord, William Lukins, Aquilla Lukins, Savilla Madara, John McLennan, Miss Pamilla Miller, Miss Emma Miller, Geo. W. Mortimer, Jr, Daniel Nagle, Sr., Enoch Neff, Catharine Neff, Rebecca Staats, Mrs. Susan M. Steck, Newton A. Steck, Miss Vallie Steck, Miss Kate D. Steck, Edwin Stewart, Amelia Stichter, Agnes Spohn, Miss Clara Shum, Miss Kate Troutman, Mrs. Margaret Ward, Calvin A. Wier, Daniel Wolf, Frank Yurrights.

In 1870.

Mrs. Bedford, Samuel Garrett, Solomon Haak, Catharine Haak, John A. Cable, Wm. B. Kurtz, Mrs. Mary Kurtz, Charles Lehe, Michael Moser, Mrs. Emma Rath, Hugh J. Scott, Mrs. Mary A. Shum, John Wolfinger, Mrs. Mary Zerks.

On the 17th of July, 1870, Dr. Steck presented the following

RESIGNATION.

To the Council of the English Evangelical Lutheran Church of Pottsville,

BRETHREN :

Allow me herewith to tender my resignation as pastor of the English Evangelical Lutheran Church, to take effect upon the First of September next.

This act is prompted by an imperative sense of duty. Without any seeking on my part, a call, given with unanimity, has come to me from the Church at Middletown, Maryland, one of the largest and most desirable charges in our connection. The support guaranteed is such as to put me entirely beyond the fear of anxiety on the question of temporal comfort. This is not the case with me here ; nor, when the people are doing all that can reasonably be expected of them, can I find it in my heart to make myself a burden to them.

But, though about to leave you, I will not cease to feel a fatherly solicitude for the prosperity of this Church. I shall not cease to remember that it is the Church of my first love.

I will do what I can, before leaving you, to aid you in the selection of a suitable pastor to succeed me. May you be so fortunate as to call a man upon whom all will unite ! In view of the present peaceful condition of the Church, this, I think, can be done.

To you, as the Council, I tender my warmest thanks for the kindness you have on all occasions shown me. In the administration of the affairs of the Church, we have, by the blessing of God, been enabled to work together in entire harmony.

And now, regretting that my ministry among you has not been more fruitful of good ; with kindness to all and malice to none ; and with the earnest prayer that the Church may yet see her most prosperous days, I hereby tender my resignation.

D. STECK, Pastor.

The following resolutions were adopted by Council :

" Whereas, the Rev. D. Steck, our beloved pastor, has tendered his resignation with the view of accepting a call from the Lutheran Congregation at Middletown, Maryland ;

And Whereas, his faithful services in our Lord's vineyard have been attended with much good, and we, who have been intimately associated with him in the Council of the Church, feel called upon to express our sorrow and regret at his departure; therefore,

Resolved, That while we regret losing the services of one so eminently adapted to unfold the teachings of God, our best wishes will follow him to his new field of labor, and that among other pleasant recollections we will ever recur, with peculiar satisfaction, to the harmony and good feeling which has characterized all our Council proceedings.' '

In a local paper, the subjoined description is given of

DR. STECK'S FAREWELL SERMON.

The Rev. Dr. Steck, Pastor of the English Lutheran Church, preached his Farewell Sermon on Sunday evening last. It was an occasion which will not soon be forgotten by those who were privileged to be present. The congregation was unusually large, every available spot in the spacious auditorium being occupied. Besides members and others accustomed to attend divine services in the Lutheran Church, the event attracted many attached friends and admirers of the retiring pastor from the general population.

The sermon was a model of appropriateness. Like all the best efforts of the speaker, it was able, forcible, and truly eloquent. It abounded in passages of uncommon beauty and pathos, which thrilled every heart. It occupied nearly an hour in delivery, yet the vast audience hung with rapt attention upon the speaker's words from the beginning to the end of the sermon. The text, Acts 20: 32, was in these words: "*And now, brethren, I commend you to God, and to the word of His grace, which is able to build you up and give you an inheritance among all them which are sanctified.*"

After a brief account of the circumstances which attended the utterance of the foregoing words by the Apostle, the speaker gave, as the first part of his discourse, a short, clear, and beautiful paraphrase upon the several members of the text. A vivid picture was drawn of the Apostle as he stood before the sorrowing band he was about to leave. Behold him (said the speaker) as with eyes turned aloft, and hand lifted gracefully toward heaven, his countenance made radiant by reason of the unearthly glow which burned in his mighty heart, how grandly he soars to the climax of his theme and opens the paradise of eternal blessedness to the view of that sorrowing band! An inheritance among the sanctified host who appeared before the throne of God in robes of white, their gemmed crowns flashing, their palms of victory waving, their golden harps ringing, and Jesus in their midst! Surely this was a prospect before which all others fade into littleness and darkness; nor do we wonder that it has so thrilled the heart of many a saint as sometimes to make him long to be disencumbered of his clay, that he might rise and bask forever amid the blessedness of which the sublime vision gives promise. Glorious heirship, immortal inheritance, reserved for the holy and happy throng who shall finally meet in those blissful realms where parting shall be no more!

Coming to this point, the speaker said he would add no more were it not not for the deep interest he felt in the continued prosperity of the Church he was about to leave. For this reason he could not, in a way so summary, vacate his place nor be in such haste to speak the parting word. He then stated that this was the second time he had stood in his present attitude before this Church; and he went on to give a brief but lively sketch of the labors and trials and triumphs which followed his first advent to Pottsville, as a missionary, in the spring of 1847, when he was in his youth, and the little flock which rallied around him were also young, and by no means rich, save that in regard to faith and good works he thought they were richer then than they had ever been since. His labors at that time, extended over a period of *eleven* years. They were years of unceasing toil, but of great and almost unalloyed happiness. Without a congregation, without a Sabbath School, without a house of worship, without a name, yet with the blesssing of God on the use of the means, it was not long before all these were granted, and the Church, when he took leave in 1858, was every way in a prosperous state. After an absence of eleven years it pleased the congregation to recall him. His second term of service, he regretted to say, was short, much the shortest of his entire ministerial life thus far—it was not quite two full years. But short as has been his stay, his labors, by the blessing of God, had been attended with encouraging results. There had been additions made to the membership at every communion ; the whole number received was *sixty-two.* Still, said the speaker, in making our estimate of the condition of a Church, whether prosperous or otherwise, it is not enough that we have regard merely to numbers. Character is quite as important. Show me a Church whose members are increasing in knowledge, who are growing in their love of the truth, who are rising by steady steps to higher and yet higher conceptions of the great end of the Christian calling, and I will show you a Church in which there is progress, even though it may not be able to make any startling exhibition so far as the mere reckoning of numbers is concerned. There is a tree of many branches ; but half of them are dead. The dead branches do not add a particle of vitality to the tree ; cut them all off, and the tree will have all the vitality it had before. So it is with a Church ; it is not prosperous in the true sense, in proportion to the number merely, but rather in proportion to the vitality, of its members. There must be unity also. Gideon, in his expedition against the Midianites, started out with an army of 32,000 men, but to put it in good fighting condition it had to be reduced to 300. The 300, because they had faith in God and were united as one man, were better than the 32,000, full of discordant elements, would have been.

In making up his mind to accept the call lately tendered him by another congregation, he was impelled to the painful decision only by a sense of duty, and he left with none but the kindest feelings for the flock it had been his privilege to serve. Said he : " I cannot cease to cherish a tender regard for your welfare. To whom should this Church be dear if not to me ? You remember the words of our Lord : ' Where your treasure is, there will your heart be also.' And if there is a sense in which service, well meant and long maintained. may be regarded as a treasure, where is the man who has put more of it into this Church than I have ! My warm regard for this Church is a necessity. It is as natural for me to love it as it is for a parent to love his child. No, brethren, I cannot forget this Church, nor put the strong desire I have for its welfare away from my heart.

There are holy, undying memories of the past which forbid it; memories of toils and prayers and tears; memories too of joy and good will and friendship such as Heaven stooped to smile upon, and which, by the blessing of God, I expect to renew in a better world. And if, because of past recollections, which remind me, among other things, of the names of some who sleep their last sleep, this Church *has* been dear to me, so must it *continue* to be for the reason that it has among its members to day many of my most cherished friends. With malice toward none, and kindness for all, there are yet here special friends who are to me as Jonathan was to David, friends to whom I feel bound by chords of love whose vibrations will make sweet music in my soul to the last hour of my life.

To the young members of this flock let me say: Be active in the Lord's work. "Quit you like men; be strong." Your activity is your best security. To deal with a slack hand is one step already, and a dangerous one, in the downward road; the next step is open neglect, and the next after that is desertion. Therefore, if you would be secure against falling, be active. Don't forget that this Church was organized and established by young people; nor fail to do your best for a cause which it will ever be your highest honor to uphold.

To the Council let me say, be faithful to your solemn trust. Be on your guard against the admission of strange customs without clear Scriptural warrant. To the erring be kind, gentle, forbearing, so long as there is hope of amendment; but when there is no longer hope, and the offender only grows worse, be firm, nor fail to exercise to the full the authority with which you are invested. Try to keep the Lord's garden clean. When there are weeds, pluck them, lest by their blighting influence they make the whole garden unfruitful. *Better that a rebellious Jonah should go overboard than that the ship should be lost.*

And now, brethren, my work among you is done. In a few days, God willing, I will be in the midst of other scenes. When I am out of your sight, and you will hear me no more, in spirit I will still be with you. In thought I will follow you to the house of God and to the homes where I have enjoyed your society. For your kindness I will cherish you while I have a heart to be grateful or a tongue to speak in your praise. We are still one in the same blessed faith and in the same heaven-appointed work; nor is this all: we are one in a common hope — the glorious hope of immortality. In this hope we part, but we meet again, not here it may well be, but in heaven, which will be far better. And that thus it may be

"When this fitful scene of life is o'er,"

is the earnest prayer of him who now bids you all FAREWELL!

LATER HISTORY.

After taking his departure from Pottsville, Dr. Steck enjoyed a pastorate of five years at Middletown, Maryland, and one of six years at Gettysburg, Pennsylvania, at which place it was the writer's privilege frequently to sit under his preaching. Here upon Friday, the 10th of June, 1881, it pleased the Lord of the harvest to call this faithful reaper to his everlasting reward.

The funeral services took place on Tuesday afternoon, June 14th, in St. James' Lutheran Church, on which occasion Rev. Dr. M. Valentine preached an appropriate sermon, and addresses were made by Rev. Dr. E. J. Wolf, of the Seminary, and Rev. Mr. Demarest, of the Pastoral Association. Revs. D. Schindler and D. C. Foulk also took part in the exercises. His remains were deposited in Evergreen Cemetery, and were followed by a large number of relatives, friends and parishioners, who united in this last sad tribute to his memory.

Doctor F. W. Conrad, Editor of the Lutheran Observer, remarks;

"Dr. Steck was endowed with more than ordinary talent, and gifts of speech, by the cultivation of which he became an instructive and edifying preacher, and took rank among our most popular pulpit orators. He was devoted to pastoral work, and prosecuted it with energy and success. He had good judgment, and proved a wise counsellor in Church matters.

He had a generous disposition and a kind heart. He was a warm friend and cheerful companion, a devoted husband and fond father. Decided in his theological convictions and devoted to his own Church, he cherished at the same time the most fraternal relations with his pastoral colleagues of other orthodox denominations. We called a few weeks ago to look upon his face once more, and to bid him a last farewell; but his physical debility was so great at the time, that we were constrained to forego that melancholy gratification. He continued to grow weaker from day to day. The day before he died he exclaimed a number of times: "O the richness of the mercy of God!" On the morning of his last day, when his son, who had watched with him, said to him, "Father, you have been sinking during the night," he replied, „Then let me to myself; I wish to be alone." These were his last words. Soon after his wife approached him, but the power of speech was gone, and at 6 o'clock on the evening of the 10th of June he calmly fell "asleep in Jesus." And as we mourn his loss as that of a brother beloved, and a true yoke-fellow in the ministry of the gospel, we rejoice in the opportunity of paying this imperfect tribute to his memory."

The *New Era*, of Lancaster, in noticing his death, says:

"His impassioned oratory is well remembered by many people of this city, and Lancaster has had few, if any, finer pulpit orators in her history. Not of a very strong physical organism, he put his whole heart into anything that he had to do, working, at times, unnecessarily hard; and this, it is thought, tended to shorten his days."

The Middletown *Register*, in an appropriate notice of the death of Dr. Steck, states also that at sunrise on the following Sunday morning the bell of the Lutheran Church was rung as a token of respect to his memory, and refers to his pulpit ability as follows:

"Dr. Steck was ranked as one of the most popular pulpit orators in the Lutheran Church. His composition was ever strong, fervid and elegant, and abounded in a beauty and grandeur of word-painting, which, when delivered in the rich sweet tones of his magnificent voice, never failed to add a charm, and to captivate and leave its impress upon his hearers."

The editor of a leading paper of Gettysburg declares:

"Dr. Steck possessed the gifts of a strong pulpit orator — an earnest nature, a commanding voice under control, a clear intellect, and the power of readily choosing expressive language. In his convictions, honestly and conscientiously formed, he was among the most decided, and no matter what consequences threatened, he defended them with all his natural ardor and manly courage. Few men equaled Dr. Steck in stirring and commanding eloquence. These characteristics placed him in the front rank of prominent divines, and the void his death creates will not soon be filled.

CHAPTER VIII.

OUR SEVENTH PASTOR.

Rev. John Q. McAtee, was born near Waynesboro', Franklin County, Pa., on the 25th of November, 1838. In the following spring his parents removed to Clearspring, Maryland. He was educated at first in a private school, and later, under the care of a private tutor, was prepared for the Academy at that place. Entering afterwards the Junior Class at Pennsylvania College, Gettysburg, Pa., he was graduated in 1858. He completed the full course of instruction in the Seminary at Gettysburg three years later, in the fall of 1861. He was at once Ordained by the West Pennsylvania Synod, at its convention in Mechanicsburg, Pa., and became pastor at Lunenburg, Novia Scotia, in the month of November. Here he remained until June, 1866. His next field of labor was Bedford, Pa., where his pastorate extended from the autumn of 1866 to the spring of 1871.

He was called thence to Pottsville, on a salary of $1500., and at first declined. But after a renewal of the call by the congregation, with an accompanying promise to build a parsonage, he accepted. There was a debt of some $2800. resting at this time upon the Church.

Rev. McAtee resided at first on the South-West Corner of Lyons and Fifth Streets. He was Installed by Rev. J. R. Dimm, D. D., on the Twenty-Fourth of September, 1871.

THE PARSONAGE BUILT.

At his first recorded presence here, at a Council Meeting on the 7th of April, 1871, a proposition was made to the Council by the Sabbath-School, to donate to them the sum of $1200. toward the building of a Parsonage upon the lot adjoining the Church, providing the Council would execute a mortgage to the Saving Fund, from whom they proposed to raise the money, the school paying the premiums on the same. The offer was "cheerfully accepted," and a Committee appointed upon plans and specifications. Upon the 10th of May, bids were received in accordance with plans and specifications meanwhile adopted, and the contract for the furnishing of all materials and work, with the exception of Excavation, Stonework, Brickwork, Plastering, and Plumbing, was awarded to Mr. Charles B. Fasolt for the sum of $1677.

Upon the following day a Building Committee, consisting of brothers Jacob Huntzinger, Peter Fasolt and Charles Lord, was appointed.

By the First of January, 1872, $4405.05 had been expended in its erection, and by the Ninth of February, 1872, the balance of $292.21 required, a total of $4697.26. Ten days later, the Council received the Parsonage from the hands of the Building Committee, and the latter were, with thanks for their efficient services, discharged.

APPEARANCE AND LOCATION.

A general idea of this Parsonage can be formed from the cut we have already given. It is a commodious three story structure, with pressed-brick front and brown stone trimmings, containing three rooms on the first floor, five on the second, and three on the third. It has a cellar furnace, kitchen range and bath room with all modern conveniences. It is located, as already indicated, immediately adjoining the Church, in one of the most pleasant parts of the town. It stands near the head of a wide oblong square, formed by the recession of two blocks on either side, between Fourth and Sixth Streets, on Market, originally containing the Market House, which has long ago been removed. After the death of the lamented Garfield, the name of this spot was altered to Garfield Square, and in the very midst of it, at the intersection of Fifth Street, a handsome Soldiers' Monument will soon be reared. We append the substance of a brief pen-picture of this monument as given in the Pottsville Evening Chronicle upon the 8th of May.

"We take great pleasure in describing in our columns the proposed memorial of the patriotism of Schuylkill County — first to respond to the Nation's call in her hour of danger; the County that had 200 men at the Capitol where secession was rife, before the ink dried on the President's Call; that gave thousands of heroes; advanced money to the government which has never been repaid. Schuylkill County should have had a memorial of this kind years ago. Its men rushed to the front in numbers that far exceed its proportion. Its women struggled as only those who saw will ever know, while their sons' best blood went out to bedew and enrich the flowery but gory field of the South.

It is right that a County having such a record should have a memorial of it, and one that will be worthy of it. In this the association has chosen from many designs with success. In its architectural outlines it is very handsome, while from an artistic standpoint it must attract the admiration of all. It is also singularly expressive and appropriate, so that there is no necessity for any inscription to designate its object, and there will be none to mar it.

The monument will be erected on Garfield Square, and is to be completed on the first of July of next year. Richard Collins has the contract to do the granite work, and August Zeller, the popular young Pottsville artist, will make the figures and historic panels.

The base is octagonal in shape, 18 feet in diameter, and will be laid on a solid foundation of native stone sunk deep enough to reach solid strata. As the monument, without the figures, will weigh 100 tons, the foundation must be of the most substantial character. The lower course of the base will be of dark Quincy granite, the water drip and margin draft being hammered fine, and the remainder left in its quarry state. On this will rest three lifts of a lighter and contrasting color of New England granite of the best quality, all the joints of which will be tied, so that there will be no displacement by the action of heat and frost. On this is the plinth of the first die, heavily moulded, highly polished, and with an elaborate cap. From this there will be four projecting pedestals upon which will be mounted four figures representing the various arms of the service. These four figures are to be cast in the best yellow bronze.

On the faces of the second or sub die will also be bronze panels representing historic incidents in the war, civil, military and naval. These panels will be executed in high relief. They will be elevated 12 feet above the street level.

On the top of this die is an elaborate cap supported by columns of highly polished Quincy. From this rises a fluted column surmounted by a Corinthian cap, the carving of which is alone a work of art. This is the end of the granite work and its top is 31 feet above the ground. Standing on the column is the "Genius of Liberty," 9 feet in height, made of yellow bronze. Mr. Zellers is now at work on his sketch figure of this piece. This sketch which is being modelled in clay, is six feet high, and he had a professional model here from Philadelphia to pose for it. She was a French woman and has since returned to her native land, her engagement here being the last she accepted in America."

A plot of ground 30 feet in breadth and extending 75 feet in length upon either side of the monument, will be kept ever green and adorned with plants and flowers. It is expected that the latter will be so arranged as to represent a Greek Cross, a Trefoil, a Maltese Cross, and a Star, the badges respectively of the Sixth, Second, Fifth and Twelfth Corps; and that two fountains will add their sparkling beauty to the scene. At its western terminus, this plot will extend almost to the line of our Church property.

The thanks of the present, and of each succeeding, pastor are surely due to Rev. McAtee for his efficiency in securing the erection of a parsonage of such completeness in a location so desirable at the time, and one which is becoming even more so as the years roll by.

A Lecture.

On March 22nd, 1872, a lecture that was delivered for the benefit of the Church, by Horace Greely, is reported to have given proceeds to the amount of $151.95.

On the first of January, 1876, the pastor reported a membership of 279.

Repairs.

On April, 13th, 1876, the Sunday-School asked permission to execute a mortgage against the Church for the sum of $1000. for the purpose of raising money to repair the Sunday-School Room, they agreeing to pay the interest and from $50. to $200. a year, upon the mortgage. At a congregational meeting, May 18th, 1876, the Council were instructed to execute such mortgage or a judgment note. On July 1st, 1876, a judgment note was given to Mr. John Haring, for $600, the amount necessary to pay for repairs that had then been completed. A new floor was put in and new seats were purchased. They were of Ash and Walnut, in the form of reversible pews. They are handsome and convenient, but a few minutes effort being needful to transform the room, as arranged for classes, into proper shape for the weekly prayer-meeting service.

Upon August 1st, 1876, the Pastor reported having received $600. from Mr. Haring, to pay for the repairs of the Sunday-School Room, and having given a judgment bond as security for the same.

On the 1st of January, 1877, the Pastor reported a membership of 297. Since the pastorate of Rev. U. Graves, there had remained a debt of $1000. It was incurred in the enlargement of the Church, and was, at this time, in the form of a mortgage held against the Church by a Mrs. Caroline Lins.

On the First of November, 1877, the Council agreed to accept from Benjamin Haywood, a loan of $2000. and to give him a mortgage against the Church for the term of five years, with interest at six per cent per annum, payable semi-annually.

The purpose of this loan, as stated at the time, was to pay Mrs. Lins the $1000. mortgage and interest accrued thereon, and to pay the floating debt of $1000. against this Church, due this date, to Rev. J. Q. McAtee, as pastor ($600.) the Haring Bond, and sundry other small bills.

On the Eighth of November, the pastor resigned.

On the 15th of November, 1877, a committee consisting of brothers Wm. R. Williams and George Rishel, reported having given said mortgage and having received $617.80 on account; that the balance would be paid as soon as the $1000. mortgage of Mrs. Lins was cancelled.

Rev. McAtee Received, Baptized, Married and Buried the following :

HE RECEIVED.
In 1871.

Mrs. Althaus, William Fasolt, Emma Fasolt, Mrs. Jacob Fox, Louisa Hetherington, Charles Keefer, Ellen Keefer, Oliver Keller, Eliza Keller, Mrs. Isaiah Kline, H. W. Kriner, Mrs. H. W. Kriner, Richard J. Lore, Amanda Lore, Franklin P. Miller, Sarah Ann Miller, Josephine Nagle, Mrs. Caroline Smith, Mrs. Sarah Steinbach, Wm. Sterner, Mrs. Wm. Sterner, Miss Sterner, Daniel R. Super.

In 1872.

Kate Betz, Jacob Bishop, Wm. Buechley, Miss Emma DeFrehn, Nora Ebert, Miss Martha Hadesty, Amanda Hadesty, Georgiana Heisler, Mrs. A. Heisler, ——— Hetherington, Louisa Herwig, Mrs. Mary Hoffman, Miss Lizzie Leffler, Miss Lizzie Lord, Henry Nagle, Mrs. Henry Nagle, Frank Reber, Mrs. Frank Reber, Miss Mary Steinbach, Lizzie Wilde, Amelia Young.

In 1873.

Minnie Auman, Emma Auman, Z. T. Becker, Mrs. Z. T. Becker, Mrs. E. Bocam, Joseph E. Bocam, Mary E. Bocam, Lizzie Bodefield, Howell Bonawitz, Miss Clara Brownmiller, Miss Bella Christian, Miss Sallie Christian, Miss Carrie Christian, Charles H. Dentzer, Mrs. M. Dickson, Keziah Douey, Mary Douey, Miss Clara Ebert, Miss Hallie Evert, Miss Mary Fans, Miss Clara Fertig, Dr. P. K. Filbert, Miss Sarah Foltz, Mrs. Mary Foltz, Emma E. Fox, Mrs. S. A. Garrett, Susanna Guers, Maggie J. Glover, Adam Gottschall, Miss Alice Hart, Emma Hehr, Mary A. Herring, Daniel Holtzman, Hannah Houp, Robert Huntzinger, Nicholas Kemp, Mrs. N. Kemp, Daniel

Keller, Daniel Kershner, Mrs. Catharine Kline, Anna E. Kline, Jacob Koble, Rebecca Koble, Jennie Koble, Simon Koser, M. C. Lord, Miss Mary Mease, Mrs. Sophia McDaniel, Mrs. Cecelia McDaniel, Winfield McDaniel, Kate McDaniel, Magaret Mortimer, Marcus H. Nagle, Miss Laura M. Nagle, Ida Nagle, Mrs. R. Reeser, Margaret Reichert, William Rishel, Geo. M. Rishel, Miss Lizzie Nagle, Miss Ella S. Rosengarten, Miss Laura Rosengarten, Charles F. Seltzer, Mrs. Rebecca Seltzer, Daniel J. Shearer, Ella V. Seiler, Miss Hannah E. Seiler, James M. Sigmund, Miss Amanda Smeltzer, Miss Mary Stichter, George Snyder F. W. Sterner, Mrs. D. R. Super, Miss Lizzie Wernert, A. J. Weigle, Agnes Whitman, Mary E. Wineland, Augustus Yost.

IN 1874.

Clara Batdorff, Mrs. Henry Betz, Mrs. Joel Betz, Frank Bock, Calvin Bonawitz, Hugh Campbell, Miss Henrietta Conrad, George DeFrehn, Peter Dunkleberger, Howard Fertig, John H. Hart, John H. Helwig, Miss Alice Heffner, Miss Carrie Hildebrand, Oscar Hoffman, Miss Alva Kirkpatrick, Solomon Lord, Henry Lord, Mrs. Henry Lord, Mrs. Susan Miller, Frank Miller, Katie Moore, Frank Nagle, John Oliver, John Reber, Mrs. Sarah Reed, Mrs. Elizabeth Reed, Flora Reichard, Christian Shum, Albert Smith, Mrs. Albert Smith, Miss Clara Stichter, Ambrose Teter, Robert Whitman, Oscar Whitman, Mrs. Rachel Young.

IN 1875.

Mary E. Bates, Jennie Beyerle, Ellen E. Bonawitz, Catharine Dimmick, George W. Farrow, A. R. H. Fiedler, Mrs. Dr. P. K. Filbert, Ida M. Fullman, Maria Grieff, Matthias Goodman, Emma Goodman, Mrs. Sarah Hower, Clara E. Jones, Miss Mary McAdams, Miss Annie McGlone, Josiah B. Meyers, Harry Nagle, Henrietta Quinn, Geo. W. Rath, Miss Elmira A. Riffert, Margaret Rosh, Edgar B. Seidel, Ellen Smith, Ida Smith, Kate F. Steinmetz, Miss E. Kate Sterner, John Teter, Mrs. John Teter, Miss Mary J. Teter.

IN 1876.

John Adcock, Miss Hannah Brown, George Frankinstine, Oscar Glassmire, J. H. Helwig, John Hower, Miss Lilla V. Loose, Miss Aurelia Loose, Miss Ella R. Loose, Miss Fannie Moore, Mrs. Vallie Nagle, Enoch Neff, Mrs. E. Neff, H. M. Oberholtzer, Harry E. Paul, Conrad Rath, Morgan R. Reed, Miss Kate E. Rishel, Miss Kate M. Roehrig, Valentine Sauppe, Mrs. V. Sauppe, Miss Libbie Stoffregen, Mrs. Hannah Spehrley, Anna Smith, Mrs. Vaughn, Laurence Zeugner.

IN 1877.

Mrs. Helen Beard, Mrs. Susan Chance, Mrs. A. Cochran, Charles DeFrehn, Anna Fegley, Sarah Finney, Charles Fleck, Mrs. C. Fredericks, Miss Emma Fricke, Eliza Haring, Miss Hannah E. Heffner, Miss Sallie E. Helms, John K. Hollenbach, Mrs. J. K. Hollenbach, Hilbert Hoops, Mrs. Caroline Hoops, Miss Mary E. Jolly, Mrs. Mary Kershner, Miss Laura E. Kershner, Mrs. Clara Kopp, Jacob Kopp, Laura Krohmer, Mary E. Lukens, Miss Matilda Margwarth, Mrs. Anna Moore, Mary Moyer, Mrs. Matilda Neff, Reuben Oxenford, Miss Mary C. Paul, Mrs. Amelia Risheill, Mrs. Ida Seltzer, John C. Seltzer, James M. Shum, Geo. W. Smith, Miss Josephine Steiger, Kate Stoffregen, Catharine Stoffregen, Annetta Strauch, Calvin Wagner, Mrs. Calvin Wagner, Mary C. Walbridge, Cordelia Warm, John Will, Wm. R. Williams.

HE BAPTIZED.

IN 1871.

Frederick H. Snyder, Howard P. Nagle, Harry P Lowthard, Emma L. Rath, John S. Crosland, Wm. Warren Crosland, Carrie M. Rishel, Clifton R. Hetherington, Emma L. Hetherington, Sallie G. Hetherington, Benj. Daniel Houser, Ida May Lenhart, Frank H. Fey, Kate Rebecca Yeiser, Robert Anderson Kurtz, Carrie Irene Kurtz, Howell Fisher Kurtz, Burd Patterson Kurtz, Wm. Augustus Kurtz, Richard J. Lore, Wm. Edward A. Lore, Franklin P. Miller, Eliza L. Huntzinger, Henry Weber Cake, Mary E. E. Miley, Jane Dentzer Miley.

IN 1872.

John L. Rath, Edward Nelson Jennings, Sarah C. Reber, Oscar Downey, Jacob Wm. Fox, Edwin F. Huntzinger, Oscar Knox Gottschall, Iva Pearl Weston, Albert L. Gottschall, Joseph A. Haring, Martha L. Hadesty, Amanda E. Hadesty, Emma R. Hinterleitner, Walter Kelison Betz, Jacob Bishop, Nellie May Sherman, Joseph Logston Williams, Charles Oscar Goodman, Isaac F. Betz, Henry W. Betz, Letitia R. Seltzer, C. Louisa Smith, Elenora Seaman, Charles Wm. Seaman, Harry Grant Crosland, Mary Ellen Smith, John Elias Bensinger, Calvin Kaup Bensinger, Cora Fertig, Laura Foltz, John S. Ulrich, —— Dentzer, Geo. F. Smith, Franklin B. Keller, Robert B. Stoul, Mary Sophia Houser, Linn B. Bocam.

IN 1873.

Henry Quinn, Henry W. Goodman, Harry Lloyd, Charles Uriah Rath, Elsie Susan Hartline, Z. Taylor Becker, Charles E. Reichard, Oscar Leon McDaniel, Matthew Hume, Anna May Cake, Valeria Super, Emma Hehr, Anna Jardine Feather, Nellie K. Beard, Nellie A. Mortimer, Howard L. Beyerle, Robert Lincoln Nagle, Sarah M. Sterner, Elizabeth Robinson, John Jacob Krebs, Esther I. Britton, John Charles Britton, James Irwin Esterly, Annie M. Hart, Zachariah East, Clara I. Heisler, Joseph W. Heisler, Ida M. Weyand, Bessie M. Zoll, Geo W. Rath, Lewis Reeser Garrett, Laura Maud Garrett, Geo. Shoener Garrett, Margaret L. Garrett, Elenora S. Kershner, George Mills, Byron F. Cotton, Sallie H. Helms, William Mott Garrett, Margaret E. Garrett, Lewis A. Wagoner.

IN 1874.

Augusta Farrell, Frederick Walter Hay, Christian E. Berdiner, Benjamin Scott Evert, Henrietta G. Wilson, Mary Nichols Heffner, Hugh Campbell, Carrie Hildebrandt, Ettie May Cruikshanks, Samuel Cruikshanks, Frank Arthur Beck, Margaret Hartman, Alice Parker, Katie Faust, William Parker, Anna Savilla Meyers, Stella Smith, Iva May Lukens, Anna Justina Lukens, Mary M. Heller, Sarah Jane Heller, James B. Heller, Sophia E. Williams, John D. Huntzinger, James Bennett Skiles, John F. Zimmerman, Harry Leslie Kating, Carrie M. Fricke, Carrie Estelle Lord, Lulu May Lord, Charles Hagar Lord, Harry Irwin Helms, Nathan James Houser, Amelia D. Dentzer, Ella F. Guers, Frank T. Bock, Edwin Hillete Bock.

IN 1875.

John Franklin May, John Wm. Candy, Robert Grant Haring, Sallie L. Shapples, Geo. W. Mortimer, Frank C. K. Toussaint, Hattie Estelle Cake, Josephine Bohn, Jules Bohn, Gertrude Fox, Charles F. Simpson, Frederic Ohnmacht, Mary Elenora Bates, John Franklin Bindley, Charles I. Hoepstine, Mary Emma Beard, Carrie Maud Reichert, George W. Foltz, Florence May Fasolt, Jeremiah Rath, Elenora Kate Phillips, Kate Barton Davis, Jean Conn Glover, Sophia Main Dengler, Allen Luther Dengler, Josiah B. Meyers, Minnie May Meyers, Caroll Brewster Meyers, Edwin Earnest Meyers, Jacob Rath, George Rath, Mary E. Wagoner, Mary Ann Pflueger, Maud I. Fasolt, Howard F. Walbridge, Cora Emily Walbridge, Elmer F. Walbridge, Claud Bender Boyer, Rella Reed Boyer, Emma R. Baughman, Ida Victoria Gillinger, Edith May Walbridge, Elizabeth Kean, Robert Wallace Gibson, Rachel Jane Gibson, James Emory Gibson, Laura Bell Kepley, Clara Kepley, Mary

Amelia Kepley, Wm. Wesley Jones, Harry Tyson Snyder, Mary Melissa Bausman, William John Bowe, Joseph Daniel Esterly, —— Keller, Chas. F. Hessenberger, Charles B. Holtzman, Frederick Samuel Glover, Francis Siddons Glover, Minnie Jean Glover, Sarah May Farrow, Harry Milton Kershner, Howard D. Kershner.

In 1876.

Claud F. Williams, Charles Franklin Neff, Bella Irene Rahn, George W. Hawkins, Elizabeth B. Temple, Elmer Meade, Fannie Moore, Lilla Virginia Loose, Aurelia May Loose, Cora May Alexander, James Alexander, Cora Edith Seltzer, Julia Camilla Hartline, Fred. Leon Beck, Frank Leib Cake, George William Fricke, Minnie Ella Krebs, Laura Annie Weston, Elmer Weston, Joseph A. McLennan, Bessie May Nagle, George R. Hummel, Maggie Sabina Weand, Harvey Ives, William Edward Lord, Mary Melissa Bausman.

In 1877.

Mary E. Ohnmacht, Emma Dentzer, Jerold Albert Koller, L. Keller Smith, Anna Moore, Florence G. Kershner, John David Miller, Clara Louisa Gottschall, Cecelia Holton, William Holton, Willie Henry Smith, Edward S. C. Smith, John McAtee Neff, Sallie Amelia Lukins, Edmund Paul Heller, Bessie Koons Nagle, Anna Lydia Gwinner, Laura May Hoffman, Emma M. Hessenberger, Samuel Hartley Garrett, James List, Emily A. Rishel, Effie Estelle Kershner, Lucetta S. Esterly, Guy Milton Eckenrode, William A. Hartline, Anna Stratton Bindley, Andrew Snyder, Theodore A. Gillinger, Alfred P. Wolder, Edwin Shoener Super, George Brown Laurence.

HE MARRIED.

In 1871.

Henry H. Hill, Martha Kirkley ; Samuel Gohe, Emma J. Fulton ; Horace K. Boyer, Sallie K. Grant ; Samuel M. Ruch, Sarah Koons ; George Gottschall, Lizzie Knox ; Albert Esterly, Clara E. DeFrehn ; David Billman, Rebecca Cramer ; Winfield Morrison, Anna Manger ; Franklin Mowry, Sabella Parker ; Valentine K. Boyer, Emma S. Murkel ; Alexander G. Jennings, Sarah Ann Evans.

In 1872.

Frank Weston, Elizabeth Wilson ; Edward Lebo, Bella Hause ; Edward Hume, Caroline A. Weir ; Daniel Finn, Elizabeth Reddington ; John E. Cake, M. Maggie Dillinger ; Wm. G. Matthews, Elizabeth Picton ; George D. Robinson, Kate Smith ; Charles Hack, Maggie Hendler ; George Heller, Sarah Moody ; Alonzo Cotton, Rebecca M. Helms ; James Goodall, Catharine Horn ; Charles E. Snyder, Emma Gallagher ; Nicholas Dennebaum, Eliza Spohn.

In 1873.

Addison G. Henry, Emma F. Gerrung ; Geo. D. Bohler, Anna M. Jones ; Augustus Shollenberger, Rachel A. Weir ; Samuel Zimmerman, Mary Critchlow ; Wm. H. Smith, Emily Boyer ; John Wesner, Katie Walker ; Bernerd G. Meyers, Emma Dewald ; Esekias Laubenstein, Anna E. Alexander ; Benjamin Bannan, Anna M. Gallagher ; John J. Parker, Alice Faust ; William Morgan, Sarah M. Hilbert ; Joseph Hoover, Clarissa Wilkinson.

In 1874.

George W. Farrow, Laura C. Evert ; C. F. Hessenberger, Mary A. Koegel ; Benjamin D. Thomas, Sarah S. Kopp ; Jabal Ohnmacht, Minnie Brodbeck ; Thomas F. Mills, Elizabeth A. Beal ; William P. Gillinger, Hannah Wommer ; Edward L. Seltzer, Nannie L. Seltzer ; William Fiedler, Emma Dohrman ; Samuel J. Simpson,

Eliza L. Krebs; Charles A. Glen, Emily E. Fox; George Rahn, Amanda Hadesty; William Kleinsmith, Mary E. Montgomery, Rev. I. N. S. Erb. Miss Ella Frailey.

IN 1875.

Guy E. Reinhart, —— Sheithauer; Levi Horlacher, Uria Broadbeck; John C. Seltzer, Ida R. Heffner; Charles B. Fasolt, Lydia Eisenhuth; George Meade, Elizabeth J. Wilde; Henry Botzman, Emma M. Floto; Gottlieb Emhardt, Amelia R. Sterner; Thomas M. Spittler, Mary E. Wiest; Winfield S. Glassmire, Isabella Koller; B. Frank Kemmery, Mary A. Goodwin; George Jones, Rebecca Robinson; George Weaver, Susan Albright; Samuel M. Ruch. Sarah A. Johnson.

IN 1876.

George Gwinner, Emma R. Krebs; George W. Ent, Clara J. Koup; Henry F. Ives, Kate Faust; George J. Thomas, Lillie McDonnel; Charles H. Runkel, Amelia R. Boyd; William H. Rishel, Ella V. Seiler; Jacob J. Kopp, Clara F. Eckenrode; J. Howard Evans, Louisa Rosengarten; John J. Fernsler, Ruellia Lloyd.

IN 1877.

Theodore J. Kershner, Josephine Meintzer; Marcus Nagle, Sallie Helms; William Haring, Emma Kepley; George W. Drehr, Maggie Williams; George W. Hummel, Caroline L. Shindel; John D. Nagle, Mary Crosland; John Jones, Mary A. Haring; Richard Llewellen, Mary Shearer; John L Evert, Elizabeth Bodefeld.

HE BURIED.

IN 1871.

William Boyer, —— Glover, William Henry Parton, Mrs. Gallagher.

IN 1872.

Mrs. Reichard, Sallie Auman, William Glassmire, Mrs. Michael Kiensle, Emanuel Russel, Jacob Bishop, Catharine Flood, Oscar Downey, Edwin F. Huntzinger, Charles D. McAtee, Mrs. Hannah Hill, Isaac Bensinger, Anna Matthews, J. Kate Zimmerman, Mary Nagle, Cora Fertig, Mrs. H. Auman, —— Shearer, Henry Wesner, —— Phillips, Mary Cohoon, Sarah Mowrey.

IN 1873.

Katie Yeiser, Walter Neil, —— Hartsock, Susan Miller, Elvina Riffert, Maudie Christian, William Glassmire, Adam Zerbe, John Boyer, Jesse Lord, Anna May Cake, Martin Smith, Samuel Young, Elenora Kershner, Fred. Conrad, Robert L. Nagle, —— McCree, Sarah Swift, Mrs. S. Shirey, Emma Gwinner, Mrs. Mary Ware, Abagail Armstrong.

IN 1874.

Henry Auman, Frederick Ohnmacht, Isaac Ward, —— Weiser, Catharine Kreamer, Ettie Cruikshanks, Maggie Hartman, Mrs. Chas. Fasolt, Isaiah Kline, George B. Reed, John Huntzinger, James B. Skiles, B. H. Heitz, Hannah Beck, Mrs Henry Shelly, Hannah Gwinner, Nellie B. Trayer, Anna M. Kirkpatrick, Mrs. Geo. Hill, John H. Fricke, Matilda R. Madara.

IN 1875.

Katie Biltz, Phœbe Frederick, Mrs. E. Allison, Peter Hilbert, J. M. Russel, Mrs. A. Heffer, Frank Wilson, Theodore Toussaint, Amanda Zoll, Charles Reed, Katie Heffner, John Rath, Mrs. A. Nagle, Mrs. P. Fasolt, Mrs. S. Holder, —— Huntzinger, George Rath, Rela Reed Boyer, George Nagle, John Evans, Dr. Koehler, Mrs. Mary Grief, Solomon Roop, Samuel Roop, Samuel Zeugner, Mary Ida Runkel, Ida May Lukens, Joseph Shaw, —— Hadesty, Harry A. Raudebush, Jacob Kline

John Grove, William Glover, ——— Boyer, Claud F. Williams, Carrie M. Fricke.

IN 1876.

Edward Lenhart, Mrs. Susan Pflueger, Amanda Kahn, Solomon Bowman, Rev. A. Yeiser, Ida V. Gillinger, F. M. Reinhart, John Jennings, Oscar Glassmire, Father Keefer, John Bretz, Cora Alexander, ——— Huntzinger, Clara Dengler, Mrs. B. Zimmerman, Eli Seiler, ——— Bowen, Mary M. Kershner.

IN 1877.

Mrs. Hannah Nagle, Richard Linn, George Bell, Louis Toussaint, ——— Cake, ——— Meyers, Allen Dengler, ——— Quinn, Bessie Nagle, Laurence Zeugner, ——— Miller.

THE RESIGNATION OF REV. McATEE

is as follows:

Pottsville, Nov. 8, 1877.

To the Council of the English Evangelical Lutheran Church of Pottsville, Pa.

DEAR BRETHREN :

I hereby tender, through you, to the congregation, my resignation as pastor of the English Lutheran Church of Pottsville, to take effect the last of the present month. I do so not from a desire to leave a people, with whom I have been so pleasantly associated for seven years, or for any want of interest in you, but wholly from a conviction that in so doing I am walking in the path of duty. A call, unexpected, unsought, and unsolicited, has come to me from the Church in Red Hook, New York, one of the largest in our connection in that State. It is a call given with *unusual unanimity*, and this, taken in connection with the support guaranteed me there, places me entirely beyond any anxiety on the question of temporal support. In consequence of the embarrassments brought on many of our members by the failure of the moneyed institutions in our midst, and the continued hard times and want of employment of others who were always liberal supporters of the Church, our revenue has been so diminished that I feel as a burden on the congregation at my present salary. I did, of my own accord, a few months ago, reduce it two hundred dollars, but I still find that the congregation is unable to pay what yet remains as my stated salary.

Viewing all these circumstances, I am satisfied that the call given to me to a new field is of God.

I regret indeed to leave you. My family entertain the same feelings. We know that we have warm places in your hearts, and believe the many declarations of regret that we hear in connection with our contemplated removal. We love you all as much, and shall always feel a great interest in your prosperity, temporal and spiritual.

We believe we can say that *a good and substantial work* has been done by me as Pastor, and you as a congregation working with me, not in our own strength, but by the grace and help of God.

The Church is in a flourishing condition, with perfect peace and harmony among its membership. I do believe I can say, *we are a unit.* I thank you as a Council for the kind consideration you have invariably shown toward me, and your willingness to assist me in every good work.

There have been those who were once among us, who are now away. The fault was neither with you or the Pastor. "They were not of us, therefore they went out from us." Their absence is no loss to the Church.

Regretting that my labors were not more productive of good than they were, but thankful that we have so many substantial tokens of some success in our work here, with earnest prayers for greater prosperity among you, I hereby tender you my resignation.

J. Q. McATEE.

RESOLUTIONS ADOPTED BY THE CONGREGATION.

"Whereas, It has pleased the Head of the Church, Jesus Christ, to call, unto another field of work our beloved pastor, Rev. J. Q. McAtee, who has ministered so faithfully unto our spiritual wants during the seven years he has labored with us ; therefore be it

Resolved, That it is with the deepest regret that we learn of his determination to sever his connection with this Church as its pastor, and, in the acceptance of his resignation, we only yield to what we recognize to be a call of Providence and conducive to the best interest of our retiring pastor.

Resolved, That we desire to express our high appreciation of his efforts to promote the spiritual and secular advancement of this congregation during his ministry, and the affection we cherish for him as a minister and friend.

Resolved, That we ask an interest in his prayers in behalf of this part of the Lord's vineyard, and that God may so direct our footsteps and guard us from the evils of life as to suffer us to be eventually gathered into his own heavenly fold.

Resolved, That it is our earnest wish that his new associations may prove pleasant, and his future work be rich in the fruits which must attend the preaching of a faithful Christian minister, and that he and his worthy family may win the esteem and confidence of those in whose behalf they labor."

HIS OTHER PASTORATES.

In November, 1877, the same month upon which he left Pottsville,

Rev. McAtee entered upon the labor of the new field to which he was called, and remained there, at Red Hook, New York, some eighteen months.

In July, 1879, he accepted a call to Cumberland, Maryland, which he remembers as one of the most pleasant he has ever had, and where during a pastorate of four and a third years, he was also attended by marked success.

In November, 1883, he became pastor of St. Peter's Lutheran Church at Barren Hill, Pa., a congregation which Rev. Henry Melchior Muhlenberg had founded, and to which he had preached as their first pastor.

Rev. McAtee is still occupying this field. It needs but a glance over the statistics of his pastorate here, to assure the reader of the tireless activity of this good brother at that time. He has carried the same energy into other fields, losing but three months out of a ministry of Twenty Seven years, and is as vigorous to day as ever.

INTERIM.

Rev. J. R. Dimm filled our pulpit on the 16th of December, 1877, and presided afterwards at a congregational meeting at which Rev. S. Henry was elected pastor. A call was extended to him on a salary of $1000. and parsonage, but upon the 1st of January, 1878, he saw fit to decline it.

On the 12th of January, 1878, it having appeared that Mrs. C. Lins desired to retain her mortgage of $1000. against the Church, which it had been the intention of Council to pay, and that she was anxious to loan $1000. additional, it was unanimously agreed

"That a Bond and Mortgage be given Mrs. C. Lins for $2000. for five years at six per cent interest; $1000. of said money to be used to satisfy her mortgage of $1000. already against the Church, and the balance to pay Benjamin Haywood the $617.80 already received upon the mortgage given to him." This was afterwards done, and the Haywood Mortgage satisfied.

CHAPTER IX.

OUR EIGHTH PASTOR.

Rev. John McCron, D. D., was born October 23rd, 1807, at Manchester, England. He came to this country in 1831.

He married Miss Martha Morse, of Vermont, and, having received in early life a good education, engaged, with her co-operation, in teaching at Mechanicsburg, Pa. He made a profession of religion among the Methodists, and became an exhorter and local preacher in that denomination. But, having become impressed with the conviction that he was called to the ministry, and having become acquainted with the doctrines and usages of the Lutheran Church, he gave them his decided preference, and entered the Theological Seminary of the General Synod at Gettysburg in 1838. He was licensed by the West Pennsylvania Synod in 1839, and called as pastor of the English Lutheran Congregation in Pittsburg. They erected a Church building a year later.

After a short pastorate here, he removed to Lancaster, Ohio. In 1843, he accepted the Chester Spring charge in Chester County, Pa. He afterwards was pastor at Pikeland, Pa., and, in 1847, of the Still

Valley Church located three miles from Easton. In 1851, he went to Norristown, Pa., in 1852, to Rhinebeck, New York, and in 1854, to Middletown, Maryland. In 1855, he was called to the pastorate of the Monument Street Church, Baltimore, and in 1860, to that of the Lexington Street Church in the same city. He received the Degree of Doctor of Divinity from Roanoke College, Salem, Virginia, in 1857.

He accepted the Principalship of the Hagerstown Female Seminary in 1873. Thither he was called to the pulpit of the Lutheran Congregation at Bloomsburg, Pa., and thence to Pottsville

By a vote of Ninety-four to Two, immediately made unanimous, he was elected on the 20th of January, 1878, as pastor of this congregation, at a salary of $1000. and parsonage. Though a widower when he came, he was married the same year to Miss Martha Bailey of Baltimore, Maryland.

At the request of the congregation, the Doctor delivered a lecture for the benefit of the Church. The proceeds were $46.75. A Festival was also held the proceeds of which were $61.89.

On Sunday, July 1st, 1879, the congregation used, for the first time, the present Communion table and handsome silver Communion vessels, the gift of the Young People's Sociable. On the 3rd of September, 1879, a Peach Festival was conducted under the auspices of the Choir, in the Lecture Room of the Church, for the purpose of furnishing the gallery with new chairs and carpet, and themselves with new music for the congregation.

The Young People's Sociable was granted permission, on the 16th of February, 1880, to hold a Supper in the Lecture Room.

On May 17th, 1880, permission was also given them to hold a Strawberry and Ice-Cream Festival in the same place.

Dr. McCron brought to this field quite a reputation as a pulpit orator, and was listened to with great pleasure by many, but for some reason the finances of the congregation in this period did not seem to prosper. At the close of the first year, a canvass of the congregation resulted in but $735. in subscriptions for support, but the salary was still kept at $1000. for the year 1879, the pastor himself contributing $50. of the amount. A canvass in December, 1879, for pledges to salary for 1880, resulted in but $600. subscribed; while at the Annual Congregational Meeting on January 5th, 1880, there were reported outstanding bills to the amount of $383.91. The pastor's support for 1880 was then fixed at $600. and parsonage, and as much more as could be raised by proper effort.

We know not, nor have we inquired very closely into all the facts in the case, but are impressed that the following causes contributed toward this state of things. The advanced age of the Doctor, incapacitating him in a large measure for active pastoral work, and preventing a wide and sympathetic acquaintance with his people; differences between members of the congregation upon the adoption of certain measures in the Church, his natural temperament leading him to espouse the views of the one side with an enthusiasm that *appeared* to the other to savor more of the spirit of a partizan than of a pastor; and a disposition, in general, less genial than that of his earlier years, because of the advancing infirmities of age, and of the sad affliction in his household—his good wife, soon after their marriage, having been affected with cancer. All of these causes, with others, combined to render his ministry in Pottsville by no means his most happy or efficient one. He has nevertheless left many warm friends among our people, and some very precious results of his ministrations yet remain.

HE RECEIVED.

In 1878.

Edward D. Bolich, J. T. B. Dengler, Miss Savilla Heilner, Miss Annie Heisler, Miss Sophia Kirkley, Miss Lillie L. Mortimer, Miss Mamie A. Mortimer, Miss Sallie Reed, George Roehrig, Mrs. H. Rosengarten, Ida C. Stoffregen, Pierce G. Teter.

In 1879.

Miss Alfarata Betz, Miss Charlotte Beyerle, Miss Kate Faust, George Good, Miss Laura Kline, Miss Laura Pflueger, John Rosengarten.

In 1880.

Miss Tillie Beyerle, Miss Ellie Beyerle, Charles T. Brown, Wm. H. Brown, Miss Minnie Brown, Mrs. J. W. Bock, Miss Celia Conrad, Miss Lou Detrick, Mrs. Rebecca Detrick, William Fertig, Mrs. Wm Fertig, Aletha Fertig, Catharine Feidler, Harry Heller, Ida Hollenbach, Mrs. Sarah Heilner, H. W. Kriner, Mrs. H. W. Kriner, Francis J. Margwarth, Edward Miller, Miss Anna Morrison, Mrs. Emily Mortimer, Miss Lydia Nagle, E. Orwig, Mrs. E. Orwig, Charles G. Reed, Miss Celia Reichart, Mrs. Risheill, Miss Emma L. Risheill, Miss Caroline Roehrig, George Scheaffer, Wilson Schwartz, Lizzie Wilson.

HE BAPTIZED.

In 1878.

Charles I. Fasolt, Bertha A. Filbert, Harry Frances Kopp, Ida A. Kershner, John Stewart Fey, Anna Bertha Fey, Frederick W. Rabenau, John Hoffman, —— Heffner, James Claud Nagle, Annette Elis Sheetz, Linda May Morrison, Charles E. Morrison, Jennie Irene Kershner, Henry R. Evans, Alvin Ives.

In 1879.

Sarah Jane Rath, Howard S. Bell, Frank R. Bell, Edna E. Bell, Lizzie Olive Haring, Jennie L. Wagner, Frank Dentzer, Martha E. Dimmick, Emma E. Meyers, Robert William Seltzer, Dora B. Glassmire, Esther L. Glassmire, William F. Orwig, Bessie M. Hollenbach, Emma L. Kershner, Thomas Peter Cotton, Alexander H. Cotton.

HE MARRIED.

In 1878.

George Bachman, Laura A. Christian; Roland Winterstein, Elizabeth Martin; John Crosland, Margery Oren; Stephen Robinson, Celia Price; Lewis Fall, Mary L. Allison; James Giles, Eleann Lowther; Ambrose Meade, Mary Alice Raeder; Israel Matthews, Olive Sutton; George F. Helms, Ida Emily Trebley.

In 1879.

John Brownmiller, Louie Hewes; Hugh J. Scott, Mary E. Bocam; Frank P. Mortimer, Clara H. Seltzer; William Bosely, Ella E. Boltz; Henry N. Wise, Mary C. Walbridge; Joel Hein, Phœbe C. Krebs; James W. Bock, Mary Miller; Benjamin Millward, Elizabeth Allen; Frank Quinn, Maggie Bobb; George K. Ketter, Elizabeth Kirkendall; August C. Floto, Anna Louisa Herwig; Clinton G. Hower, Maggie I. Marsh; Thomas H. Wardel, Louisa Kohler.

In 1880

Charles Smidley, Annetta Shett; Harry K. Connor, Mamie C. Wren.

HE BURIED.

In 1878.

Eliza Krebs, Mrs. Kline.

Upon the First of August, 1880, Doctor McCron read from the pulpit

His Resignation,

with the request that action be taken thereon so soon as he could make it convenient to leave. It was accepted by the Council, August Fifth.

Doctor McCron, upon leaving Pottsville, took charge of the Lutherbaum Congregation in Philadelphia, in which city, having reached the midst of his 75th year, he died upon the Twenty Sixth of April 1881.

His funeral services took place in St. Matthew's Lutheran Church, Philadelphia, Rev. W. M. Baum, D. D., pastor, on the 29th of April. Rev. Drs. M. Sheeleigh, E. Huber, W. M. Baum, L. E. Albert, and S. A. Holman participated in conducting the sad rites, and Revs. J. H. Menges, J. H. Steck, S. Laird, and Seiss, were present, as also members of the Lutherbaum Mission and other Lutheran Churches of Philadelphia. He was laid to rest in Fernside Cemetery, West Philadelphia.

Among the tributes to his memory that the news of his death elicited were two that appeared in the columns of the Lutheran Observer from the pens, respectively, of the Rev. Drs. George Diehl and Reuben Weiser.

Doctor Diehl states: "Doctor McCron came to the Theological Seminary at Gettysburg when I was connected with the College. I had but a slight acquaintance with him then. I remember his appearance. He had not the robust and ruddy look which a few years of active work in country Churches gave him, six or eight years afterward. When a theological student, he was rather slender and pale, with indications, however, of moderately good health. He had a refined and gentlemanly air — more scholarly in appearance than the average theological student. His face and form and manners would attract attention at once. He was then a married man about thirty-one years of age. Seeing him in a group of students, the question naturally arose, ' Who is that intelligent and sprightly young man ? ' He seemed to form few acquaintances among the citizens and the college students, partly because he did not remain the entire time of the years then given to the Seminary course. Although not personally acquainted with him, almost every one knew Mr. McCron by sight. His reputation among students and citizens was that of a more than ordinarily talented man. I know of only one public performance by Mr. McCron while a student, outside of the Seminary chapel—a temperance lecture delivered at the request of prominent citizens of the town, near the close of his student life. It was an address of marked ability, complimented by Thaddeus Stevens, and pronounced by Robert Goodloe Harper, the scholarly editor of the *Sentinel*, as the finest temperance speech he had heard.

I was a near neighbor of Doctor McCron when he was pastor of the Still Valley Church, and again when he was at Middletown, Maryland. At the former place I saw him every week, and heard him frequently. He was then in the prime of life, in vigorous and robust health, capable of much work, full of vivacity, exceedingly genial, entertaining and witty in conversation, very popular with the people, and doing a large amount of pastoral work in his large country parish. No minister in that region could draw such large congregations. No pastor did his pastoral work in a more acceptable manner. He was especially popular at weddings, and had more than his share of marriages.

I was well acquainted with his methods of work. In his country or village Churches he usually preached extemporaneously. His sermons were then characterized by plain, direct and forcible truth, delivered in an animated manner. He was always ready and fluent. When he preached before Synods, or in the city Churches, his discourses were more elaborate — often overstrained. Those special efforts were not his best. They lacked the gospel simplicity and unction of his preaching among his own people in country Churches. I was frequently with him in services held every night for a week, in several villages—Finesville, Springtown, Harmony, and Stewartsville—lying several miles from Still Valley Church, although belonging to the central congregations. In those services he gave the best sermons I ever heard from him. Forgetting himself, and aiming solely at the spiritual good of his hearers, his discourses were extremely felicitous, adapted to the occasion and the audience, abounding in Scriptural truth, direct appeals to the conscience and the heart, full of tenderness, unction and power, and always fluent, although many of them unpremeditated. When listening to those fervent and powerful addresses, the regret often arose in my mind that Dr. McCron did not preach in the same strain when he came before great audiences in large towns, and before ecclesiastical conventions. If Dr. McCron had made Addison and Dr. South his models in style, instead of the Johnsonian grandiloquence, probably taking Chalmers and Melville as his models, his preaching would have been more popular among educated people. He was a man of more extensive reading and information than some have given him credit for. His memory was remarkably retentive, and the movements of his mind rapid. He had a good knowledge of some of the mathematics, and a decided taste for such studies. Although not of a philosophic or analytic turn, he possessed logical ability, and his arguments were sometimes keen and strong. He was highly imaginative, and his elocution was excellent. His pictures were often strong and vivid, yet sometimes lacking delicacy of fancy and taste. Had his great intellectual powers been subjected in youth to the severe dicipline of a university or college training, the style of his oratory would have been more conformed to the taste of the learned. As he was, he has few equals in his own peculiar department. It was a customary remark of Dr. Steck, a few years ago, that, for readiness, fluency, fervid intellectuality, and glowing oratory, Dr. McCron stood without a rival.

He was of a highly social nature. None enjoyed good company more than he, and none brought to the social circle a more genial flow of good spirits, sparkling conversation, and pleasant wit. His merriment was sometimes overflowing. He had a delicate regard to the feelings of others — never wounding one's sensibilities. However gushing his exhuberant spirits, or keen his wit, it was always in a vein of good nature. He was a man of quick sensibilities, and when he suspected a wrong to himself, his indignation would flash out. About the time of his accepting a call to the First Church of Baltimore, unfortunate circumstances alienated him from some of his brethren. He labored under a suspicion that some persons made a combined and persistent effort to disparage him. This produced some constraint. Yet he had warm friends and admirers all the time. During the five years of his pastoral connection with the Third Church, and for six or eight years in the Lexington Street Church he drew crowded houses. Among the popular preachers of different denominations in Baltimore during the last forty years, there have been few who drew larger houses for a longer time. Among his ardent admirers were men of high professional and literary ability. In the death of Dr. McCron, many of our ministers have lost one of their most trusted and cherished friends, and the Lutheran pulpit has lost one of its most brilliant ornaments.

Doctor Weiser says :—

"I first became acquainted with Dr. McCron in 1837, when he was a student at Gettysburg. He was a good English scholar before he went to the Seminary. He wrote a beautiful hand, equal to copperplate. He had a most tenacious local memory, and a wonderful flow of language. His articulation was clear and distinct, his gestures graceful and becoming ; in short he was a natural orator. In 1838, he went to Pittsburgh as missionary of the West Pennsylvania Synod and took charge of the mission in that city, which had been commenced by Father Heyer. In 1839, he came East to collect money for the building of the Church at Pittsburgh. He visited, among others, my churches at Woodboro. The people were everywhere carried away by his eloquence. He made a deep impression wherever he went, and raised a good deal of money. In the spring of 1839, our General Synod met in Chambersburg. Brother McCron was there. I had been appointed by the Synod of Maryland to visit some of the Western states as an exploring missionary, and brother McCron and I made arrangements to go as far as Pittsburgh together. We traveled in a private carriage, and preached alternately in all the towns along the road. We had a pleasant time of it. When I came to Pittsburgh I found that brother McCron was very popular there, and was looked upon as the most brilliant orator in the city.

Brother McCron was full of life and animation, but like all men of his temperament, had his times of gloom and depression. He was a cheerful companion, and was fond of jesting — so much so that some thought it bordered on levity. He was a pure-minded and good-hearted man, and brim-full of good humor. He believed in the motto — 'Laugh and grow fat.' And yet he was at times serious, and even grave, without being morose. He was honorable and dignified, polite and affable in his intercourse with men. His mind was well stored with the knowledge of English literature; he was well acquainted with the best English writers. His theological learning was not very profound, as his mind did not run in that direction. He paid more attention to the beautiful and the ornate than to the profound. Thousands who read this article, will recall his beautiful and finished sermons.

As an old friend of nearly half a century, I wish to hang this chaplet upon his monument, and thus to add my testimony to the talents and virtues of my departed brother. It is natural for us all to wish after we are dead, that some friendly survivor may say a word in our favor. We would all rather have a few flowers scattered over our graves, than to have naught but the cold waves of oblivion roll over them.

I do not know the particulars of his death, but I know that he who lives right, will die right. I have no doubt, that blessed Saviour whom he preached so long and so faithfully, sustained him in the hour of death. I have often heard him quoting those sweet lines:

> 'Jesus can make a dying bed,
>   Feel soft as downy pillows are,
> While on his breast I lean my head,
>   And breathe my soul out sweetly there.'

He would not be likely to forget this in his last struggle! He used often to quote with thrilling effect, a passage from Henry Kirke White:—

> 'Yet Jesus, Jesus, there I'll cling—
> I'll crowd beneath his sheltering wing;
> I'll clasp the cross, and holding there,
> E'en me—O bliss! his wrath may spare.'

We all know how often and beautifully he quoted poetry. But he is gone; he has finished his course, and has received his crown in the better land. Peace to his ashes!"

INTERIM.

A succession of supplies and of candidates now filled the pulpit for a season, two of whom were consecutively balloted for upon the 26th of September, 1880, but without an election — the vote standing 33 to 29 against the first, and 34 to 29 against the second. The result of the next effort of this kind will be revealed in the following chapter.

CHAPTER X.

OUR NINTH PASTOR.

The Author of this volume, the ninth and present pastor of the English Lutheran Church, was born at Harrisburg, Pa., on the Fourth of May, 1856. In the fall of 1865 he removed with his parents to Gettysburg, where his father had been called to a seat in the Faculty of the Theological Seminary of the General Synod. He there received his education, passing successively through the Preparatory Department of the College, the College proper, and the Seminary, from which he was graduated in June, 1878.

On the 29th of July, 1878, he received a call to the pastorate of the St. James' Evangelical Lutheran Church of Huntingdon, Pa, and, on the 21st of August, entered upon its duties. Upon the 16th of September, 1879, he was married to Laura Ella, daughter of Washington Buchanan, of an Elder of his Church. On the 26th of October, 1880, he received a request from the Council of the English Lutheran Church, of Pottsville, to fill their pulpit upon the following Sabbath, October 31st. In compliance with this invitation, he arrived upon Friday evening, October 29th, and was cordially welcomed and kindly entertained at the home of Mr. Joseph

DeFrehn, 300 South Second Street. He had hoped to see something, before the Sabbath, of the place and of the people. But the rain fell in torrents on Saturday morning, and was not much less copious in the afternoon. Somewhat inclined to carry his point when possible, he concluded to venture forth in the afternoon. His host would have accompanied him, but he would not hear of it. He found his way down Second to Market, and up Market to Fifth. This, he thought, must be the Lutheran Zion. The door was open and he met a fair damsel descending the stairway who dispelled his illusion, informing him that this was the Second Presbyterian Church. He found at last the Church he sought. He entered its open door. He paused not at the audience-chamber, but clambered on to the gallery. He saw — room for a large congregation, a carpet and pulpit furniture decidedly the worse for wear, and away down there at the altar-railing, a solitary woman wielding the weapons of her warfare — broom and dust-cloth. Through her kindness he learned — well, let the conversation pass. She told nothing but the truth, and nothing but what he saw fit to ask. Some facts received were not the most encouraging.

Still he had learned before this that the real *Church* anywhere, is not the building but the worshippers. And these he found, on Sabbath, to be attentive and devout. They were also cordial, and he thought he could see a future for the Church if pastor (whoever he should be) and people should abide together in harmony and love.

He visited the Sunday School also upon that day. The reader will note that it was Reformation Sunday, October 31st. He spoke briefly to them of the great Reformer and his work. Upon inquiry he learned that a large number of these young people had as yet made no profession of their faith. Here thought he is certainly a grand field for *someone* — "White unto the harvest."

Upon the Seventh of November, 1880, a congregational meeting was held for the election of a pastor, and the writer the day afterwards received, at Huntingdon, the following:

Pottsville, Pa.
Nov. 8, 1880.

DEAR BROTHER :

After services last evening the Church Council of the English Lutheran Church of this place held a special meeting, and authorized me to write to you and say that you were duly elected pastor of our Church, (as per enclosed certificate), and to formally ask you to accept, and let us know at once when we may expect you to be with us, and take charge. We have, as per last report, 179 Communicants ; 127 Contributing Members. We have a debt of $2,000. on the Church (I believe the parsonage is free from debt). We also owe a note of $150. to Bro. Yost, but we are only required to pay him the interest during life. We are free from *all* debts, except the above named, and have less than $5.00 in the Treasurer's hands at this writing. The fuel, light, &c., that you will require at the parsonage will be at your expense.

Yours fraternally,

E. L. ORWIG, Sect'y.

The following Certificate of Election accompanied the above communication.

POTTSVILLE, NOV. 8, 1880.

REV. E. G. HAY,
        Dear Brother :
                We certify that, at the congregational meeting of the English Evangelical Lutheran Church of this place, held yesterday, you were elected pastor by a vote of Seventy-One (71) for, to Six (6) against. The election was, on motion, made unanimous.

The salary was fixed at Six Hundred Dollars a year, and the use of the parsonage — you to pay the water-rent, $19.60 per year, and allow the Church the water she may need, free.

Chairman of Congregational Meeting,

C. H. DENGLER.

Attest, E. L. ORWIG.
        Secretary.

Under the same date, the two following letters were also received :

SCHUYLKILL HAVEN, PA., Nov. 8. 1880.

DEAR BRO :
        I preached at Pottsville yesterday, and was present when you were elected pastor. There was apparently great unanimity of feeling in favor of you, and you may consequently expect a hearty welcome.

Pottsville is a good field for work, and a devoted man may look for success. The salary at present is not large, but will no doubt be increased in time.

As your nearest neighbor, I bid you welcome to this region, and express the hope that we may be mutually helpful to each other.

Fraternally Yours,

J. A. SINGMASTER.

POTTSVILLE, PA., Nov. 8, 1880.

REV. E. G. HAY,
        Huntingdon, Pa.
        DEAR BROTHER :
                I regret that I saw so little of you while you were here. I have but time to write a few lines. Will leave again in half an hour for Baltimore.

We had a very interesting congregational meeting after services, and you were unanimously elected pastor. I say unanimously. There were a few scattering votes against you, but the interest was decidedly for you; and I will further say, that *I never saw a more unanimous and harmonious feeling.* I trust you will accept. I know there is a large field for usefulness here.

In haste,

C. H. DENGLER.

These different communications, and the views of the situation arrived at after visiting the field, led to the following response to the call of the congregation.

HUNTINGDON, PA.
Nov. 11, 1880.

Brethren of the Council :

After mature and prayerful consideration, I have concluded to accept your call, and will inform you at an early date, of the time when I can enter upon my duties as your pastor. The promptness and unanimity of your decision has greatly moved me, and furnished to me an additional indication of the will of Divine Providence in this matter.

Yours in Christ,

E. G. HAY.

Arriving upon the 22nd of November, we were entertained temporarily by the same kind family, at 300 N. Second Street, who had taken good care of the writer upon his first visit.

The parsonage, however, by the assistance of strong and willing hands was soon made habitable, and the fourth night of our sojourn was spent beneath its roof. Several delightful evenings during this week (Wednesday and Thursday, the 25th and 26th), were spent by the pastor and his wife at Centennial Hall, where a Paper Festival, conducted by the Sunday School, was in progress. Paper flowers, of every description, paper head-dress and regalia upon those who had charge of the tables, paper ornaments and articles of various design and utility, were leading features of the scene, but substantials and delicacies for the inner man were also there in great profusion, and were heartily enjoyed. The beginning of many precious friendships was there made, and more than once, as we looked over the multitude of young and happy faces, did we in heart exclaim with joy "To how promising a field of effort has the Lord in his goodness called us !"

Believing that Installation services should always be held as nearly as possible at the beginning of a pastorate, and not, as is now so often the case, some six months or more afterwards, we had arranged for these services upon the First Sabbath after our arrival.

Upon the 28th of November, therefore, these services took place, Rev. F. W. Conrad, D. D., of Philadelphia, presenting the reciprocal duties of pastor and people, and Rev. C. A. Hay, D. D., of Gettysburg, reading the liturgical service, propounding the usual questions, and declaring the pastoral relation duly ratified.

In the afternoon a Children's service was held, and addressed by the visiting ministers. Doctor Hay occupied the pulpit in the evening.

Upon the 5th of December, the Sabbath following, our introductory discourses were preached, the Rev. Doctor G. W. Smiley, and his people of the Second Presbyterian Congregation, honoring us with their presence at the evening service.

FIRST WEDDING.

On the 24th of December we performed the first of what, to say the least, has been a very pleasant series of ceremonies in the parlor of 515 Garfield Square, uniting in the bonds of wedlock, Mr. D. C. Freeman, of Rochester, New York, and Miss Kate Rishel, of this place.

CHRISTMAS.

The proceeds of the Sunday School Festival, already described were $258.79. Of this the School donated $100. to the Church, and spent $125. upon a Christmas treat for the children. On Saturday Morning, December 25th, at half-past ten o'clock, they gathered in the main audience room, where, after brief exercises appropriate to the day, each scholar received an ample share of the good things provided. If memory serves us aright there was a quart of peanuts, an orange and a pound of the best mixtures for each.

EASTER.

Of our services upon Easter Sabbath, April 17th, 1881, the following description appeared in the Lutheran Observer from the pen of brother Charles H. Dengler.

"What a glorious season Easter is, and how fondly memory clusters around the word—Easter! the day that Christ arose! Surely we ought to rejoice that 'He not only died, but rose again, and ever liveth to make intercession for us.' This season of the year is especially precious to those reared in the Lutheran Church, as the ingathering into the fold is, as a general thing, larger than at any other time of the year. This was the case in our Church in Pottsville to-day. The day opened bright and clear, and nature was in accord with it. The birds seemed to warble 'The Lord is risen indeed,' and our hearts are still making music with the service and exercise of the day. Many hearts were made especially glad, not only those who for the first time partook of the Sacrament of the Lord's Supper, but those who have been in the service for many years. On the evidence of one who had been in the Church for thirty-four years, there has never been a time of such general interest in our Pottsville Church as at present. When our young pastor, Rev. E. G. Hay, was installed four months ago, there were grave doubts in the minds of many whether he, being so young, was the proper person for this field. The result is amazing and gratifying beyond all expectation, and we feel to-day like telling to others what the Lord has done for us—not in a spirit of vain glory, but in the spirit of the disciples who, when Christ left them at Emmaus, returned immediately to Jerusalem, and finding the eleven, assured them the 'Lord had risen indeed,' relating the circumstances of the meeting and saying, 'Did not our hearts burn within us while he was talking with us by the way?' Yes our hearts, too, were made glad to-day, by the accession of Seventy persons into our Church—Nineteen by certificate. Nine members of other Churches were received by the hand of fellowship; Five others were baptized, and Thirty-Seven were confirmed. The floral decoration about the chancel was beautiful, reflecting great credit on the designers. Altogether, it was an event in the history of our Church which will be long remembered."

The figures above given are correct with a single exception, there being but Sixty-Nine receptions, one less confirmation than here reported. Of these services the Chronicle remarks:—

"At the English Lutheran Church yesterday forenoon, the services were of a specially interesting character. Instead of a sermon, the time was given up to the reception of new members, an addition to the Church of Sixty-Nine in all. Such an event naturally delighted the older members, and pleasure was expressed on every lineament of their countenances. The altar was beautifully decorated with flowers, the music was apropos and well rendered, and the Church was crowded. After all who desired it had been received into membership, the Sacrament of the Lord's Supper was administered. In the evening, Rev. E. G. Hay, the pastor, preached an appropriate sermon to a large congregation."

The Sunday-School Convention of Lebanon Conference held its sittings in our Church on the 16th and 17th of June.

A VISITOR

arrived at the parsonage on the 24th of June, who is still with us. We can ask no greater blessing from Heaven than that he may follow the usual course of "preacher's sons," living to serve the Lord in the grandest of all occupations—the " Ministry of Reconciliation."

After hearing of the death of Rev. Dector D. Steck, the founder of our congregation, a sermon appropriate to his memory was preached upon the morning of the 24th of July. All the facts of interest it contained have already, in substance, been given to the reader.

On the 18th of August our Sabbath-School picnicked at Railway Park.

Our hearts were made glad upon the Fourth of September, by the unsolicited and generous gift of Brother James Matter, of Scranton, Pa., of the sum of $200. towards the liquidation of our debt.

On the 18th of September, at a Congregational Meeting, the Pastor was authorized to extend to the Synod of East Pennsylvania a cordial invitation to convene the year following in our Church. The invitation was duly presented, and unanimously accepted by the Synod at its meeting at Lancaster.

CHILDREN's MISSIONARY SOCIETY.

We had the pleasure of organizing, on the 13th of November, a Children's Missionary Society in our Sunday-School, with a membership of One Hundred and Ten. Its members have scattered somewhat and its number been diminished by removals; but it still exists, and is cheerfully doing good work.

RE-UNION.

On the 27th of November, a Sabbath-School Re-union was held, of which the Miners' Journal gave the following account:

" A Reunion of old and young members of the English Lutheran Church and Sunday-School was held in the Church on Garfield Square, yesterday afternoon. It was very largely attended. In fact, had there been any more applicants for admission, the ushers would have found it difficult to accommodate them. The meeting was opened by Rev. E. G. Hay, pastor of the Church. He spoke to an audience composed of the youngest as well as the oldest members of his Church. The exercises were of a very interesting character. The choir was led by Professor Alexander. The singing was very good. An address of welcome was delivered by Charles H. Dengler. Henry Kurtz, of Shenandoah, one of the oldest members of the Church, and a hearty worker in the Sunday-School cause in his own town, spoke in a very interesting manner of the time when the English Lutheran Church was not so solidly founded as it is to-day. When ' Brother' Heisler was called upon to speak, he informed his audience that, he was like an alarm clock, wound up to talk until notified to stop. The Rev. W. L. Heisler is now of Bendersville, this State. Many years ago he was a member of the iron firm of

Heisler and Clemens of this place. In the course of his remarks he said : ' I am, by about three days, the oldest worker in the Sunday-School of the English Lutheran Church. The congregation was organized in 1848 with eleven members. Four of them are dead. Another, I am afraid, is nearing her end. The rest are scattered. One is in Colorado, two in Shenandoah, one in Shamokin, one in Pottsville, and one in Bendersville, Adams County. We organized the Sunday-School in 1848. We were small at the start, but gradually grew. We were all interested in the work. We went out on the street to find children, and we found them. They are not hard to find in the coal region. There is no place like it for children. There is no place where Sunday-School work is prosecuted with more vigor than in the coal region. Outsiders have a queer opinion of you. To some of them you are all Mollie Maguires, even to the children. They think you are wild and uncivilized here, and that it is not a safe region to visit. They believe all they hear about the region, and more too. The members of the Church worked hard. We were almost satisfied that any child taken into our Sunday-School would, in time, become converted and a member of the Church. A goodly number have gone out from this School, and are now ministers of the Gospel. Something which all of you do not know is that this congregation owes its beginning to one long gone. In 1842, God's providence sent a man here from Northumberland County. He was every inch a man. At that time there were few in the Lutheran Church who spoke English. The Rev. Mr. Mennig could not preach in English. He applied to the mother Synod for an English Lutheran Mission. The German Lutheran Church was the feeder of all the Churches in Pottsville. The younger element in the Church spoke English and wanted to hear English in the pulpit. No wonder the formation of the English Lutheran Church was opposed here. The good man of whom I spoke found his way to the German Lutheran Sunday-School. He was in a short time elected Superintendent of this Sunday-School. He was a man of influence because of his goodness. The school, under him, became influential. In 1843 there was a revival in the German Lutheran Church. Nathan Haas was the name of this man. He died soon after Mr. Steck came among us. His influence never died. The speaker was followed by Mr. Heil, of Shamokin, one of the 11 members spoken of by Mr. Heisler. He was followed by Jas. W. Nagle, at one time Superintendent of the Sunday-School. The closing speaker was Edwin Nagle. The exercises proved of such an interesting character that the large audience would have been quite contented had they been more extended."

OUR IRON FENCE.

On the Second of March, 1882, Messrs. J. B. and J. M. Cornell, of New York City, presented the congregation with the handsome iron fence which now stands in front of the Church. They did so at the solicitation of brother C. H. Dengler, who, with his Sabbath-School Class, proposed to meet also the cost of its erection. This, according to their ideas and plans at the time, could be done for about $13. They paid this, we understand, to a party who first attempted the task—but who labored about two weeks in vain to reach an acceptable result. The Church Council then undertook its erection and, at a cost of $116.19, secured an excellent result, having it placed, not on separate columns, as had been attempted, but on a heavy brown stone foundation, several feet in width, which rested, in turn, upon a concealed wall of brickwork. The space between the fence and Church was also re-paved at this time at a cost of $32.50.

GOOD-FRIDAY AND EASTER.

Upon the morning of Good-Friday, April 7th, 1882, and at our Easter Communion, April 9th, Rev. C. A. Hay, D. D., of Gettysburg, filled the pulpit of our Church, assisting the pastor. He also preached, in the evening, a discourse appropriate to the day. The pastor had the pleasure of receiving 46 persons into membership at the morning service. Three others were admitted during the year.

BIRTHDAY CALLERS.

Upon the anniversary of the Pastor's birth, on the Fourth of May in this year, while he was engaged in uniting Mr. John H. Hart and Miss Mary J. Teter in the bonds of matrimony at the home of the bride, the parsonage was invaded by some eighty of the congregation. The pastor and his wife were sent for, in the midst of the festivities, and told that someone wished to see them at the parsonage. We made our excuses as best we could, while a number laughingly suggested that perhaps another wedding was on hand. We received a cordial welcome upon our arrival. Brother George M. Rishel arose and, in the name of the congregation, uttered many expressions of their good-will to our little family, asking us to accept, as a token of the same, an envelope containing Seventy-Eight Dollars. To say that we were both pleased and touched by this kind act on the part of our people, is but faintly to express the feelings of the hour. Other gifts of value and usefulness were also discovered by us when we found our way at length to the dining room. Looking back now after six years upon the scene, we still say as fervently as then, God bless the givers!

The East Pennsylvania Synod.

From the 20th to the 26th of September, 1882, this body convened in our Church. A Directory furnished the members was voted a great convenience at the time, and enables us now to acknowledge, in this more permanent form, the kindness of such as contributed to their comfort and pleasure while here.

The following persons entertained visitors at their homes :

Mr. Charles Baber, Rev. E. H. Delk; Rev. A. R. Bartholemew, Rev. J. H. Leeser and Mr. C. P. Haehnlen; Mr. L. S. Boner, Mr. H. S. Boner ; Dr. F. W. Boyer, Rev. C. Riemensnyder and Mr. Hartman ; Mr. N. Brownmiller, Rev. D. F. Koser and Mr. G. P. Hilbert; Mr. Frank Carter, Rev. R. W. Hufford and Rev. J. W. Finkbiner; Mr. Thomas Cooch, Rev. Wm. Kelley and J. W. Cline ; Mrs. Mary A. Dougherty, Rev. H. S. Cook and James Dauman ; Mr. Daniel DeFrehn, Rev. Emil Meister and Mr. John Ochs; Mr. C. H. Dengler, Rev. W. M. Baum, Rev. J. R. Dimm, Rev. W. H. Dunbar, Rev. W. H. Steck and Mr. E. T. Coxe; Mr. Benjamin Evert, Mr. W. W. Richard ; Dr. P. K. Filbert, Rev. P. C. Croll and Mr. P. Spang ; Mrs. T. Garrettson, Rev. S. Stall and Mr. J. B. Martin ; Mr. T. Geier, Rev. J. A. Singmaster and Prof. G. W. Weiss; Rev. E. G. Hay, Rev. C. A. Hay, D. D.; Mrs. Sarah Haywood, Rev. Dr. L. E. Albert, Rev. W. P. Evans and Rev. P. Raby; J. A. Hazen, Esq., Rev. S. A. Holman; Mrs. Hannah Heffner, Rev. Dr. E. J. Wolf, Rev. J. H. Weber, Rev. F. W. Stahley, Rev. O. H. Melcher, Mr. J. Trauger and Mr. G. H. Helfrich ; Mr. G. K. Hoffman, Mr. William Strickland; Major Levi Huber, Rev. E. Huber, D. D. and Rev. H. B. Wile; Mr. Wm. Kennedy, Rev. P. Willard ; Mr. Wm. H. Knoll, Rev. J. M. Dietzler and Mr. R. Steinmetz; Mr. H. W. Kriner, Rev. T. C. Billheimer; Mrs. Dieffenderfer, Rev. W. H. Lewars ; Mr. Charles Lord, Rev. G. C. Henry, Rev. J. J. Weber and Rev. W. S. Porr; Mr. Charles Roehrig, Rev. A. B. Erhart ; Mr. George Rosengarten, Rev. William Mennig; Hon. James Ryon, Rev. J. H. Menges and Mr. J. Mosteller ; Mr. J. H. Super, Rev. H. M. Oberholtzer; Mr. P. W. Shaefer, Rev. J. A. Wirt and Mr. J. Garman ; Col. William Thompson, Dr. W. M. Baum and Mr. E. H. Delk, Sr.; William B. Wells, Esq., Rev. M. Sheeleigh and Mr. J. W. Lenhart ; Mr. Wm. R. Williams, Rev. S. Dasher, and Mr. J. A. Dukel ; Mr. R. T. Williams, Rev. I. P. Neff and Mr. J. H. Kurtz.

The following members of Synod were entertained at Hotels or Boarding Houses :

At Mrs. Sarah Beyerle's, Rev. M. Fernsler, Rev. J. Peter, Rev. F. T. Hoover, Mr. C. P. Bittle, Mr. Joseph Royer, Mr. N. W. Long, and Mr. I. S. Carpenter ; at Mrs. J. B. Hoffman's, Rev. J. T. Kendall, Mr. R. J. Gruver, Mr. C. Buzzard ; at Mrs. Kate A. Jones', Mr. B. W. Holtzman and Mr. F. C. Gottschall ; at the Merchants' Hotel, Rev. E. S. Henry, Rev. C. L. Ehrenfeld and Mr. H. J. Keim ; at the North-Western Hotel, Rev. T. C. Pritchard, Mr. J. C. Cassel, Mr. Charles Bensinger, Mr. Levi Felty and Mr. J. S. Young ; at the Pennsylvania Hall, Rev. A. H. Studebaker, Mr. Daniel Eppley and Mr. J. H. Boyer.

The persons who provided for the entertainment of the above are as follows :

Mr. John Adcock, Misses Bannan, Rev. Dr. Belville, Mrs. Annie Betz, Mr. Wm. Bock, Mr. L. S. Boner, Mr. James Bowen, Mrs. A. B. Cochran, Mr. Joseph DeFrehn, Mr. George DeFrehn, Dr. P. K. Filbert, Samuel A. Garrett, Esq., Mr. James M. Hadesty, Mr. John H. Hart, Mr. Louis Heller, Mr. John H. Helwig, Mr. Harry Hill, Mrs. J. B. Hoffman, Mr. Daniel Keller, Mr. Nicholas Kemp, Miss Tillie Kimmel, Mr. H.

W. Kriner, Mr. Francis Marquarth; Mr. G. W. Mortimer, Mrs. Elizabeth Nagle, Rev. B. F. Patterson. Mr. George Rishel, Mr. George M. Rishel, Mr. Andrew Robertson, Mr. Henry Rosengarten, Mr. W. R. Simons, Mr. Fred. Spaecht, Mr. Harry Sterner, Mrs. Valentine Stichter, Mr. Henry Strohmeier, Mr. John Teter, Rev. B. T. Vincent, Charles W. Wells, Esq., Mr. John Weinreich, Mr. Wm. M. Zerbey.

On the Morning of September 26th, the Synod was treated to a ride upon the Reading Railroad to the famous Brookside Colliery. The trip is thus described by a Chronicle Reporter who accompanied us :

"Dominies are not such bad fellows to be out on a lark with after all. Some of them are, of course, prosaic and went-to-sleep-when-a-boy sort of fellows, but others are wide awake, crisp and jolly. A majority of the Lutheran pastors who made up the excursion yesterday, were of the latter sort. They had a good time and came home with faces broadened by many a hearty laugh. So did the laity who accompanied them. Brother Menges was particularly in excellent spirits even with the damper put on him at the depot before starting. He tells a first-class cat story. He repeated it several times during his week's stay. The members of the Synod seemed to fear that they were in imminent danger of being afflicted with it again. They nipped it in the bud. 'Menges,' shouted one, 'Dengler here has a story.' 'What is it?' asked the Philadelphia parson. Dengler commenced : 'It's about a cat—.' He got no further. Menges fled amid a chorus of lusty shouts. One of the three cars kindly furnished by the P. & R. Company was appropriated by the smokers of the party. Those who were not addicted to the weed soon discovered that they had business in another car. The smoke became thick enough to cut with a knife, and rank enough to kill cats. The latter quality was attributed to the character of the cigar smoked by Bill Heimer, as the President of the Synod was affectionately called. The familiarity with which the ministers addressed each other was somewhat of a surprise to the lay members. "Hello, Finkey" was only one of the numerous expressions that startled the uninitiated. The train stopped for a little while at Auburn, Pinegrove and Tremont. At the latter place a stop of half an hour was made —long enough to visit the Lutheran Church. Brookside colliery was reached at a quarter past ten o'clock, the scenery en route being greatly admired from the back platform. The party who occupied the the latter, was composed principally of non-clericals. They got to talking base-ball. The Rev. Studebaker was in the crowd. He soon opened fire, and those who heard him learned that he was not only an old ball player himself, but still an enthusiastic admirer of the game. At the colliery, exploration parties visited the dirt banks, breakers, and the mouth of one of the slopes. Some of the more venturesome wanted to go inside. The ladies were unanimously in favor of this. The arrangements were finally completed. Cars were procured and the 'locy' took some thirty into the tunnel to the foot of the walking way, which was climbed in good order. The solidity of the roof rock was a wonder and admiration. The sights were very enjoyable, and the return trip, via the Mine Hill road, was not the least interesting. The lunch basket was discussed at this time with as much satisfaction as any part of the trip. A quartette occupied one car and delighted the other passengers with their melodies. The knowledge gained on the trip will be of much service to all, while the pleasure of it was a fitting climax to the work of the week.

SUPPLY OF PORT CARBON.

On the 10th of November, 1882, at the solicitation of the Port Carbon Lutheran Congregation, the writer consented to supply them with preaching, for a season, giving them one service every other Sabbath in the afternoon. This was as much as they had been accustomed to for years. Although the request of Conference had been coupled with the appeal of the congregation, and the full consent of Council had been given to this step, we felt from the first the disadvantage to the work *here*, of an enforced absence of the pastor at such frequently recurring intervals. Yet the needs of a worthy people constrained us to continue until January 17th, 1886. In that interval they were relieved of some $300 of debt and made improvements to their Church property amounting to $600.

The congregation is unfortunately situated — far away from the central part of the town, and, with such occasional services, could not expect a rapid growth. Still we were enabled to do something for them — having found a membership of but Thirty-Two and adding Twenty-Eight. The record of our pastorate upon their book is as follows : —

RECEPTIONS.
IN 1883.

Robert L. Biebelheimer, Miss Lillie May Crouse, Miss Phoebe Krebs, Miss Carrie Koppf, Thomas Mellington, Miss Lena Shoean, Miss Lena Zerbey.

IN 1885.

Mrs. J. Eisenach, Miss Etta A. Fricke, Miss Gussie S. Fricke, Mrs. Sarah Hilbert, Miss Emma J. Hilbert, Henry William Hummel, Miss Rose Hummel, Mrs. Albert Krebs, Mrs. Wm. Krebs, John Jacob Krebs, Mrs. T. Mellington, Mrs. Harriet Rummel, Miss Mary E. Rummel, Miss Laura A. Rummel, Miss Clara J. Rummel, Philip Shoean, Miss Charlotte Shoean, Mrs. C. Snyder, Mrs. Samuel Tiley, Albert Traynor, James E. Wilson.

BAPTISMS.

IN 1883.

Ida Amelia Runkle, Eva Marion Auer, Lewis Arthur Hain, Joseph S. Harron Mary L. Simpson, Carrie M. Gellinger.

IN 1885.

Ida G. Simpson, Emma Louise Stokes, Elenora May Brown, George Edward Tiley, Oscar E. Rummel, Walter R Rummel, Herbert E. Rummel, Freddie C. Bomm.

FUNERALS.

Joseph Smith, Mrs. C. Zerbey, Mrs. Sarah Hilbert.

Several months after we ceased to supply this congregation, they felt able, with assistance of $200 from Conference for one year, to attempt to sustain a pastor of their own. They are still supporting him though Conference is no longer giving aid.

CHRISTMAS, 1882.

The Chronicle of December 26th thus describes our services : "Yesterday morning the Sunday School children of the English Lutheran Church had a very pleasant time. The auditorium was very handsomely decorated. A gilt bell was suspended from the centre of the ceiling, with festoons of evergreen extending to the corners of the room. Two large Christmas trees arose, one on either side of the pulpit, glistening in silver sheen, and were surrounded with piles of satchels of elegant candy. About 456 of the latter were distributed to the children, who in turn presented to the teachers many handsome tokens of affection. The Choir sang very prettily and the responses by the school were very effective. The occasion was one of the most joyous in the history of the School."

PAYMENT OF DEBT.

On the 23rd of February, 1883, the pastor had the pleasure of accompanying the Trustees to the Court House and witnessing the cancellation of a mortgage of $2,000. which was resting upon the Church when he came. It will always be interesting to our people to remember, and may be satisfying to the general reader to know, how this amount was secured.

As early as the Sixth of December, 1880, a special meeting of the Church Council was held, to devise means for liquidating this indebtedness. It was agreed "That we prepare petitions and present them to the members of the congregation for specified weekly contributions from them *until the debt should be paid,* the signers, in each instance, to designate whom they desire as collector, and the one suggested to hand the petition, with signatures, no later than the 26th instant, to either brother E. L Orwig, Daniel DeFrehn or J. H. Helwig," a committee then appointed, and authorized to carry into effect the plan stated.

On the 6th of January, 1881, at regular Council meeting, it appeared that these brethren had met with so little response to their suggestion that they had become disheartened, and were disposed to abandon the attempt. The pastor did not feel so. He had thought the movement an excellent one from the start; he had endorsed it from the pulpit against the advice of some of the brethren, who wished him success, and feared that the possible failure of the experiment would compromise him if too closely identified with it. Reluctant to discard this advice, he yet had done so for the good that might ensue, nor was he willing now to see the effort dropped without a greater struggle for success. These are facts which Council will readily recall. He urged continued effort and secured the co-operation of a Committee more hopeful than the others. Books were prepared by them and placed in the hands of Collectors, who were at the time as follows:

COLLECTORS FOR THE SINKING FUND.

J. W. Bock, John Shum, W. H. Brown, Mrs. Albert Esterly, William Rosengarten, Tillie Fredericks, Joseph DeFrehn, Henry Hart, Laura Rosengarten, Katie Nagle, Mary Teter, Sallie Reed, Minnie Rishel, Ettie Conrad, Mrs. C. Smith, Calvin Wagner, Mrs. R. Reeser, Mrs. Wm. Bensinger, Harry Heller, Charles Wright, N. Brownmiller, Mrs. E. L. Orwig, Alice Jolley, Mrs. Britton, Mrs. Wagner, J. D. Rice, Mrs. C. H. Dengler, John Brownmiller, Charles Lord, and William R. Williams.

FUNDS SECURED.

In tracing the history of this, and all our financial efforts, the writer has availed himself of the Semi-Annual Reports of the congregation, and proceeds by stages according to the dates of their publication, upon April First and October First of each year.

By the First of April, 1881, the sum of $108.90 had been raised by these Sinking Fund Collectors. By the First of October, 1881, they added to their number Mrs. S. Beyerle, Paul Dengler, Dr. P. K. Filbert, J. H. Helwig, Mamie Heller, Sadie Heller, Lilla Loose, G. W. Mortimer, Laura Pflueger, Carrie Rosengarten, Nellie Rosengarten, and Henry Strohmeier, and placed in the hands of the Treasurer $234.74 more. This sum was now increased by the generous gift of $200 by brother James Matter of Scranton, and by $100 from the treasury of the Ladies' Mite Society, making an aggregate of $643.64.

APPEAL.

Desirous of securing as much as possible by our first year's effort, the following appeal was then addressed to the people:

M . . . .

It is thought that the Collectors of the Sinking Fund will raise about $500 in the present year.

The Ladies' Mite Society has contributed $100 in this direction. Mr. J. Matter of Scranton, an absent member, has given $200 more. This will give us, for the year, about $800 upon our debt of $2,000.

Is it not worth while to endeavor to reach the round $1000 since we will come so near it ?

It can easily be done, if each family in the congregation will give something, *according to ability*, above what has already been given or promised.

If you are able and willing to give something for this purpose by the First of January, 1882, please notify me at once of the amount, in the blank below, enclosing this paper, thus filled out, in the accompanying envelope.

E. G. HAY, Pastor.

I promise to give, at the time mentioned $ . . . . . .

M   . . . .

RESPONSES.

Responses came, in the envelopes which had accompanied the above appeal, from Mrs. L. Beyerle, Mrs. A. Betz, Mrs. J. A. Bowen, L. S. Boner, Mrs. R. Cotton, Mrs. C. Dimmick, Mrs. J. D. Detrick, Lou. Detrick, A Friend, Mrs. J. E. Fredericks, Sarah Foltz, Mrs. R. Fernsler, Edward Fox, Mrs. Edward Fox, Elias Faust, Charles Fleck, Amelia Gallagher, Mrs. E. Garnsey, Earnest Gross, Annie Goldsmith, William Haring, Mrs. L. Heller, Henry Hart, John Hart, Sarah Haller, Martha Hadesty, Mrs. J. Hower, John Hollenbach, Mrs. M. Jones, Alma Jones, Nicholas Kemp, Charles Kershner, Minnie Kurtz, Mrs. W. Lorriman, S. B. Morgan, Mrs. F. Miller, Mrs. John Miller, Mrs. Mary Miller, Mrs. J. G. Miller, C. Mader, F. Marguarth, M. H. Nagle, Mrs. E. Nagle, Ellen Nagle, Philip Nagle, Byron Phillips, Mrs. Byron Phillips, Allen Paul, G. M. Rishel. Mrs. S. Steinbach, Frederick Spaecht, Emily P. Snyder, Mrs. H. Smith, Annie Simmons, Mrs. Wm. Saylor, Wilson Swartz, John Teter, Ellie Wildermuth, Joseph Yost, Mrs. L. Bocam and George Rishel.

These amounts, together with the gatherings of the Collectors already mentioned, among whom in this interval and afterwards, was Irvin Esterly, reached by the First of April, 1882, the sum of $347.74, giving us a total very near the $1000.00 at which we had aimed, or $991.38 in all.

Prior to this, however, in the month of January, 1882, we paid $800 upon the mortgage, all that we could prevail on Mrs. Lins to accept at the time. The moneys collected were intended to meet the principal only of our indebtedness, and we so provided, meanwhile, for the interest, that only at this time did we use any of these funds to meet it. The payment of $800 upon the mortgage, the printing and mailing of the above "appeal" and the payment of $25 upon interest, left a balance on hand, April 1st, 1882, of $162.23.

Miss Jennie Goldsmith and Miss Martha Hadesty appeared with the Collectors in the next six months, and on the First of October, 1882, $150.17 more had been gathered together, or a total, with the balance from April, of $312.40.

Prior to the 23rd of February, 1883, $174.37 additional was secured by the Collectors, and $226.00, the proceeds of an Oyster Supper, held January 24th and 25th, 1883, had been given to this fund, giving us $712.77 in hand.

CONCURRENT EFFORT.

As far back as May, 1882, almost immediately after the payment of the first $800 of the mortgage, the pastor had called a special meeting of the Council and offered the following, which was unanimously adopted:

"Whereas, There is now resting upon the English Lutheran Church of Pottsville, a debt of $1200.00, which it is highly desirable to liquidate by the Sixth of February, 1883, therefore,

Resolved, That we, the Council of the aforesaid Church, being assembled in special meeting this 11th day of May, 1882, do unanimously agree,

First, That the time has arrived when it is expedient to make a special effort to provide for the liquidation of said debt within the specified time.

Second, That the Pastor having volunteered to endeavor to secure the amount by personally requesting contributions to that end from all parts of the congregation, over and above what they have already pledged themselves to do through the Sinking Fund — said pledges to be payable by the First of January, 1883 — we accept the proposition.

Third, That, in the prosecution of this work, he shall choose such time in the near future as he deems suitable, and that he may depend upon us for our assistance to the full extent of our ability."

RESULT.

The result of this effort had been the securing, before the 23rd of February, 1883, of $427.75, which, with the $712.77 above, amounted, on that date, to $1140.52.

The Young People's Sociable now came forward with a donation of $140.04, giving us a total of $1280.56, with which, upon the

Twenty-Third of February, 1883, we paid all remaining interest, and cancelled the mortgage of $1200.00.

EASTER.

On Easter Sabbath, March 25th, 1883, Sixteen persons were admitted into membership with our Church. Two others were received during the year.

PASTOR'S SALARY RAISED.

At a congregational meeting held May 13th, 1883, at the close of the regular services, the salary of the Pastor was raised from $600 to $800, to take effect from the First of April, and the Church assumed, for the future, the payment of the water-rent, $19.60 per annum. It is needless for the writer to add that the kindness of the congregation was highly appreciated.

OUR LUTHER CELEBRATION, NOVEMBER 10TH, 1883.

DESCRIBED BY LOCAL PAPERS.

"The year 1883 will be remembered as an important one in the closing years of the nineteenth century, as commemorating the birth of the great German preacher and reformer, an event which occurred on the 10th day of November, 1483. The various Lutheran Synods in this and other States have recommended the setting apart of one day by the separate congregations of that denomination or by the union of the Churches of one or more Counties. In conformity with this recommendation, commemorative services have already been held in various parts of the State. In this County a large celebration was recently held at East Mahanoy Junction, but the location could not be conveniently reached by a large proportion of the Lutheran congregations of the County. It was therefore deemed advisable to hold a celebration at the County Seat. The matter was taken in hand by committees from the English and German congregations of Pottsville, and invitations were extended to all the Churches in the County, and to convenient congregations in adjoining Counties to participate. Yesterday was the day set apart for these services. It was originally intended to hold them in Railway Park, but the weather was so inauspicious that the committee thought it best to take the Academy. The day turned out so pleasant, however, that after holding the morning services in the Academy, it was concluded to spend the afternoon in the park.

There were few Churches in the County that were not represented, and some sent large delegations. From Ashland and the Eastern end of the County there was a good representation, and from the West end about one hundred and fifty. These representations were met at the depots by a committee and escorted to the English Lutheran Church, on Market street. About 10 o'clock they formed into line and marched down to the Academy of Music in the following order :

Third Brigade Band.
Rev. Hinterleitner and visiting ministers.
Committee.
Sunday School.
Choir.
Congregation.
Rev. Hay and visiting ministers.
Committee.
Sunday School.
Choir.
Congregation.

At a few minutes past 10 o'clock the exercises were opened by a voluntary by the band, which was followed by a hymn by the united choirs of the English and German Churches. This company of singers was under the leadership of Dr. Filbert and A. D. Kopp, while Misses Emma Krebs and Aurelia Loose performed at the organ.

A fervent prayer was offered by Rev. E. S. Henry, of Pinegrove, after which the German hymn, "*Erhalt uns deine Lehre,*" was sung by the entire audience.

Rev. J. Weishans, of Philadelphia, was then introduced. He spoke in German, taking as his theme "Luther Lives."

The address of Rev. Weishans was unintelligible to the reporter, but it was pronounced by the best German scholars present as one of the finest discourses they ever listened to. Rev. Weishans is one of the best German scholars in the country, and one of the leading divines in the Lutheran Church. While his theme on this occasion is suggestive of his train of thought, it was a source of regret to his English hearers that they could not understand him.

At the conclusion of Rev. Weishans' address, the English hymn, "Before Jehovah's Awful Throne," was sung by the entire audience. This was followed with a selection by the band entitled "*Volkslieder Klænge.*"

Rev. Dr. J. Fry, of Reading, was then introduced.

DR. FRY'S ADDRESS :

He said that the occasion which had brought the audience together was no ordinary one, but one such as the world seldom witnesses—the commemoration of the four hundredth anniversary of the birth of one of the greatest men the world has ever known. These services were not intended to canonize a human being. They were simply intended to do honor to the memory of a great and good man, and to recount the services he has rendered to human kind. For the same reason that the American people celebrated the birthday of the Father of his Country, did the Protestant world commemorate the birth of Martin Luther. The one was honored for his heroic services in the cause of civil liberty, the other for his courageous and successful battle for religious liberty. He believed that God raised up men for special purposes. That Martin Luther was a special instrument in God's hands, no one could doubt. The Reverend gentleman then traced the various steps in the career of Martin Luther, from his birth up to the time he became the leader in the Reformation. He tried to make the relative geographical position of the several towns connected with the life of Luther plain to his hearers by taking Pottsville as a centre, and making other towns in the State identical with those in which Luther lived and worked. The straightened circumstances of his parents; his insatiable thirst for knowledge; his abandonment of the law for the life of a recluse; his awakened conscience and investigation of the truth for himself; the promulgation of the results of his investigation; his arraignment, trial and persecutions; his firm and unalterable adherence to his convictions, and his final triumphs — all were briefly alluded to. If asked who Luther was, he would reply: 1. That he was a child of poverty, and as such was a counterpart of all great reformers. When God wants to raise the race, he doesn't take a man from the top, but from the bottom, that in lifting himself up he may be the better prepared to raise others. 2. He was a child of piety. He had the advantages of religious parental training. The parents' influence in forming the basis of a great and good life could not be overestimated. 3. He was a man of a vigorous constitution, and took pains to preserve it. Strong and healthy men were not necessarily good men; but a sound mind in a sound body might be put down as almost an absolute condition of success in any great work. In conclusion, the speaker said that, notwithstanding all opposition, the work started by Luther was still going on, and would continue to move forward until the grand consummation was reached.

"The name of Luther is known all over the world already, and there will be few Centennials of Luther's birth, before every tongue in every land will acknowledge as he did, that God alone can save."

Prayer was offered by Rev. J. H. Weber, of Ashland, after which a collection amounting to $50 was lifted. While the baskets were in circulation the band played "*Festlied, mit Chor.*" Then the battle hymn of Luther, *'Ein Feste Burg ist Unser Gott,'* was sung by the entire audience, accompanied by the Third Brigade Band. The hymn was printed both in German and English, so that all could join in its singing. The effect was grand, as the audience was composed of nearly a thousand persons.

The audience was then dismissed for the morning with the Benediction by Dr. Fry.

AFTERNOON EXERCISES.

It was 2.30 o'clock before the exercises were opened at Railway Park. The number of people present was much larger than at the Academy in the morning. The exercises were opened with a voluntary by the band, being a selection from Mendelssohn. The united choirs then sang 'All Hail the Power of Jesus Name,' at the conclusion of which Rev. W. Miller, of Shenandoah, offered up a prayer. An English hymn, 'I Love Thy Zion, Lord,' was sung by the entire audience with fine effect.

Rev. J. H. Weber, of Ashland, was then introduced.

REV. WEBER'S ADDRESS.

The theme of the speaker was 'The great work done by Martin Luther.' He said that after the lapse of four centuries, surrounded as we are with the incomparable blessings of civil and religious freedom, it was impossible for us to appreciate religious despotism, and consequently the value of Luther's work. He then briefly referred to the condition of the Church in Luther's time, and the evils charged by the Reformers upon the earthly head of the Church. The world was just beginning to emerge from the gloom of the dark ages, and Luther, he said, but grasped the reins of Progress that Providence seemed to have put in his hands. The hardships endured by Luther were particularly referred to. It was an easy matter, he said, for a soldier to fight the enemy when backed by the moral as well as the physical force of a community, but to stand *alone* in opposition to the whole religious, as well as civil powers of the government, required a courage that it is impossible in these times to appreciate. After briefly summarizing the work of Luther as comprehended in the success of his doctrines enunciated in the Augsburg Confession, the speaker closed with the hope that the memory of Luther would be preserved by his followers, not so much in eulogizing his deeds, as in living out his principles.

An English anthem was then sung by the choir—'Rejoice in the Lord'—followed by a selection by the band, and a hymn in German.

Rev. John Kuendig, of Reading, was introduced, who spoke briefly in German.

REV. KUENDIG'S ADDRESS.

The theme of the discourse was 'The Blessings Bequeathed by Luther.' His argument was that the success of Martin Luther involved more than mere religious franchises and tenets. That these were primarily the ends secured, but remotely the civil blessings which have not only crowned the Fatherland, but have spread into all countries where the seeds of Lutheran principles have been planted. The gentleman then showed the different ways in which this had been effected. He spoke forcibly and eloquently.

A very interesting part of the programme was the reading of an original poem, in German, by Rev. Thomas Duensing, of Tamaqua. The title of the poem was 'Luther's Grave.' After the reading of the poem the same gentleman offered a prayer, when the Reformation hymn was again sung by the whole audience, with accompaniment by the band. The exercises were closed with the Benediction by Rev. Daniel Sanner, of Tremont, followed by the Doxology.

The occasion was one of great interest and was certainly a successful and happy affair. The day could not have been more delightful nor all the circumstances attending the celebration more propitious.

MINISTERS PRESENT.

Among the ministers present were: Revs. E. G. Hay and G. A. Hinterleitner, Pottsville; J. H. Weber, Ashland; P. C. Croll, William Kuntz, Schuylkill Haven; E. S. Henry, Pinegrove; W. Miller, Shenandoah; Daniel Sanner, W. L. Heisler, Tremont; F. Weishans, Philadelphia; G. W. Guensch, Minersville; Dr. J. Fry, J. Kuendig, Reading; J. Reihsteiner, Mahanoy City; H. Wendel, St. Clair; Thomas Duensing, Tamaqua."

MEMORIAL DISCOURSE.

On Sunday morning, November 11th, a service was held, of which the Miners' Journal speaks as follows :—

"Services commemorative of the great work of the German Reformer were held in the English Lutheran Church of this place yesterday morning. The services were conducted by Rev. E. G. Hay, pastor. There was a large congregation present including many of other denominations.

After the preliminary services, Rev. Hay delivered an interesting discourse, reviewing the growth of Protestantism and sketching briefly the life of the Reformer. He said it was natural to hesitate in venturing upon the task of a fitting review of the Reformation, when intelligence upon the subject is within reach of every household. The followers of Luther, however, could not be too thoroughly acquainted with the character of the Reformer and the value of his labors. The work begun by Luther could only be carried on by men who were imbued with a like spirit and devotion. The character of Luther must therefore be analyzed, if we would understand the man. The first element in his character to which he desired to call attention was that *he was a man of prayer*. From his earliest childhood to his latest breath, this was a marked characteristic. It is said that Luther devoted at least three hours a day to prayer, and when he prayed, it was with an implicit faith in God's promises. He then quoted some examples of Luther's earnest appeals to God for help and deliverance. It was here that history, as it were, ' raised the veil of the sanctuary and disclosed to view the secret place whence strength and courage were imparted to this humble instrument in God's hands.' In the second place Luther was *studious*. It was no ignorant man whom God had selected to accomplish such wonders. God often, it is true, makes the foolish things of this world to confound the wise ; but he everywhere encourages and honors intelligence. The history of the Reformation, he said, showed that it was the ignorant who were fanatical ; the intelligent who stepped to the foreground in the march of progress. Luther was not a superficial student ; was not merely content to know what others had written and said, but as he studied the thoughts of others he weighed them in the balance of his own judgment. Where others had but taken off the surface, he delved to the bottom and brought up new discoveries from the mine of thought. Luther did not study to be consistent. No great mind which pursues a course of educational investigation for a long period will be found to be completely consistent in all its views. New revelations often necessitate the abandonment of previous opinions. But there are certain underlying principles as the ground work in every field of labor, and to these Luther was as true as the needle to the pole. His life was a continual exemplification of his belief. His was a religion of the heart, and he could not dissemble, nor avow one thing and practice another. Luther was also preeminently *a man of courage*. His stand before the Diet of Worms was a proof of this, and is generally referred to as one of the severest tests of the Reformer's courage. The speaker, however, cited other instances to show the moral and physical courage of Luther. But that feature of his life which explains and continually sustained all others, was his *faith*. This was strikingly exhibited in the Wartburg and elsewhere in the treatment of the divine Word, and in his constant consciousness of a divine protection and guidance. When about to venture forth from the Wartburg, he writes to the elector George : ' Be it known to your Highness that I am going to Wittenberg under a protection far higher than that of princes and electors.'

These outlines of the character of Luther were filled up with sketches in exemplification of each, and were highly interesting as well as instructive."

NEW PULPIT FURNITURE.

On the Sabbath just described a new and complete set of pulpit furniture was placed in the Church. The pastor had secured $194.-50, the amount needful for this, by personal solicitation. The following are those who contributed to this "very spontaneously," as the need was so manifest that all wanted to help. As we were then engaged in raising funds for a still larger object, the pastor stopped collecting when he had enough.

Mrs. A. M. Bannan, $5.00, Mrs. William Bensinger, $3.00, Mrs. L. Bocam, .50, Mrs. Mary Bock, $5.00, L. S. Boner, $10.00, Mrs. J. W. Bowen, $2.50, Mrs. Mary Buchanan, $5.00, Mrs. A. B. Cochran, $5.00, John Conrad, $2.00, Daniel DeFrehn, $2.00, George H. DeFrehn, $5.00, Mrs. R. Detrick, $3.00, Mrs. Albert Esterly, $2.50, Thomas J. Erdman, $5.00, Dr. P. K. Filbert, $10.00, Mrs. Edward Fox, $2.50, Mrs. J. E. Fredericks, $5.00, Thomas Geier, $10.00, Henry Hart, $2.00, E. G. Hay, $10.00, L. F. Heller, $2.50, J. H. Helwig, $10.00, Nathan Houser, $5.00, Mrs. Robert Howell, $1.00, Daniel M. Keller, $5.00, H. W. Kriner, $5.00, Mrs. Samuel Morgan, $5.00, G. W. Mortimer, $10.00, Mrs. Daniel Nagle, $5.00, Mrs. James Nagle, $5.00, Byron Phillips, $2.00, Mrs. R. Reeser, $5.00, Frank Roehrig, $2.00, Mrs. H. Rosengartên, $5.00, Harry S. Sterner, $10.00, John Teter, $5.00, William R. Williams, $10.00, Mrs. Martha Wolfinger, $2.00, Joseph Yost, $5.00.

The framework of the old sofa and chairs, rehabilitated, now grace the chancel of the Lutheran Mission Church at Shenandoah, Pa.; while the former pulpit is now used in the Lecture Room of our own Church.

ENVELOPE SYSTEM.

Upon the First of March, 1884, measures were taken to introduce, by April First, the beginning of our fiscal year, an Envelope System for the reception of money for Pastor's Salary and Current Expenses. Our former system it is needless to describe. It was doubtless serviceable, but we find the plan adopted at this juncture to work better and to be more convenient. Each member now receives in advance of each quarter, three envelopes to be used during its continuance, one on the First Sabbath of every month. They are placed on the collection plate, and a full report of all contributions is given in a Semi-Annual Report. The town is districted, and members of the Council see to the distribution of these envelopes among the people, and inquire into the reason of any delinquencies, reporting to the whole Council, quarterly, the condition of the districts under their charge. Annual subscriptions are taken upon pledge-cards sent out and returned with the envelope for the First Sunday in April.

Together with these envelopes is sent to each member every quarter another, in which a contribution for Missions is given upon Communion Sabbath. With proper urgency, which the best of systems require, this plan is as simple and effective as any of which we know.

FESTIVAL.

At Centennial Hall, on Wednesday and Thursday Evenings, March 5th and 6th, 1884, a Festival and Oyster Supper was conducted under the auspices of our Young People's Sociable, for the benefit of the Church. The proceeds were $226.00.

EASTER.

At our Easter Communion, April 13th, 1884, Thirteen persons were admitted to membership. Eight others were received during this year. Our evening services were appropriate to the day.

OUR PIPE ORGAN.

On Friday Evening, May 16th, 1884, a Sacred Concert was given in our Church. It was the occasion of the Opening of a large and beautiful Pipe Organ which had just been erected by the congregation. Of the character of the entertainment afforded those who attended it, as well as of the appearance, construction and location of the instrument, and the opinions of eminent judges as to its quality, we will permit another to speak. The Miners' Journal says, "The organ, without disparagement to any other instrument in the city, is as handsome as any in the County. It stands sixteen feet high to the top of the centre pipe, is ten feet three inches wide, and seven and a half feet deep. It has seventeen stops and five hundred and forty seven pipes. The bellows, instead of working with a mere lever, work with a lever and wheel. The case is solid walnut, and the pipes are of a superior metallic composition. The organ is placed to the right of the pulpit with the face fronting the congregation. The ornamental pipes are very handsome, and the eligible location of the instrument shows off their beauty to great advantage. It was built by Mr. Samuel Bohler, of Reading, and cost $1,225, all of which has been paid."

In a later issue the same writer remarks: "At the Organ Recital and Sacred Concert in the English Lutheran Church last night, the musical qualities of the new instrument were tested. For this purpose some of the best musicians in the State were invited to be present, among the number Profs. Wood, of Philadelphia, and Becker and Alexander of Pottsville. They were all loud in their praises of the general excellence of the organ. The concert was opened by Prof. H. A. Becker with a 'Voluntaire and Grand Offertoire,' which was executed in a masterly manner. The 'Grand March' (Schubert,) and the 'Overture to William Tell,' by Prof. Wood are skillful performances, in which the abilities of the distinguished musician are shown to perfection. 'A Sabbath Evening's Reverie.' by Prof. J. I. Alexander, was a beautiful collection of sacred melodies which captivated the house. The entire programme included twelve numbers and occupied about two hours time. It was a period very delightfully spent by all present."

ORGAN DEDICATION.

On Sunday, the Twenty-Fifth of June, Rev. Doctor Conrad of Philadelphia preached a sermon to the congregation upon the subject of Sacred Praise and then set apart the organ from all secular and profane uses, dedicating it exclusively to the service of song in the house of the Lord.

The services of the day are thus described in a local paper. "Special services were held in the English Lutheran Church yesterday, Dr. F. W. Conrad, of Philadelphia, editor of the *Lutheran Observer*, dedicating the new organ in the morning and preaching to large audiences both then and at night. His subject in the morning was 'Sacred Praise,' his remarks being based upon Eph. 5: 19, " Speaking to yourselves in psalms and hymns and spiritual songs, singing and making melody in your heart to the Lord." The doctor is a most able and fluent speaker, and the brief outlines appended can give but a faint idea of the subject matter presented. On the subject of Sacred Praise he said: 'God has conferred the capacity of praise upon every rational creature. It is a talent which each is bound to cultivate and for whose neglect or perversion he is responsible. The purpose for which this capacity is bestowed is to make melody in our hearts unto the Lord, to enable us to give suitable expressions of the gratitude awakened by his goodness. There is necessity that we attach due importance to both the *letter* and *spirit* of sacred praise. Each has at times been exalted at the expense of the other. After speaking at length of the *power* of music — its essence and manifestations — the objections that have at times been raised against instrumental music as an accompaniment to sacred praise, were successively presented and answered — the scriptural arguments for its use held up and the position of the Lutheran

Church commended, in that she retained it from the very first as over against the Anabaptists and others. In conclusion the doctor emphasized the following facts: That sacred praise in the Christian Church belongs to the free development of her system of worship. That it has proved a barrier to the propagation of heresy and a promoter of sound orthodoxy. That through it the sanctification and progress of the Church has been ever advanced. That its continuance is one of the chief employments of heaven for the promotion of its bliss and glory.'

At the evening service the Doctor took his text from 1 Timothy, 6: 13, 14 "I give thee charge in the sight of God, who quickeneth all things, and before Christ Jesus, who before Pontius Pilate witnessed a good confession, that thou keep this commandment without spot, unrebukable, until the appearing of our Lord Jesus Christ."

'Luther and the Reformers as Confessors of the Truth' was the theme presented. After dwelling upon the need of confessions, both ordinary and extraordinary, it was asserted of Luther and his coadjutors in the time of the Reformation: That they made the Scriptures the ultimate umpire in the decision of all religious questions; declared the true principles of Protestantism, involving the right of private judgment and liberty of conscience; restored justification by faith alone to its central position in the Gospel of Christ; reformulated the orthodox system of theology; adopted conservative principles and methods of reform, and laid down an ecumenical basis upon which the true unity of the Church and Christian fellowship could be safely maintained. In conclusion, it was said that we are called upon to recognize the hand of God in raising up and qualifying Luther and the Reformers for the accomplishment of the Reformation. To cherish their memory and imitate their example, to carry forward the work which they inaugurated and prosecuted. The exalted position and extensive influence which the Augsburg Confession exerted upon the creeds of the Reformation and orthodox Protestantism was dwelt upon with great clearness, and the discourse concluded by apt and stirring quotations in exaltation of the attainments and work of Luther, from a host of the most distinguished critics, historians, divines and statesmen."

THE PURCHASE MONEY.

The cost of our Organ has been given as $1,225. But the expense of its erection upon a raised platform upon the right of the pulpit, and alterations in connection therewith, aggregated $1440.73. How this amount was secured so soon after the liquidation of the debt, it will now please us to recall.

Before the actual payment of the last installment on the debt, but after they saw they had secured enough to meet it, Council passed, on the First of February, 1883, a series of resolutions, thanking all whose efforts had conspired to that result, and determining to continue the Sinking Fund with a view to obtain money for the purchase of an Organ.

By October First, 1883, the sum of $85.00 had been raised in this way.

By April 1st, 1884, this sum had increased to $384.08; the Port Carbon Church had paid, for our former organ, $100; the Sunday-School had contributed $100; the Ladies' Mite Society, $47.65; and the Young People's Sociable, $717.31; a total of $1349.04, and this despite the $194.50 secured in the same interval for Pulpit Furniture. This gave us more than was needful to pay for the Organ itself, and before our next, or October Report appeared, all expense incurred in its erection had been met, leaving a balance in the Sinking Fund.

And, indeed, before that date, we were already thinking of other needful things and taking measures to secure them.

AN APPEAL

Was sent forth to all our members as early as the close of September, 1884, which read as follows:

POTTSVILLE, PA., September 25th, 1884.

Dear Friend and Member of the English Lutheran Church:

We should be thankful that God has thus far blessed our united efforts for the improvement of our condition as a congregation, as seen in the payment of our debt and the securing of an organ — so helpful in our service of praise. Yet it needs but a glance to see that other improvements, such as frescoing, painting, and re-carpeting, are still needed. Let me ask of you a contribution toward this purpose, *to be paid into my hands on or before the first of January,* 1885.

Please name the amount you are willing to give upon the enclosed card, signing it when thus filled out, *and placing it in the collection basket within two weeks,* in the accompanying envelope. Each member of the congregation has been thus addressed. With such sacrifices God is well pleased.

Your affectionate pastor,

F. G. HAY.

ANOTHER OYSTER SUPPER.

In City Armory Hall, on Wednesday and Thursday Evenings, November 12th and 13th, 1884, our capacity for the enjoyment of the toothsome bivalve again was tested, and right merrily did we partake of the feast the Young People's Sociable had prepared. The proceeds seem to have been $179.22.

CHRISTMAS, 1884.

A pleasant service, consisting of Responsive Readings, Singing and Recitations, was held by our School upon Christmas evening. The Scholars were indulged also in candies, at an outlay of $80.

The Appeal above quoted, which was measurably' successful, shows the purposes entertained at the time, but other objects of equal worthiness now claimed our attention While unable to secure sufficient, at this juncture, to purchase *great* improvements, we were enabled before long to gain some lesser ones, which were just as badly needed.

STAINED GLASS WINDOWS

Were secured and inserted, prior to our Easter Service in 1885, the following year. This was purely the result of a personal effort upon the part of the pastor. He felt that ere long the entire interior would need renovation and feared that there might be some hesitation *then* to make the effort so thorough as to include the windows. If this could but be done in advance, he felt that a substantial gain would be made. In less than two weeks the amount needful — $397.02 — was secured. The following is the list of those who contributed toward the windows, and of those who responded to the September "Appeal."

Mr. Geo. C. Arbogast, $1.00, Mrs. Geo. C. Arbogast, $1.00, Mrs. C. Bensinger, $3.00, Mrs. Sarah Beyerle, $5.00, Mrs. L. Bocam, $2.00, William Bock, $27.35, L. S. Boner, $10.00, Mrs. Jas. Bowen, $5.00, Daniel DeFrehn, $27.35, Joseph DeFrehn, $27.35, Geo. H. Dentzer, $1.00, Mrs. C. Dimmick, $2.00, Mrs. J. Ebert, .50, Mrs. E. Fredericks, Mrs. Severn and John Wolfinger, $27.35, Mrs. K. Eisenhuth. $1.00, Daniel Esterly, $1.00, Miss Mary Faus, $3.00, Dr. P. K. Filbert, $27.35, Edward Fox, $30.00, Miss Amelia Gallagher, $3.00, Mrs. C. Gilbert, $1.00, Wm. H. Haring, $2.00, Hart (family) $27.35, E. G. Hay, $5.00, L. F. Heller, $4.00, Harry Heller, $1.00, J. H. Helwig, $5.00, Mrs. S. E. Holt, $1.00, Miss Lilla V. Loose, $5.00, Mrs. Henry Lord, $1.00, Miss Carrie Lord, $1.00, Mrs. Eliza Miller, $1.00, Geo. W. Mortimer, $27.35, Miss Ellen Nagle, $1.00, Mrs. Elizabeth Nagle, $6.00, Miss Katie Nagle, $5.00, Allen Paul, $2.00, Byron Phillips, $3.00, Mrs. R. Reeser, $27.35, Rishel (family) $27.35, Miss Charlotte Schrader, $1.00, Miss Louise Schrader, $1.00, Miss Alma Seitzinger, $2.00, I. H. Severn, .50, Miss Katie Snyder, $1.00, Miss Emily P. Snyder, $1.00, H. S. Sterner, $10.00, Allen Sterner, $1.00, Mrs. Val. Stichter, $5.00, John Teter, $27.35, J. H. Uhler, $5.00, Wm. R. Williams, $37.35, Cash, $1.00. Total, $451.85.

The Windows bear the following worthy names:—

Mrs. William Bock, Lewis Reeser, Mrs. Martha Wolfinger, Henry Hart, John Teter, Nicholas Brownmiller, G. W. Mortimer, Jacob D. Rice, Mrs. Albert Esterly, Mrs. Daniel DeFrehn, William R. Williams, George Rishel and Rev. Daniel Steck, D. D. The latter name is upon the large central window in the Church-front, and was contributed by his friends in the congregation. Another window, partially concealed from view by the Organ, bears simply the inscription, 1885, the year of insertion.

EASTER, 1885.

At our Easter Communion, April 5th, 1885, Twenty Eight new members were received. Seventeen others were admitted during the year. At this service the present practice was introduced, of using cards as certificates of participation in the Sacrament. Due care had always been taken to secure, for the record, the names of communicants, but the former plan to accomplish this, the distribution of pencils and papers beforehand in the pews, was needlessly troublesome.

The cards now introduced are sent to each member with his envelopes, bearing his name and, as they can be returned, after the record is made, in advance of the next quarterly communion, need only occasionally be renewed when mislaid or accidentally destroyed.

The services of this day were thus described by the local press:—

"Easter Sunday was of more than ordinary interest to the members of the English Lutheran Church of which Rev. E. G. Hay is pastor. There was an unusually large attendance at communion. The decorations were elaborate and beautiful. The morning text was from Rom. 5: 10: ' If, when we were enemies, we were reconciled unto God by the death of his Son, much more, being reconciled, we shall be saved by his life.' The pastor spoke *first* of *God's willingness to save* those already reconciled, dividing the thought of the Apostle as follows: 1. If God so love us as to *begin* the work of salvation in our hearts, we may be assured he is willing to *complete* it. 2. If he began it while we were *enemies*, he is surely willing to complete it *since our enmity is slain and we are his friends.* 3. If he began it by *great sacrifices*, he is certainly willing to complete it since the full price of our salvation has been paid, and there remaineth *no more sacrifice* for sin. 4. If Christ in apparent *weakness and defeat* made possible the beginnings of Christian life, His present renewed *life of victory and power* is sufficient pledge that its completion is possible.

He spoke *secondly* of *God's agency in saving* the reconciled — the present life of Christ. ' We shall be saved by his life.' We have a *living* Saviour, and through His life only our salvation shall be completed.

1. We advance in our love to God by communion with Christ. 2. We advance in victory over sin — by the strength derived from Christ who dwelleth in us. 3. We shall triumph over death through Him — 'Because He lives we shall live also.' 4. We shall be welcomed into heaven by the voice of Him who shall be our Judge — 'Who liveth and was dead and is alive forevermore.'

In conclusion — 1. If reconciled and lost we alone are responsible. God is willing to save. 2. To reject such a salvation stamps the soul with the stigma of unspeakable folly.

The services at the English Lutheran Church last evening were of special interest. The Sunday School was present in a body, and despite the distracting influence of the fire alarm a few moments before service, the Church was filled. The service was conducted by the pastor, and consisted of an address on the subject of the day's lesson by Mr. George Rishel, Assistant Superintendent, a short explanation of a Scripture promise by the pastor, who wrote his several illustrative statements on the blackboard as he spoke, and the repetition of a number of God's promises by the various classes of the school. These exercises were interspersed with frequent singing by the school and the offering of brief prayers, and were heartily enjoyed by all present."

A Tin Roof

Was ordered as early as the 25th of April in this same year and paid for in full in the month of July. It cost $260.08.

Our Insurance.

Some time previous to this, longer indeed than the writer cares to acknowledge, our insurance upon Church and Parsonage had expired. Some few were none too heartily in favor of its renewal, pressed as we were for outlay in so many other directions. We could not feel perfectly at ease in this state, however; and when, during the early part of June, 1885, a series of alarming fires in quick succession had stirred the fears of the people, moved forward in the matter at once and at the cost of $88, gladly contributed, insured our entire property for three years to the extent of $10,000.

Renovation Of Audience Chamber.

At the meeting of Council, November 5th, 1885, it was decided to proceed with the refurnishing of the audience room, and a committee of four, of which the pastor was Chairman, was appointed to devise all necessary means to accomplish it. They were also given power to add to their number at discretion. The pastor appointed brothers H. W. Kriner, G. M. Rishel and J. H. Helwig, and the committee afterwards asked the co-operation of brothers H. S. Sterner and J. C. Adcock. A canvass of the congregation was made at once and at the next regular meeting of Council a subscription of $725 was reported as already secured. The payment of these subscriptions was requested by the canvassers in five monthly installments, for which envelopes, bearing the names respectively of the months November, December, January, February and March, were placed in the hands of subscribers.

CHRISTMAS, 1885.

The anniversary of this day was celebrated by suitable exercises by the Sunday-School. They rendered a printed Service entitled Christmas Greeting.

PRESS DESCRIPTIONS OF IMPROVEMENTS.

Concerning the renovation attempted, as it approached its completion, in March, 1886, one of the local papers states:—

"The pastor, Rev. E. G. Hay, and the officials of the English Lutheran Church, are to be congratulated upon the spirit of improvement which they have infused into the congregation. We have been noticing periodically some addition to the Church paraphernalia. Some time ago it was a new organ and pulpit furniture; later, handsome stained glass windows were put in, and now they are about completing more extensive improvements, which will make the English Lutheran Church edifice one of the most inviting in town. The gallery, which extended across the rear end of the room, has been removed, new walnut pews have been put in, the walls have been re-papered, and a Brussels carpet will complete the renovation. The auditorium will be re-opened for service on Sunday March 28th, with appropriate ceremonies. Rev. J. H. Menges, pastor of Grace Lutheran Church, West Philadelphia, will preach on the occasion."

Another expresses itself thus:

"The main audience room of the English Lutheran Church has been greatly improved by the removal of the gallery, which extended across the rear. The old pews have also been taken out and new and graceful pews of walnut and oak substituted in their place. The walls and ceiling have been papered in tasteful fresco designs, and the floor is being covered with a handsome brussels carpet. These new improvements, in connection with the stained-glass windows, which were put in last spring, and the new organ which stands to the right of the pulpit, are certainly beautiful and harmonious in design and color, and have converted the Lutheran Church into one of the most pleasant and handsome auditoriums in town. Extensive improvements have also been made in the lower story of the Church, in which rooms for the Infant School and the Bible class have been set apart. The pastor is to be congratulated on the successful completion of his plans of Church improvement; and in those congratulations the entire community may join, for the adornment of the Church is a matter in which every citizen may feel a just pride."

As is usually the case in such efforts, the Committee attempted considerably more than they had thought of at the beginning, but did so in the belief that the congregation would sustain them. In one item, indeed, the alterations made in the pews, they obtained the sanction of a special congregational meeting. As the day of Re-Opening approached, it was found that at least $800 more than that which was already subscribed would be needed to cancel all obligations assumed. But the pastor had his eye on the man for the occasion, and the sequel reveals that his confidence was not misplaced. The improvements, above alluded to, in the lower story of the Church, consisted of re-papering handsomely the chamber originally used by the Infant Department. A portion of it on the West Side had, shortly before this, been separated by glazed doors from the remainder — sufficient in size for the actual needs of the department at this time. This room was now needed by the class of brother Sterner, and a similar one was formed on the East Side by the erection of other doors, where the Infant Department has since been accommodated. Thus what was originally one large room was converted into two, leaving an intervening hall extending from the vestibule to the main Sabbath-School room. Half the expense of papering these rooms was met by brother Sterner's Class and half by the Ladies' Mite Society.

RE-DEDICATION.

According to announcements duly made, Rev. J. H. Menges assisted us at the Reopening of our audience Chamber on Sunday March 28th, 1886. Another has thus described, in one of our local papers, the occurrences of the day:

"Yesterday was a joyous day for Pastor Hay and his English Lutheran congregation, at their house of worship on Garfield Square. The late renovation and general improvement of the interior renders this one of the neatest, most comfortable and attractive Church edifices of its dimensions in this section of the State, a fact which people of other congregations readily admit. Yesterday was the day set apart for its Re-dedication, and as a matter of course the members of the congregation were out in full force and hundreds of outsiders sought admission to the various services, but some were necessarily disappointed on account of lack of room for so many people. At the morning service Rev. J. H. Menges, pastor of Grace Lutheran Church, West Philadelphia, occupied the pulpit and delivered a most interesting discourse appropriate to the occasion, his text being from Haggai 2 : 9, 'The glory of this latter house shall be greater than of the former, saith the Lord of Hosts.' The deductions were finely drawn and the sermon so compactly put together that no synopsis we might make would do the eloquent divine justice, and we regret not being able to give it in its entirety.

Referring to the beautiful structure in which the congregation was then worshiping, he gave them the closing application of the text — which was that there was nothing detracted so much from the beauty of God's house as a heavy incumbrance, and he did not want to see this structure defaced by any such unsightly object. He proposed therefore to raise in the audience the sum of eight hundred dollars, which would cancel every cent of obligation. After a short and pleasant speech on the subject, by which the congregation was wrought up to a liberal frame of mind, when the cash and subscriptions were counted it was found that every cent of indebtedness was extinguished. The preacher was greatly pleased. Rev. Hay looked as if he was spending the happiest day of his life, and the congregation seemed delighted. The whole improvement cost over $1,500.

At half-past three in the afternoon, in order that the children of the Church might have their especial share in the events of the day, a service was held for their benefit, at which appropriate addresses were made by Rev. J. Wesley Sullivan, Rev. J. H. Menges, Rev. A. R. Bartholomew, Rev. Dr. Lawson and Rev. P. C. Croll. The attendance was large and the young folks enjoyed the occasion very much.

At the evening service Rev. J. H. Menges again occupied the pulpit, delivering another interesting sermon, taking for his text, 'Oh, Lord, thou son of David, have mercy on me,' the case of the woman pleading for the restoration of her child. The power of prayer was the theme of the discourse, and it was listened to with great delight and profit by the large congregation.

At the conclusion Rev. E. G. Hay, pastor, performed the dedicatory service, which closed one of the most auspicious days in the history of this old and popular house of worship, which through the energy of its pastor and the generosity of its congregation sets out upon a new career of usefulness in the community."

SUNDAY-SCHOOL CONVENTION.

On Monday and Tuesday, March 29th and 30th, the Schuylkill District Sunday-School Convention of Lebanon Conference convened in our Church, and another friendly voice is heard to say:

"The Lutherans, of this city, have been enjoying quite a revival season in increased interest in their Church and Sunday-School affairs the past three days. The Re-Dedication of their handsome Church on Sunday was an event in which every Lutheran took great delight, and the following of the session of the Schuylkill County Lutheran Sunday-School Convention in the Church which took place yesterday and today was another event successful in every particular. May this Church go on indefinitely on the tide of prosperity and usefulness which appears to have beset it!"

EASTER, APRIL 25TH, 1886.

Concerning these services the Chronicle states:—"At the English Lutheran Church, Rev. C. A. Hay, D. D., addressed the communicants, and the pastor received Thirty-Three new members. At the morning service Seventy-One Dollars were contributed for Missions: At the evening service between Eight Hundred and One Thousand people were present. Mrs. George Rishel presided at the organ, and was assisted by a Cornetist. The Sunday-School, and especially the Infant Class, acquitted themselves with much credit.

Rev. Dr. Hay addressed the Sunday-School at this service. A collection of nearly $30 was lifted to defray, in part, the cost of One Hundred and Seventy-Five copies of "The Augsburg Songs" just issued by their Publication House and ordered by the School; while the service entitled 'Chimes of the Resurrection' was rendered with fine effect by the scholars."

Besides the admissions to membership in the morning we were pleased to receive Fifteen others during the year.

A FESTIVAL AND OYSTER SUPPER

Held by the Young People's Literary Society in Centennial Hall on the 17th and 18th of November, for the benefit of Church and Sabbath School secured over $200.

THANKSGIVING DAY.

On the morning of Thursday, November 25th, 1886, twelve of our sixteen protestant congregations united in a common service of thanksgiving. The sermon was preached by the writer, from Psalm 147 : 20. "He hath not dealt so with any nation." In the evening Rev. J. H. Menges delivered a lecture on "Blunders," in our English Lutheran Zion, to a full house.

VISIT OF THE SECRETARIES.

On the 21st of November our pulpit was filled in the morning by the Rev. J. C. Zimmerman of York, Pa., the Secretary of the Board of Church Extension of the General Synod, and in the evening our people had the opportunity of hearing also the Rev. J. A. Clutz, Secretary of the General Synod's Board of Home Missions. A special meeting of the Sabbath-School in the main audience chamber in the afternoon was also addressed by both of these brethren. Their visit is remembered with pleasure by all. It was followed up by the pastor with an effort to circulate the "Missionary Journal," and to organize a Women's Missionary Society. Of the former, 120 copies were put in circulation within the month. The latter attempt also was successful, an organization having been effected upon the First of December.

OUR CHURCH PAPER—THE ENGLISH LUTHERAN.

At Council Meeting on the Fifth of December, 1886, on motion of brother J. H. Helwig, a committee of two were appointed to co-operate with the pastor in making arrangements for the publication of a monthly paper in the interest of the Church. Said committee consisted of brothers J. H. Helwig and J. C. Adcock. The first issue appeared in the same month under the title of The English Lutheran. A twelve page pamphlet, with an issue of five hundred copies at first, it soon became sixteen pages, with a circulation of eight hundred copies monthly. Sent through the Sunday-School and in other ways into every family belonging to the congregation or represented in the School, it is a great help in many ways in the work of the Church. It is edited by the pastor, and conducted without any expense whatever to the Church. Our only wonder now is how we ever did without it.

CHRISTMAS, 1886.

Of our services on this occasion the Chronicle remarks:

" Last evening the English Lutheran Sunday-School had a delightful Christmas Entertainment. The programme consisted of very pleasing recitations by the little folks, interspersed with singing of a very high order by the Choir and Scholars, together with a closing address by the Pastor. It was one of the most pleasant occasions the Scholars have experienced for years, due soley to their united efforts to make it the success it was."

Among the many surprises of Christmas Day was the gift to the Pastor, by the ladies of his Bible Class, of a Rogers' Group, entitled "Neighboring Pews." A gentleman is courteously leaning forward and pointing out to a young lady in the seat in front the place in the Hymn Book—and gratitude, if nothing more, is beaming in her face. An older lady at her side does not look very approvingly on the transaction. But we can hardly imagine any disapproval on the countenance of the Pastor. Let the scene be constantly re-enacted *in our pews*. Be courteous to strangers. Proffer them Hymn-Books should you see they have none, for that is a worse dilemma for them than momentary failure to find the hymn announced. Do more than this. Take them by the hand after service. Do not only let them *suppose* they are welcome there. *Tell* them so. If utter strangers to you—the greater need. Learn their names, and place of residence. Above all do not fail at once to tell your Pastor of the knowledge gained. Singing, sermon, and praying may be all they should be, but no congregation can prosper, for none ever did, without courtesy upon the part of its membership to those in the Neighboring Pews.

Repairs To The Sabbath-School Room.

Sunday, the 6th of February, 1887, was a red-letter day for our School. It marked the completion of important improvements.

"For several weeks previously the School Room was in the hands of the painters and paper-hangers, and when they had put on the finishing touches the room presented a very attractive appearance. The ceiling is laid out in four panels of handsome design with appropriate decorations, the ground being of rich gilt paper. The side walls are done in fine gilt paper with a handsome wide border. The floor, which at various places near the wall had sunken, was raised and repaired, the pews were sand-papered and given a coat of varnish, and the wainscoting was similarly treated. New and beautiful chandeliers have taken the places of the less modern ones, a feature of this renovation not thought of at the beginning, but toward the purchase of which, when it was suggested, the School contributed, with but one week's notice, almost $52.00.

The doors and library were grained in the highest style of the art. and with the re-arrangement of some of the classes, and the more advantageous position of the Superintendent's desk, the school presents a complete appearance. The re-opening was signalized with attendance of almost four hundred, and a contribution of over ten dollars."

Y. M. C. A.

On the evening of the Ninth of February, our Young Men's Christian Association was organized, whose work and progress will be described in our chapter on Societies.

ANOTHER SURPRISE.

Our hearts were again touched by a kindly evidence of good feeling upon the part of our people, in an unexpected inroad of smiling faces and laden hands on Wednesday Evening, the 9th of March. This time it was the pastor's wife who was especially thought of, and there was presented to her by Brother H. S. Sterner in behalf of all, a beautiful rocking chair in which she might refresh herself after clambering over hill and dale. The chair was of walnut, elaborately finished and upholstered with figured garnet silk plush. It was also ornamented with a handsome Pongee Silk Scarf with outline decorations in tinsel.

As nearly as could be ascertained, some ninety-three were present and partook of the abundant provision for the inner man which they had brought with them and the general good time that followed.

They departed some time on Thursday Morning, and we took up of that which remained several baskets full.

May God bless the kind friends for this evidence of their continued interest in me and mine—and aid their pastor in a more faithful and earnest discharge of his pleasant duties among them.

PLEDGES REDEEMED.

On the Twenty-Fifth of March, 1886, at our service of Re-dedication, the people were given one year in which to make the payments then pledged. When received in full they were as follows:

George C. Arbogast, $5.00, John H. Arbogast, $2.50, Amelia Auman, $1.00, John Adcock, $15.00, Mrs. Chas. Adcock, $1.00, Mrs. John Bell, $2.00, Mrs. E. Bell, $2.00, Mrs. Geo. Bensinger, $2.50, Mrs. Wm. Bensinger, $7.00, Mrs. H. W. Betz, $5.00, Howard Betz, $5.00, Mrs. L. Bocam, $4.50, Wm. A. Bock, $5.00, Mrs. Wm. A. Bock, $10.00, James W. Bock, $10.00, L. S. Boner, $25.00, Jas. W. Bowen, $10.00, Mrs. Jas. A. Bowen, $5.00, Mrs. E. Britton, .11, Mrs. M. J. Brown, $2.25, Miss Minnie Brown, $1.25, Charles T. Brown, $10.00, William H. Brown, $3.50, Nich. Brownmiller, $5.00, Miss Bessie Burnett, $1.50, Mrs. A. Billington, $6.00, Mrs. John Bolich, $1.00, P. G. Brendlinger, $25.00, Mrs. L. K. Beyerle, $5.00, P. Brenneman, Jr., $10.00, R. Bergeman, $1.00, R. Bruce, $2.00, Mrs. A. B. Cochran, $20.00, Wm. Cochran, $5.00, Choir, $25.00, C. F. Conrad, $10.00, Miss H. C. Conrad, $2.00, Mrs. John Conrad, $5.00, Miss Carrie Christian, $5.00, Cash, $2.00, J. Cheetham, $5.00, Daniel DeFrehn, $15.00, George DeFrehn, $15.00, Chas. Defrehn, $15.00, Joseph De-Frehn, $20.00, Mrs. Joseph DeFrehn, $10.00, Mrs. Catharine DeLong, $1.00, Mrs. George DeLong, $1.00, Geo. H. Dentzer, $5.00, Mrs. H. G. Dentzer, $2.00, Chas. Dimmick, $2.00, Mrs. C. Dimmick, $5.00,

Mrs. H. Dillinger, $1.00, Mrs. Dennebaum, $5.00, F. E. Deisher, $40.00, Mrs. Carrie Deibert, $1.00, Mrs. Daugherty, $5.00, Fred Emhardt, $5.00, Thomas J. Erdman, $15.00, D. L. Esterly, $10.00, Mrs. Benj. Evert, $1.25, Miss Mary Faus, $4.00, Mrs. J. E. Fredericks, $5.00, Dr. P. K. Filbert, $50.00, Bertha Filbert, $5.00, Edward Fox, $35.00, Miss Fertig, $2.00, Chas. Fleck, $2.50, Mrs. L. Fleck, $2.00, J. W. Fleet, $5.00, Friend, $1.00, E. W., $1.00, Mrs. S. A. Garrett, $10.00, Lewis & Samuel Garrett, $2.00, Mrs. E. C. Garnsey, $7.00, Thomas Geier, $50.00, John A. Gilger, $5.00, Mrs. Edward Green, $4.00, Jacob Guers, $1.00, Mrs. Gaue, $2.00, Mrs. Glassmire, $5.00, E. G. Hay, $25.00, Master E. B. Hay, $1.00, John H. Hart, $15.00, Henry Hart, $10.00, Mrs. Henry Hart, $2.00, Miss Alice E. Hart, $5.00, J. H. Helwig, $14.00, Lewis Herwig, $5.00, A. Hillstram, $1.00, Mr. & Mrs. L. F. Heller, $15.00, Harry Heller, $4.50, Miss Minnie Heller, $2.50, Mrs. H. H. Hill, $30.00, Miss E. Hollenbach, $3.50, Mrs. Robert Howell, $2.00, Mrs. John Hower, $2.00, Jas. W. Hoepstine, $2.00, Mrs. T. C. Heilner, $2.00, James Hodgson, $5.00, Mrs. Geo. J. Heisler, .50, Wm. H. Haring, $10.00, Miss Martha Hadesty, $2.00, Mrs. George Hamilton, $3.00, Miss Mary Hartman, $5.00, Mrs. Joseph Holt, $5.00, T. J. H. $5.00, Mrs. Ketner, $5.00, Daniel Keller, $7.50, Mrs. C. Kepner, $5.00, Nicholas Kemp, $11.00, H. W. Kriner, $10.00, Mrs. John Knerr, $2.00, Chas. Kopitzsch, $5.00, Mrs. C. Klare, $5.00, Mrs. Charles Lord, $10.00, Miss Lizzie Lord, $5.00, Miss L. V. Loose, $5.00, Miss Annie Livingood, $1.33, A. S. Lillie, $1.00, Levi Laubenstine, $5.00, Mrs. M. Levy, $2.00, G. W. Mortimer, $40.00, M. Michael, $25.00, Dr. G. M. Miller, $15.00, Frank A. Miller, $10.00, Mrs. F. P. Miller, $1.50, Mrs. John Miller, $5.00, Mrs. Eliza Miller, $1.00, Miss Pamilla Miller, $1.00, Mrs. S. B. Morgan, $10.00, M. Moser, $5.00, Miss Mary Moser, $5.00, Mrs. Medler, .25, G. Wesley Mortimer, $3.00, Thomas Montgomery, .50, Mrs. Wm. Musket, $5.00, Mrs. Jas. E. Nagle, $16.00, Mrs. Daniel Nagle, $10.00, Howard P. Nagle, $3.00, Miss Ellen Nagle, $1.00, Philip Nagle, $1.00, J. H. Olhausen, $10.00, Allen S. Paul, $7.50, Byron Phillips, $5.00, Mrs. Mary Pflueger, $1.00, Miss Laura Pflueger, $1.00, Daniel Pugh, $1.00, Miss Anna Pyle, $1.25, John Parton, $2.00, George Rishel, $25.00, G. M. Rishel, $5.00, Charles L. Rishel, $2.50, Mrs. Risheill, $5.00, Miss M. Reber, $1.00, Mrs. H. Reber, $1.30, John Reber, $2.00, Mrs. R. Reeser, $5.00, Frank Roehrig, $5.00, Mrs. F. Roehrig, $5.00, Miss Carrie Roehrig, $2.00, Mrs. H. Rosengarten, $15.00, Arthur Rosengarten, $5.00, Wm. H. Rosengarten, $10.00, Emily Roehrig, $1.00, Andrew Robertson, $25.00, Morgan Reed, $5.00, Mrs. William Sabold, $4.00, Mrs. William Saylor, $1.00, Misses C. & L. Schrader, $4.00, Mrs. S. Schlaseman, $5.00,

Miss Alma Seitzinger, $2.00, I. H. Severn, $4.00, Mrs. Frank Smith, $2.00, J. H. Shellhammer, $10.00, Mrs. Chas. Snyder. $10.00, Miss Catharine Snyder, $3.00, Miss Emily P. Snyder, $1.00, F. D. Sterner, $10.00, Harry S. Sterner, $20.00, Mrs. Val. Stichter, $5.00, Miss Libbie Stoffregen, $1.00, Miss Ida Stoffregen, $1.00, Miss Mollie Sterner, $5.00, C. M. Sterner, $1.00, O. Sterner, $1.00, Mrs. H. Spehrley, $4.00, Fred Spaecht, $3.00, Winfield Scott, $1.00, Miss A. Smeltzer, $1.00, Miss B. Shollenberger, $5.00, Mrs. C. Sheetz, $5.00, Mrs. & Miss Mary Steinbach, $10.00, Mrs. J. Simmons, $1.00, John Teter, $15.00, Mrs. John Teter, $7.00, J. H. Ulmer, $7.00, Jacob Ulmer, $25.00, J. G. Ulmer, $1.00, Mrs. John Wagner, $2.00, Horace Walbridge, $2.50, Frank Wagner, $1.00, Benjamin Wagner, $1.00, Mrs. George Weiderhold, $1.00, Mrs. A. N. Wetzel, $5.00, W. R. Williams, $100.00, Charles Wright, $1.00, Thomas Wright, $1.00, R. G. Weston, $6.00, Mrs. M. Wolfinger, $1.00.   Total, $1502.99.

EASTER, APRIL 10th, 1887.

In connection with the Communion Service on this day, Forty-Eight new members were admitted. Twelve others were received during the year. Says the local press:—"Over Three Hundred people communed. Many beautiful and fragrant flowers were tastefully arranged about the pulpit by the young ladies of the Sunday-School, reminding one of a beautiful flower-garden in midsummer with flowers in full bloom. As special services had been announced for the evening, long before the time of opening people were turned away from the doors unable even to secure a glimpse of the closely packed room, every available space being occupied.

The services were opened with a voluntary by the Choir, which was followed with a prayer by the pastor, Rev. E. G. Hay. The beautiful Easter-Service, entitled 'Christ the Exalted,' was then rendered by the members of the Sabbath-School, to the number of Four Hundred and Seventy, during which the singing by the Choir and School was very inspiring. The services were interspersed with recitations by Jennie Conrad, Laura Weston, Sallie Bindley, Emma Shoenaman, Callie Smith, Sophie Dengler, Stella Deisher, Amy Parker, Lizzie Wilde, Mamie Kirkpatrick and Willie Brownmiller, all of whom did credit to themselves and afforded much pleasure to the large audience."

The day indeed has passed, but pleasant and precious memories remain. Precious the memory of the ingathering of a harvest of many souls, of the multitude that gathered round the Communion board; of our Savior's presence with us at his table; of the ringing anthems of the Choir, so delightful and inspiring; of the glad ho-

sannahs of the whole vast congregation unto him who liveth and
was dead and is alive forevermore;

"Who captive led captivity,
Who robbed the grave of victory,
And took the sting from death."

And pleasant indeed will ever be our recollection of that evening
service — the enthusiastic singing of the children to the children's
Friend; the floral offerings so emblematic of the transforming and
beautifying impulses and power of God; the gift of the class of Mrs.
Frank Smith to the Sabbath School, that excellent and handsomely
framed portrait of the Great Reformer Martin Luther whom the
world delighteth to honor; the complete happiness of our worthy
Superintendent, brother Harry S. Sterner in the proffer of this gift
through him to the School and the reception for himself, from the
School and friends, of the handsome Elgin gold watch; and last but
not least, the manifest interest and pleasure of the entire audience
that packed every available corner of our large room, and filled even
the open door-ways and vestibule to overflowing. Truly "the Lord
hath done great things for us, whereof we are glad!"

The Miners' Journal thus describes our services upon

CHILDREN'S DAY, JUNE 12th, 1887.

"At the English Lutheran Church every seat was occupied and
many people were turned away unable to gain admission. The altar
was beautifully decorated with laurel and other plants, and numerous bouquets and pot flowers adorned the chancel. A special programme was prepared and distributed through the audience. It
consisted of a greeting song, Scripture reading and invocation, followed by a variety of exercises by the scholars and teachers.

The Infant Department also assisted quite materially in the singing, rendering several very beautiful selections. The exercises were
all very appropriate for the day and were well performed. The occasion was a gratifying success in all its phases. A very interesting
feature of the evening was the presentation of a beautiful gold watch
to George M. Rishel, Assistant Superintendent of the school. The
affair was a complete surprise to Mr. Rishel. The presentation
speech was made by the pastor, Mr. Hay, in a few well-timed remarks.
Mr. Rishel responded in a feeling way, and there was no mistaking
the fact that he appreciated the testimonial, which is certainly a deserving one, as Mr. Rishel has been a conscientious and faithful
worker."

A STRAWBERRY FESTIVAL.

On Wednesday and Thursday evenings, the Fifteenth and Six-
teenth of June, we held a Strawberry Festival in Centennial Hall.

The proceeds were devoted to meeting expense incurred in improvements upon the Eastern side of the Church. The wall on this side is of stone, to the height of some eight or ten feet above the foundation. It had been originally plastered, but this had fallen away, exposing the rough stone-work, and admitting much moisture to the injury of the papering on the interior of the Lecture Room. This wall was now neatly cemented and the whole side of the Church painted. The foundation wall was also cemented and the drainage greatly improved.

Although coming in at about the end of the Strawberry season, and after several similar assemblies that had been well patronized, our Festival, if we may trust the judgment of our visitors, was in every way a success. Expressions of gratification were heard from them on every hand, and of themselves were so hearty as to more than repay the committee for all the labor expended. The decorations which, by the kindness of Mr. J. E. Rice, had been gratuitously furnished for this purpose, were especially admired. The stage was carpeted and bordered with mountain laurel — while from either of the projecting corners rose a magnificent century plant, and varieties of palm. In the rear were three large easels, bearing handsome engravings elaborately framed and surrounded with drapery of flags. Immediately in front of the stage was the Japanese Table. The cover was of material that corresponded with the wares, and the latter were of every variety. To the left of this, in the corner of the room, behind a window-frame of laurel set in a curtain formed of a large banner, the Lemonade Well was discoverable — while the adjoining Flower Table and Candy Table are easier imagined than described. In the centre of the room was a table arranged in the form of a Greek Cross. From the centre rose a pyramid of fruit surmounted with flowers, while the remainder of the surface was covered with tempting cakes of every description. The handsomest of these was eventually placed, as a gift, in the hands of the pastor's wife, as were also numerous other enjoyable and useful articles, it having been discovered that it was her birthday.

Among other attractions were the Fancy Table, the Picture Table, a large Music Box, a Fountain, and not least of all, the Table of General Supplies. The programme of the literary exercises was, on Wednesday Evening: Miss Carrie Stoffregen, Instrumental Music; Mr. R. J. Calm, Recitation; Miss Mamie Ohnmacht, Instrumental Music; Peter Helms, Violin Solo; Miss Jennie Conrad, Instrumental Music; Mr. J. H. Reichert, Recitation; Miss Katie Keiser, Instrumental Music; Miss Gertie Fox, Instrumental Music; Mr. S. C. Kirk, Recitation; Peter Helms, Violin Solo; Miss Callie Smith and

Miss Laura Moser, Duett. On Thursday Evening: Miss Minnie Heller, Instrumental Music; Mr. S. C. Kirk, Recitation; Miss Tenie Toussaint, Instrumental Music; Mr. J. H. Reichert, Recitation; Peter Helms, Violin Solo; Miss Tillie Fredericks, Select Reading; Miss Elsie Geier, Instrumental Music; Miss Sallie Reed, Select Reading; Miss Mary S. Miller and Miss Elsie Geier, Vocal Duett; Mr. R. J. Cahn, Recitation; Peter Helms, Violin Solo.

The proceeds of this Festival were $216.44. The Miners' Journal remarks: "The ladies of the English Lutheran Church spent a great deal of time preparing for their Festival last evening; but the grand success of the affair amply repaid them for their labors. Centennial Hall was beautifully and elaborately decorated for the occasion, and the tables were provided with the delicacies of the season suitable for a warm June meeting. The literary part of the programme consisted of several recitations and musical selections, which were all well performed and highly appreciated by the large audience."

The Evening Chronicle says: "It was the general opinion last evening that the Flower Table of the English Lutheran Festival *is the most beautiful ever exhibited* in Centennial Hall, and the interior of the Hall is more handsomely decorated than on any former occasion."

ANOTHER INCREASE OF SALARY

On the morning of the Twenty-First of August, at the close of the regular services, a congregational meeting was held at which it was decided to increase the pastor's salary Two Hundred dollars a year, making the support afforded him what it now is, namely One Thousand Dollars and Parsonage. Like all kind and worthy deeds, it blesses both receiver and giver. The receiver is surely glad to know that, happy as he may be in this renewed evidence of appreciation of his humble efforts, they who have given it are happier still, for "It is more blessed to give than to receive." Aside from personal considerations, we are glad for the credit of the Congregation that it has taken this step, for while not wealthy, it was abundantly able to do so. In fact, so far as our knowledge of it extends, it never has really tried to do anything that it failed to accomplish.

LECTURE COURSE.

On the evenings of October 17th, November 1st, November 18th, and December 6th, 1887, a Course of interesting Lectures was given in our Church by Rev. Dr. T. C. Billheimer of Reading. The subjects presented were Paris, Florence and Venice, Switzerland and Rome. The Lecturer described the interesting places in these cities which he himself had visited, and illustrated his remarks by the presentation to his hearers of beautiful stereopticon views of large size and great brilliancy. Our people were greatly pleased and profited.

SECOND DEPARTMENT.

Early in the present year, 1888, it became the firm conviction of the pastor and others, that the organization of a Second Department was not only possible, but necessary, if the natural development of our Sabbath School work were not to be hindered. Our already large room was becoming uncomfortably overcrowded, and we had knowledge of still others who were willing to attend. We decided to meet the welcome emergency by the organization of a Second Department, to meet in the upper chamber and have opening and closing exercises there, similar to those in the First Department. On Sunday, February 26th, in the name of our God did we set up our banners, and a goodly number gathered round us.

Brother George M. Rishel led the singing and opening exercises, the pastor the closing ones. Mrs. Hay presided at the organ, and brother E. J. Skelly, previously appointed as teacher in this Department, conducted the study of the lesson. Fifty-one persons composed the class.

The following appointments were soon afterwards made: Organist, Miss Martha Hadesty; Choir, Mr. William Rishel, Mr. John Brownmiller, Mrs. Theodore Heilner, Mrs. Byron Phillips, Mrs. George F. Weaver, Mrs. Theodore Batdorff, Mrs. D. C. Freeman; Secretary, Mr. Robert H. Weston.

The inauguration of this movement, which, if properly fostered, cannot but be permanent, was so far from proving any detriment to the original School, that the latter on that day had also fifty more scholars than the Sabbath preceding — giving us a total increase of One Hundred and One in one week. The Lord grant that we may grow in grace as we have in numbers, and the Lord strengthen and establish this good work!

A NEW BUILDING ERECTED.

The growth of our Sabbath-School has been such in recent days, as to require not only the organization of a Second Department, but also better accomodations for the Infant School.

At the regular meeting of Church Council upon April the 5th, a committee, consisting of brothers H. W. Kriner, H. S. Sterner and the Trustees, J. H. Helwig, W. R. Williams and J. C. Adcock, was appointed to present plans, and an estimate of the cost, of such a building as was desired for this purpose. At the next regular meeting of Council, May 3rd, this committee recommended as the place of the new building the South-West portion of our present

Church property, partially occupied now by a short wing, entirely unused save as an additional means of access to the main audience chamber, and a very poor place for the storing of coal.

The building they suggest is one that shall have a large‑cellar beneath it, with ample room for storing of coal and accumulation of ashes. Both of these will be advantages of some moment, as we have been compelled to pay more for our coal through the necessity, heretofore, of getting it in very small quantities, and for the hauling of ashes, because forced to remove them frequently, hitherto, in the midst of the winter season.

The committee proposed that the approach to the audience chamber above should, with a few alterations, remain. A plan of the whole structure was presented to Council, and after full discussion of its merits, the committee who had furnished it, whose names have already been given, were appointed to have a building erected as speedily as possible in accordance with the plan. This building will probably cost not far short of a thousand dollars, an expenditure which our congregation of nearly 500 souls will cheerfully make, thanking God for the prosperity which calls for the outlay. The Pastor was instructed to appoint a committee of three, with himself as Chairman, and with power to increase their number, who should conduct the financial portion of this new enterprise to a successful issue. Brothers Wm. R. Williams and H. S. Sterner were appointed, and brother Daniel Christian was afterwards 'elected by the committee, to share in their counsels and efforts.

The first movement of the Finance Committee was to inaugurate, through action of Council, a Strawberry Festival. The following persons were appointed an Executive Committee for that occasion. to co-operate with the pastor in making it, if possible, a success :

H. S. Sterner, S. S. Newcomer, J. H. Helwig, Geo. M. Rishel, H. W. Kriner, Wm. Rosengarten, Allen Paul, J. A. Rinck, Chas. T. Brown, George H. DeFrehn, Mrs. T. Geier, Miss C. Schrader, Mrs. Edward Fox, Mrs. J. E. Fredericks, Mrs. Edward Green, Mrs. A. B. Cochran, Mrs. L. K. Beyerle, Mrs. A. L. Phillips, Miss Mollie Sterner, Miss Katie Hutchinson.

EASTER, APRIL 8th, 1888.

We had the pleasure of receiving Forty-Four new members upon this occasion, an increase of Fifty-Two since the First of January. The Sacrament was received by large numbers, sixteen crowded tables being supplied with the Bread of Life. Our evening services were thus described by another :

"The English Lutheran Church on Market street, near Sixth, was crowded with people last evening, whose most sanguine expectations were more than realized. The exercises were entitled 'Portals of Glory,' and were participated in by the choir, Sunday-School and congregation. Mrs. Geo. Rishel was organist, and Mr. Zac. Pugh accompanied the choir on the cornet. The programme included hymns, readings and exercises by the Sunday-School children, who acquitted themselves handsomely. They were in charge of Mrs. A. L. Phillips, Miss Mollie Sterner, Mrs. L. K. Beyerle and Miss Emma Adcock. The remainder of the programme follows : Recitations by Stella Deisher, Katie Snyder and five little three-year-old tots, viz., Carrie Nagle, Vera Wagner, Susie Hoepstine and Nettie Heffner ; Singing by the Infant Class ; Recitations, May Beyerle and Vera Wagner ; Responsive Recitation by five little girls, Carrie Dentzer, Sadie Heilner, Jesse Heller, Carrie Weiderhold and Jennie Heilner ; Essay, 'The Resurrection,' Miss Carrie Holt ; Responsive Recitation, five little girls, Carrie Warm, Lulu Roehrig, Dora Batdorff, Hattie Hill, and Vergie Jungkurth ; Recitations, 'He is not Here,' Florence Kershner ; 'The Easter Story,' George Kirk ; 'Whispers of Love,' Katie Cooper ; select reading, 'The Coming of His feet,' Amy Parker. Little Vera Wagner delighted all present with the clearness of her enunciation and grace of delivery. All of the others are worthy of particular mention, and the manner in which they acquitted themselves speaks highly for the work of the Superintendent of the Sunday-School, Harry Sterner, and his efficient corps of assistants."

On the afternoon and evening of this day special collections were lifted for the purpose of securing

A NEW SABBATH-SCHOOL ORGAN.

We received almost Sixty Dollars, and a week or two later purchased for $100, a handsome Miller Chapel Organ which gives general satisfaction. Our former organ, still of some value, is used for the present by the Second Department.

WHITSUNDAY, MAY 20th, 1888.

Our Easter admission over, we thought of a few others who would probably join our congregation upon Whitsunday, and began to make inquiry and effort in that direction. But there were more than we had thought, near to the kingdom of heaven, and when the Pentecostal Sabbath dawned, no less than Twenty-Seven stood forth and testified to their humble yet confident faith in Jesus. Seventy-Nine in all have thus cast in their lot with us during this year. Eighty-

Six since the last annual meeting of Synod. May God bless them all, and keep them faithful unto death!

INSURANCE.

Good things do not usually last very long. And our insurance of $10,000 on our Church property expired upon the Twenty-Ninth of June, after a brief life of three years. Anticipating this occurrence as one of the few certainties of the future, we took all necessary precautions for its reanimation and on the first Sabbath of June made a quiet effort to secure the needful amount. Did we get it? What a question! To be sure we did, and if we live three years will get it again.

OUR FESTIVAL.

Once more it becomes our pleasant privilege to record the success of an English Lutheran Festival. On the 13th and 14th of June, Centennial Hall was arrayed in all its glory. Flags and festoons of the "red, white and blue," greeted the eye upon every side—flowers breathed their rich fragrance upon the air—ornamental trees added their tropical beauty to the scene—the atmosphere was aquiver with music and faces were radiant with joy. The Fancy and Japanese Tables were laden with articles of usefulness and beauty, and of every curious design; the Cake and Fruit Table attracted many longing glances; the Lemonade Well poured forth its refreshing streams; and the contrasting colors of the snowy Vanilla and the scarlet Strawberry adorned the tables everywhere. The proceeds reached the sum of $263.22. This gives us a nice start toward the payment of the sum demanded by the erection of the New Building.

An episode occurred upon the first night of our festivities which is worthy at least of passing notice. It happened to be the evening chosen to convey the monument of the 96th regiment from the shop of the sculptor to the cars. In its passage thither it was borne immediately in front of the Hall in which we were assembled. As the magnificent array that preceded it, to the sound of martial music, was sweeping past the Hall, the balcony of the second story suddenly became alive with Lutherans of the gentler sex in festival attire, and all the handsomer for that, waving a multitude of star-spangled banners in the air. Suddenly, from their very midst, a beautiful bouquet arose in air, overarching the dense throng upon the pavement below, and falling just beside the wheels of the monumental car with its ponderous load. It was but the work of an instant for the thoughtful attendant to grasp the tribute and place it immediately before the face of the reclining but watchful figure in stone, while a shout from the gratified balcony made the welkin ring. Those nearest imagined that the very *soldier* smiled.

The thanks of our people are due, and hereby most cordially tendered, to all who by their presence or assistance in any form contributed to the success of this effort. Among these we think should be especially mentioned Messrs. Reichert and Hostetter, W. H. Mortimer, J. D. Rice and S. A. Holmes.

Among the closing scenes of the second evening, was a quiet one unobserved by many but enjoyed by a few, as all kind acts are enjoyed by those who perform them—the presentation, to the pastor's wife of a beautiful apron which had been quite an attractive feature upon both evenings at the fancy table. It was kindly given by members of the Church and Sabbath-School. It is highly prized and was very gratefully received, as were also several other handsome gifts, from individuals, conferred upon the same occasion.ʼ

CHILDREN'S DAY.

Sunday, June 24th, was observed by us this year as Children's Day. The pulpit was never more prettily decorated, a new feature having on this occasion been introduced. This was a large fountain upon the centre of the pulpit platform, sending its sparkling and cooling streams from twelve to fifteen feet into the air. It was flowing during the opening and closing services of the morning, and throughout the evening exercises by the School. A printed programme of responsive readings interspersed with singing from the Lesson Book and the Augsburg Songs, and with recitations by the younger scholars, was followed by the School.

The children who recited were Frank Batdorff, Jennie Billman, Amy Parker and Minerva Christian.

The Pastor addressed the school upon the subject of Our Orphan's Home at Loysville for whose benefit a collection of $12.17 was lifted, and also congratulated them upon their numerical standing, being at least one hundred, in enrolled membership, above all other Schools in the community. Addresses were also made by brothers S. S. Newcomer, who spoke of Christ's interest in the Children, and H. S. Sterner, who spoke of the frequency with which water is used in Scripture to designate the blessings of salvation, and the willingness of Christ to give of this living and satisfying water unto all. The Choir then sang with fine effect "Jesus the water of life will give." A solo by Miss Elsie Geier, and the singing of the Infant School, were also highly enjoyed.

PROPHECY REACHING FULFILLMENT.

Our prophecy, on an earlier page, that the New Building for our Infant Department would be cheerfully paid for, is already reaching on toward its fulfillment. On the First of July the Sunday-School was supplied with some two hundred small wooden barrels, to be used for a short time as savings-banks, and on the 12th of August a number of these were returned. Others are still being handed in, and the amount thus far received is but little short of $100. In addition to this, $100 has been pledged by the Sunday-School from its own treasury. These sums, with the amount from the recent Festival already mentioned, and anticipated contributions from the Ladies' Mite Society and the Young People's Literary Society, will afford us something more than one half of the One Thousand Dollars needed. And now a subscription list has been started, headed by most of the members of Council, already amounting, with the pledges of a few others, to more than $200. We hesitate not to prophesy still further, that when all have been visited, the most ample provision will be made with ease for all expenditure required.

We close this somewhat lengthy chapter with a copy of the official records of our pastorate, and an item of interest which mysteriously dropped out of its proper place in the continuous narrative already printed.

WE RECEIVED.

In 1880.

Mrs. Hattie Barlet.

In 1881.

George Arbogast, John Arbogast, Mrs. Laura H. Bell, Miss Catharine E. Betz, Lamie W. Bocam, Mrs. Rebecca Bolich, Miss Carrie M. Burnette, Miss Bessie Burnette, Miss Katie Burnette, Miss Christina Conrad, Mrs. Rebecca Cotton, Mrs. Henry G. Dentzer, Geo. W. Dentzer, Geo. H. Dentzer, Miss Maggie Dimmick, Miss Carrie M. Foltz, Mrs. Edward Fox, Miss Amelia Gallagher, Mrs. Emma Garnsey, John C. Gross, Mrs. J. C. Gross, Earnest Gross, Mrs. E. Gross, Miss Clara E. Heffner, Miss Carrie Heilner, Louis F. Heller, Mrs. L. F. Heller, John Hollenbach, Mrs. R. Howell, Mrs. Ellen Jolley, Miss Alice Jolley, Miss Minnie Kurtz, Miss Carrie Laubenstine, Miss Almeda A. Loose, Miss Emma E. Lutz, Miss Sophia Miller, Mrs. Annetta Morger, Miss Mamie Moser, Miss Katie Nagle, Allen Paul, Mrs. F. Pflueger, Byron D. Phillips, Miss Louisa Reichart, Miss Minnie Rishel, Frank Roehrig, Miss Clara Rosengarten, Arthur Rosengarten, Mrs. Wm. Sabold, Miss Annie Sabold, William Sabold, Miss Katie Schartel, Mrs. Sarah Schlaseman, John L. Schlear, Mrs. J. L. Schlear, Miss Annie Belle Simmons, Miss Emma L. Skeen, Frederick Spaecht, Mrs. F. Spaecht, Miss Josephine Steiger, Miss Mollie E. Sterner, Henry Strohmeier, Mrs. H. Strohmeier, Elmer E. Teter, Miss Lillie Teter, George Unger, Mrs. George Unger, Miss Katie Ward, Miss Ellie Wildermuth, Mrs. John Wagner, Miss Amanda F. Heilner, Mrs. Eliza J. Christian, Mrs. Hannah Dillinger, Mrs. J. H. Skeen, Harry A. Skeen, Miss Kate Cruikshanks, Jacob Guers, Mrs. Wm. Haring, Mrs. Kate Huntzinger, Mrs. Julia A. Jacobi, Christian Mader, Miss Emily P. Snyder, Mr. L. S. Boner, Mrs. Emma Lorriman, Mr. C. Schnerring, Mrs. C. Schnerring, Miss Annie Goldsmith, Miss Jennie Goldsmith.

In 1882.

Mrs. Catharine Kepner, Miss Amanda Kepner, Mrs. Geo. Bensinger, Miss Ellie L. Brown, John Clay, Miss Lizzie Day, Miss Annie Duey, Jerome Duey, U. Grant, Ebert, Miss Carrie Fleck, James M. Hadesty, Mrs. J. M. Hadesty, Miss Annie M. Hart, Miss Laura Heffner, Miss Mamie C. Hoffman, Miss Emily B. Hollenbach, Robert Kepner, Jacob C. Kepner, Charles A. Kershner, Mrs. C. A. Kershner, Mrs. M. Levy, Miss Carrie E. Lord, Miss Mary Reber, Miss Emma M. Reed, Edward J. Robinson, Mrs. E. J. Robinson, Miss A. G. Rowe, Miss Mary K. Schlaseman, Elmer F. Schlaseman, Miss Alma E Seitzinger, Miss R. A. Seigfried, Miss Minerva Shollenberger, Miss Bertha Shollenberger, John G. Shum, Miss Lizzie R. Snyder, Walter R. Snyder, Reuben Snyder, Miss Clara K. Spaecht, Charles M. Steidle, Harry S. Sterner, Mrs. H. S. Sterner, Allen W. Sterner, Miss Ida M. Sterner, Miss Louisa Van-Dorn, John Weinrich, Robert Weston, Mrs. R. Weston, Miss Mary E. Zerbey, Miss Mary Hartman.

In 1883.

Andrew P. Smith, Elmer E. DeLong, William B. Bannan, Miss Clara Conrad, Thomas J. Erdman, Thomas Geier, Mrs. T. Geier, Miss Clara Kershner, Miss Lottie Michael, Miss Mary Michael, George W. Nagle, Charles L. Rishel, Clinton D. Rishel, Miss Emma R. Roehrig, William H. Rosengarten, Isaac Harvey Severn, Miss Carrie Snyder, Charles J. Wright.

In 1884.

Miss Amanda R. Hill, Miss Flora A. Hill, Charles C. Hill, Mrs. George Barker, Miss Kate Noecker, George S. Dunkleberger, Mrs. Sarah E. Holt, Miss Catharine A. Snyder, William Henry Beyerle, Harry Walter Beyerle, Howard Betz, Miss S. Clara Bock, Mrs. E. Heisler, Miss Anna Pyle, Miss Emma Schaeffer, Mrs. C. Schropp, Miss I. Schropp, Brinton M. Schropp, Miss Maggie Smith, Miss Emma L. Strohmeier, Mrs. L. J. Treichler.

In 1885.

Miss Sallie **Burnette**, Theodore Batdorff, Mrs. T. Batdorff, George W. Hamme, Mrs. G. W. Hamme, Frank E. Deisher, Mrs. F. E. Deisher, Henry Clay, Miss Katie Dentzer, Charles B. Ebert, Frederick Emhardt, Miss Laura Foltz, Miss Mary Gottschall, Miss Minnie Heller, Mrs. Harry Hill, Daniel Hill, Mrs. Daniel Hill, Mrs. Alfred E. Lee, Miss Annie Livingood, Miss Minnie H. Lord, Miss Lulu M. Lord, Howard P. Nagle, Miss Ida Nagle, George E. Pyle, Harvey Sabold, James M. Shellhammer, Miss Amelia C. Shoean, Miss Tillie Sillyman, Robert F. Sterner, Miss Minnie Stichter, Howard F. Walbridge, Miss Cora E. Walbridge, Horace B. Walbridge, Miss Ella H. Walbridge, Thomas J. Wright, Miss Emma L. Strouse, Miss Julia Bernet, John A. Gilger, Mrs. J. A. Gilger, Charles E. Kirkpatrick, Mrs. Chas. E. Kirkpatrick, Miss Ellen Wythe, George Richards, Mrs. Phoebe Helms, John Lugan.

In 1886.

Mrs. W. Gane, Mrs. A. Billington, Miss T. Sallade, Mrs. A. Bindley, Mrs. P. Bowers, Miss Sarah Bowers, Miss Annie V. Brown, Miss Ida Deisher, Charles O. Dentzer, George F. Egolf, Mrs. C. F. Frizzle, Miss Clara Elsie Geier, Mrs. George P. Heller, Mrs. James W. Hoepstine, Stephen Lauck, Mrs. Stephen Lauck, Miss Bertha Matthews, Miss Maggie Matthews, Charles G. McDaniel, Mrs. M. Michael, Miss Lottie Michael, Miss Mary Michael, Mrs. Kate Neff, Miss Mary Neff, Frederick Pflueger, John B. Rath, Miss Ida Rowe, Miss Tillie Scheaffer, Stanley M. Schlaseman, Henry L. Scott, Mrs. H. L. Scott, William M. Schroyer, Miss Katie R. Schroyer, Miss Callie

L. Smith, Miss Iva Pearl Weston, Miss Laura Weston, Edward Boyer, Albert Bowers, Mrs. A. Bowers, Mrs. Joseph DeFrehn, Miss Carrie M. Glassmire, Albert Gottschall, Miss Sallie L. Reber, John F. Spaecht, Elmer E. Walbridge, Mrs. Catharine Weiderholt, John Weiderholt, Mrs. C. H. Meck.

IN 1887.

J. H. Deisher, Mrs. J. H. Deisher, Mrs. Susan Holt, Mrs. Joseph Parker, Mrs. Clara Zeiders, Mrs. E. Barth, Robert S. Bashore, Mrs. George G. Beck, Miss Mary Beltz, Miss Lizzie G. Bindley, Mrs. Charles T. Brown, R. J. Calm, Mrs. C. Carter. John Conrad, Mrs. John Conrad, J. George Dengler, Miss Eva M. Dengler, Mrs. George H. Dentzer, James M. Dieffenderfer, Mrs. J. M. Dieffenderfer, John Fertig, Mrs. H. L. Gardner, Mrs. A. A. Greenawalt, Mrs. Lizzie Griner, Miss Carrie A. Gross, Miss Jennie Harner, Miss Minnie Heisler, Geo. P. Heller, Mrs. J. S. Helms, Miss Maggie Helms, Miss Agnes M. Johnson, Mrs. Mary Kerbel, Miss Christie Kerbel, Mrs. J. C. Krohmer, Anthony Mader, Mrs. W. H. Miles, S. E. Moore, Mrs. S. E. Moore, Mrs. George F. Moore, Miss Ada A. Paul, Miss Clara M. Pfeifer, Miss Carrie E. J. Schimpf, Miss Nettie E. Sheetz, Hiram Shugars, George F. Smith, Mrs. John G. Stevenson, Miss Maud A. Stevenson, Miss Lena A. Stutz, Miss Lizzie Stutz, Mrs. George Wilde, Mrs. D. L. Williams, Thomas Williams, Miss M. Zimmerman, Michael G. Snyder. Mrs. Emma Reichert, Jacob Reichert, S. S. Newcomer, Mrs. Joseph Summons, E. J. Skelly, Mrs. E. J. Skelly.

IN 1888.

Mrs. Charles Forseman, Mrs. Harry Hight. Prof. G. A. Transue, Mrs. Albert Schock Miss Kate Schultz, Miss Vienna Reed, Miss Carrie Stachle, Miss Ella Zimmerman, Miss Emma Adcock, Amos Billman, Mrs. Amos Billman, Mrs. Emma L. Cable, Miss Mary A. Cable, Mrs. Frederic C. Currier, Mrs. Charles W. Diliplane, Miss Nora A, Dengler, Joseph F. Dengler, Elmer Dentzer, Walter M. Engel, Edward Fox, James E. Gilger, Miss Elsie G. Hartline, George W. Hamilton, Miss Nellie A. Hill, Miss Clara May Hill, Charles I. Hoepstine, Miss Katie Hutchinson, Miss S. Josephine Keer, Charles Kull, Mrs. Aaron Moore, Miss Sallie R. Moore, Heber T. Moore, Miss Laura A. Moser, Mrs. Frank Mowrey, Mrs. Sarah Moyer, Samuel B. Moyer, Mrs. Samuel B. Moyer, Frederick Ohnmacht, William K. Parker, Miss Hattie C. Pfeifer, Mrs. Robert H. Reith, Edward Spaecht, Valentine Stichter, Frederick E. Wagner, Mrs. Frederick E. Wagner, Mrs. Harriet E. Walbridge, Miss Fannie B. Walker, George C. Welker, Mrs. George C. Welker, Mrs. Oscar P. Whitman, Harry L. Wilde, Miss Bertha L. R. Work, Mrs. C. J. Arbogast, Miss Emma Behney, George D. Beyerle, Clarence E. Beyerle, Edward Billman, Mrs. John N. Brownmiller, Mrs. Matilda S. Cruikshanks, Miss Annie E. Detzner, Mrs. H. C. Dysinger, Robert F. Fegley, George W. Gise, Mrs. Mayberry B. Heffner, Robert C. Henry, James W. Hoepstine, Miss Emma Hubley, Mrs. Lucy A. Keer, Charles H. Lord, Murray Morgart, Mrs. Daniel M. Pugh, William H. Pugh, George W. Rath, Mrs. Susan Reichart, John M. Rowe, Mrs. Wm. H. Sands, Edward C. Smith, Miss Mary Thomas, Mrs. George F. Weaver, S. M. Enterline, Mrs. S. M. Enterline, Miss Emma R. Carter.

WE BAPTIZED.

IN 1881.

May Estelle Betz, Ellsworth L. Nagle, Laura Belle Haring, Kate R. Schroyer, William M. Schroyer, Mary Snyder, Ella Snyder, John Raymond Bell, Frank E. Walbridge, Bessie Foltz, Mrytie Lee Bachman, Sarah G. Wagner, Annie May Wagner, Sylvester Schlear, Lillie Schlear, Marcia Allen Fox, Horace P. Christian, Mary M. Christian, William H. Christian, Maud L. Christian, Jessie Louisa Heller, Caroline Dentzer, Frank Spohn Seltzer, Jessie Guers, Sadie May Heilner, Jennie Shay Heilner, Clayton Smith, John Smith, Bessie H. Rosengarten, Sallie May Bindley, Wm. H. Brownmiller, Lulu M. Dunkleberger, Jessie May Oliver, George Seiler Rishel, William B. Wolff, John M. Dillinger, Maggie Cake Kepley, Charles A. Hoepstine, John Charles Conrad, Gertrude I. Simmons, Mary M. Eichenburg, Katie E. Hoover, Franklin E. Gross, Tillie Clara Gross, Catharine B. Simmons, Bessie L. Reichard, Caroline M. Henry, Ida Eva Daubert, Harold M. Daubert, William C. H. Werntz.

In 1882.

Wensil Troy, Louis A. Kershner, Emily E. Nagle, Walter H. Robinson, Carrie Irene Jones, Bertha Louisa Smedler, Harry Cake Dewald, Francis W. Bensinger, Reuben D. Bensinger, Isaac E. Bensinger, Emily I. Hadesty, Jennie Weinreich, Louisa Weinreich, Eddie Gross, Benjamin A. Christian, Mary Ann Morris, Charles A. Michael, Lulu May Bocam, John W. Fernsler, Mary L. Schlear, Bertha Belle Aregood, Edgar Adam Heckler, Jacob A. Huntzinger, Clarence K. Dengler, George Boyle Stichter, Sophia M. D. Stichter, Clara S. Entwistle, Thomas Henry Leib, Sarah Jane Leib, Geo. G. Dunkleberger, Helen B. Bonawitz, Hugh Harrison Hood, Bessie A. Beyerle, George W. Kientzle.

In 1883.

Carrie E. Schnerring, Roy Stichter Moore, Emma Agnes Bedford, Carrie E. Nagle, Harry Ohnmacht, Katie Ohnmacht, Emmie Britton, Louise Alice Hart, Alfred J. Shollenberger, Leroy C. Shollenberger, Violet Shollenberger, John Franklin Musket, George W. Kershner, Charles K. Robertson, Ida Louise Roehrig, Sylvania Huntzinger, Lucy S. Hoepstine, Frederick Hoover, Frederick Walter Held, Josie E. Steinberger, William Kohler, C. May Wildermuth, Maud Annie Hughes, Annetta M. Turner, Edward W. Oliver, Charles F. Adcock, George C. Arbogast, Elizabeth Ellen Troy, Chas. H. Eichenberg.

In 1884.

Edward H. Hodgson, Charles W. Kershner, Hiram D. Moyer, Harry Nicholas Gross, George Frederic Stout, Marion Eva Rishel, William H. Rishel, May Berger, Robert Joseph Holt, Minnie Elizabeth Holt, Anna Barbara Lugan, Charles F. Deibert, Frank P. Mortimer, Ellen Amanda Sabold, Bertha Sabold, Lottie Elizabeth Meck, Anna Laura Fauth.

In 1885.

Harry Lorne Freeman, Edith May Freeman, Annie Charlotte Hart, Joseph Troy, May Beyerle, Ella Elizabeth Nagle, Daniel V. Connor, William G. Forseman, Elsie M. DeLong, Benjamin F. Derr, Mary Matilda Turner, Howard A. Wetzel, Kate Anna Nagle, Kate Elizabeth Klare, Melvin E. Wagner, Charles D. Emhardt, Jacob C. Arbogast, Henry H. Kershner, Benjamin Jacob Fisher, Clyde Ayres Bell, Frederick S. Bell, Robert Roy Bell, Jennie May Kohler.

In 1886.

William H. Haring, Mary A. Kirkpatrick, Frances B. Kirkpatrick, William S. Entwistle, Erma Ann Freeman, Linden K. Hadesty, Harold Edwin Snyder, Edward F. Hoepstine, Charles R. Heller, Mary M. Sheere, Bessie M. Schum, Charles C. Schnerring, Robert C. Brown, Thomas R. Gillespie, Lettie Sallie Teter, Charles Miller Bock, Charles E. Fauth, Emma Mary Meck, Louella E. Detrick, Linn Isaac

Rhoads, Mark John Nelson, John C. Strohmeier, Benjamin Ciltz, Elmer T. Rhoads, Guy St. Clair Rhoads, Frederick F. Rhoads, Clara S. Rhoads, Sarah G. Rhoads, Elizabeth Watts, Freddie Watts Frank Watts, Sallie Ann Watts, Harry Dunkelberger, Harry J. Lafferty, Edith May Lafferty, Annie Lafferty, Sadie Lafferty, Martha Lafferty, George C. Bensinger, Mary M. Robertson, Annie B. Werntz, Mazie Ellen Werntz, Georgie Ohnmacht, Edward Sell Filbert.

In 1887.

George H. Huntzinger, Marguerite S. Mortimer, Grace Bessie Parton, Elizabeth M. Bausman, Lewis H. Gardner, Areba M. Gardner, Clarence S. Gardner, Maggie Zeiders, Martha May Roehrig, George Edgar Hart, George Snyder, Walter David Stout, William S. Brobst, Raymond S. Brobst, Sarah May Meade, Lettie Musket, John William Shaw, William Irvin Rowe, Howard P. Hille, Mary E. Gilger, Madeline S. Gillespie, Ursula E. Bowers, Harry Thomas Ketner, Joseph George Bocam, Stanley P. Walbridge, Elsie M. Thompson, Ferdinand John Humbert Fleck, Walter Edward Fonderwhite.

In 1888.

Robert Barges, Walter Elmer Staehle Gross, Adele Union Hight, Louis Frederick Heller, Camilla Ida Bock, John Henry Liddle, Edith Kirkpatrick, Walter Mortimer Engel, Florence Jamella Greenawalt, Edward George Dentzer, Laura Eva Helms, Edward Billman, Jennie Billman, Laura Benedict, Frederick Edward Turner, Thomas Walter Duey, Mary Edith Smith, Carrie Pearl Leiser, Ida Mary Wildermuth, Frank McLennan.

WE MARRIED.

In 1880.

D. C. Freeman, Miss Kate Rishel.

In 1881.

John A. Whetstone, Miss Hattie Cowley; Uriah G. Leffler, Miss Emma R. McQuade; George F. Moore, Miss Mary W. Foulk; David C. Smith, Mrs. Martha Cummings; John M. Goettler, Miss Amelia Hoffman; Uriah George Batdorff, Miss Ella Rebecca Loose; Wm. W. Fausht, Miss Emma L. Deblanc; John H. Lugan, Miss Clara E. Brownmiller; James Schrader, Miss Clarissa Wilkinson; Cornelius Schnerring, Miss Tillie Clay; Henry Albert Lord, Miss Mary E. Strauch; Joseph Bocam, Miss Mary E. Collier.

In 1882.

Frank C. Palmer, Miss Annie M. Sheetz; Charles E. Kirkpatrick, Miss Lizzie C. Troutman; Charles J. Christian, Miss Mary C. Leffler; Frank V. Roehrig, Miss Dollie L. Kirkley; William Musket, Miss Tillie Stouffer; Joseph H. Hoover, Miss Annie Kelly; Noah Fenstermacher, Miss Mary Alice Oyster; William F. Shum, Miss Victoria Lambruskini; Adam T. Daubert, Miss Caroline C. Frantz; John Henry Hart, Miss Mary Jane Teter; Andrew D. Robertson, Miss Clara E. Heffner; George Francis Davis, Mrs. Sallie Turnbull; Samuel Edward Moore, Miss Alice Hahn Stichter; Samuel R. Kepner, Miss Mamie A. Mortimer; George C. Woll, Miss Clara L. Speakman; John C. Adcock, Miss Lizzie Wernert; George Arbogast, Miss Arabella Christian; Frank L. Nagle, Miss Laura I. Rosengarten; John G. Fox, Miss Clara E. Bausum; David Hughes, Miss Lillie Werley.

In 1883.

William Turner, Miss Anna Margaret Morger; J. G. Dotterweich, Miss Amanda F. Heilner; Jesse Watson Fleet, Miss Aletha Bertha Fertig; Harry Nagle, Miss E.

Kate Sterner; Harry P. Herwig, Miss Ida M. Eckenrode; William F. Green, Miss Emma E. Guttabaum; John R. Sparks, Miss Lizzie L. Huntzinger; Charles M. Meck, Miss Emma E Gottschall; Elias Leonard, Miss Sarah J. Newcombe; Christian L. Shum, Miss Carrie A. Hilderbrandt; Francis Monaghan, Miss Sarah Miller; Elmer E. Teter, Miss Sue M. Gore; George W. Glenn, Miss Alice Moyer; George H. Kienzle, Miss Lucy M. Pounder; A. E. Hossler, Miss Bessie Hadesty; Charles D. Thompson, Miss Annie M. Knittle; John L. Knebler, Miss Hallie D. Evert; William Aincham, Mrs. Jane Oliver; John H. Arbogast, Miss Lousia VanDorn; Joseph E. Schrader, Miss Ellie Swingert; George Fisher, Miss Minnie Kurtz; George W. Hamilton, Miss Mary M. Stichter.

IN 1884.

Jacob F. Fauth, Miss Amanda R. Hill; Willard Holland, Miss May Patterson; Richard Hirst, Miss Eva E. Spotts; William M. Furman, Miss Dollie R. Deihm; Geo. R. DeLong, Miss Lizzie R. Snyder; Andrew Klinger, Mrs. H. E. Reamer; William M. Brown, Miss Carrie Kopp; Albert Nathan Wetzel, Miss Annie Belle Simmons; Charles Snyder, Miss Ada Flammer; William F. Werntz, Miss Mary M. Clarkson; Frederick Emhardt, Miss Lillie C. Teter; Alfred Lloyd, Miss Bertha Fernsler; Evan T. Jones, Miss Emma R. Potts; Horace B. Walbridge, Miss Carrie M. Foltz; Edward Jenkins, Miss Lizzie Francis; George M. Rishel, Miss Aurelia M. Loose; William S. Parton, Miss Elmira Eyster; Charles Fleck, Miss Ida M. Hollenbach; Harry Detrick, Miss Sallie Baker.

IN 1885.

John C. Artley, Miss Annie Brown; Ambrose S. Teter, Miss Sallie M. Christian; Thomas T. Gillespie, Miss Millie C. Engel; Frank H. Williams, Miss Annie Bast; William F. Bausman, Miss Emma L. Strouse; Charles T. Brown, Miss Sallie F. Pugh; Peter Hill, Miss Alice Schultz; Joseph W. Reichard, Miss Jennie Thomas; C. W. Olewine, Miss Celia F. Bigler; John Frederick, Miss Kate Heaton; James E. Stephens, Miss Ettie Conrad; Ellwood P. Gerhard, Miss Clara Krebs; Ephraim H. Mattern, Miss Hattie E. Wier; Walter J. Reinhard, Miss Carrie Meinhold; John William Miller, Mrs. Helena Hartman; Philip Arbogast, Miss Kate Jenkins.

IN 1886.

Dr. John S. Miller, Miss Callie Roehrig; P. B. J. Carter, Miss Mary A. Mease; John Logan, Miss Mary C. Wagner; Prof. W. R. Baker, Miss Lilla V. Loose; G. Walter Brown, Miss Laura E. Kershner; Albert J. Hunsicker, Miss Mary L. Miller; Joseph Woomer, Miss Laura A. Rummel; Preston Hille, Miss Laura Kepley; Albert F. Faust, Miss Agnes Sterling; Lewis G. Spohn, Miss Susie M. Derr; John G. Rosengarten, Miss Lizzie Dehner; Andrew H. Wilson, Miss Thresa Mallan; William O. Daubert, Miss Clara Shindle; J. Harry Heller, Miss Christina Conrad; John J. Till, Mrs. Mary A. Young; William W. Martin, Miss Sophia B. Miller; Frederick Barchet, Miss Mary A. Harris; Morgan Thomas, Miss Kate Struble.

IN 1887.

Walter Alexander, Miss Mary Noon; Jacob Weber, Miss Mary Rupert; Albert Kanp, Miss Lizzie C. Moody; George H. Dentzer, Miss Tillie R. Coover; William Gordon, Miss Sadie Bock; John Kaiser, Miss Emma Zechman; A. Lincoln Phillips, Miss Kate Anna Nagle; Harry W. Mortimer, Miss Savilla Heilner; James Leib, Miss Mary Treyon; August Botzer, Miss Elizabeth A. Coover; James M. Shellhammer, Miss Minnie H. Lord; Charles A. Flail, Miss Lillian Falls; Alexander L. Fager, Miss Sallie E. Reed; Albert L. Wildermuth, Miss Mary K. Schlaseman; David

A. Geiger, Miss Amy Stutz; Christian Grimm, Miss Sarah Watkins; Edwin C. Griscom, Miss Emma E. Brandt; John A. Rice, Miss Miranda S. Hubert.

IN 1888.

John E. Benedict, Mrs. Amelia Barges; George J. Smith, Miss Laura E. Patterson; George K. Wells, Miss Lottie E. Michael; Daniel F. Kaufman, Miss Amanda J. A. Bankes; William H. Sabold, Miss Emma E. Lilly; Frank E. Speigel, Miss Minnie Wertz; Edward A. Fronk, Miss Amanda C. Miller; Charles W. Zeiders, Miss Sophie Dewald; Smith Martin, Mrs. Sarah Collicot; George Pyle, Miss Mary E. Becker; Thomas W. Parker, Miss Matilda A. Feist; Louis A. Oland, Miss Araminta K. Miller; Earnest A. Meyer, Miss Katie A. Weller; Jacob Bosche, Miss Mary May Beltz; David E. Becker, Miss Mary Elizabeth Loy.

WE BURIED.
IN 1881.

Mrs. Hattie Barlet, William Burlee, Ada L. Galbraith, Mrs. Mary Rath, Charles E. Nagle, Frank S. Seltzer, Jeremiah Reed, Charles A. Hoepstine, Mrs. A. Gallagher, Lizzie O. Haring, George Unger, Mrs. Jeremiah Reed, Albert Huntzinger, Mrs. Hassman, William Bensinger, Jacob Miller, Mrs. Calvin Wagner, Nettie Wilson, Howard D. Kershner.

IN 1882.

Mrs. Lindenmuth,* Mrs. Mary Nagle, Mrs. S. A. Kurtz, Lillie May Reber, John M. Miller, Frank E. Walbridge, Harry C. Dewald, Miss Clara Rumple, Mrs. Emma L. Fausht, Adolphus Walbridge, Mrs. Catharine Erdman, Charles A. Michael, James M. Moore, Edgar A. Heckler, Winfield S. Glassmire, Hugh Allen, Mrs. Rose Huntzinger, George W. Keintzle, Mrs. E. J. Christian, Nicholas Madara, Gertie Dentzer, Harrison Hood.

IN 1883.

Samuel Heffner, Mrs. Caroline Saylor, Andrew P. Smith, Mrs. Catharine Fox, Florence Spohn, Sarah C. Snyder, Edward Fair, Daniel Edward Hill, George W. Kershner, Clara S. Lyons, Josie E. Steinberger, Maud A. Hughes, Nathan DeLong, Mrs. Margaret Spohn,* Wensil Troy, Daisy Bock, William M. Wagner, Mrs. George Brownwell, Mrs. Mary Berger, Mrs. Varena Fox, Mrs. Elizabeth Bennet, Mrs. Clara Esterly.

IN 1884.

Mrs. Mary Hause, J. H. Rosengarten, Miss Sarah Haller, Mrs. Rev. M. Troxell, John Doeble, Mrs. Lizzie Scott, Henry Shelly, Emma Dentzer, Rev. Joseph McCool,* Harry Nicholas Gross, Mrs. Ellen Jolley, Miss Sarah Foltz, Charles W. Kershner, Joseph Yost, William H. Rishel, Zachariah East, Thomas P. Cotton, Jennie Fox, John F. Muth, Mrs. Sarah Reed, John F. Simmons,* Clyde B. Olhausen,* Ellen Amanda Sabold, Mrs. Susan Schlear, Albert Esterly, Mrs. Jessie Lord, Roy Stichter Moore, Mrs. Samuel Heffner.

IN 1885.

Miss Sallie Rumple, Willie Gane, Mrs. Catharine Gilbert, William Bobb, George Huntzinger, Mrs. Rebecca Cotton, Morgan Mortimer, Samuel Beyerle, William Olhausen, Ella Dieffenderfer, Miss Lizzie Leffler, Howard A. Wetzel, Kate Elizabeth Klare, Daniel Krebs, Mrs. Jeremiah Seitzinger, Mrs. Dollie Kalbach, Miss Jennie Kauffman, George Richards.

IN 1886.

Jacob D. Rice, Mrs. Elizabeth Schartel, Mrs. H. Walbridge, Erma Ann Freeman

James Moore, Mrs. C. Shollenberger, Louis Dentzer, Charles Rosengarten, James Jolley, Bessie Foltz, John Wolfinger, Mrs. Ambrose Teter, Thomas R. Gillespie, Mrs. Mary M. Heller, Jeremiah Snyder, Linn Isaac Rhoads, Samuel Morgan, Solomon Lord, Raymond Thomas, Mrs. Rev. S. V. Dye, Benjamin Wagner.

IN 1887.

Mrs. Sarah Wilde, Miss Annie Hart, Mrs. C. W. Klare, Carrie Dieffenderfer, Carrie Heller, Samuel S. Kauffman, Joseph Lindenmuth, George H. Stichter, Katie M. Gross, Mrs. M. J. Brown, Elmer F. Walbridge, Maud G. Reichart, Miss Maggie Dimmick, George F. Snyder, George Wilde, Mrs. Ellen Glenn, Lettie Musket, Charles Glenn,* Tommie Kline, Clinton B. Nagle, Mrs. Henry Dentzer, Paul Parker, Mrs. Henry Blatt, Herbert Fleet, Miss Kate Olhausen,* Jacob Aurand, Ursula Elmira Bowers, Elsie May Thompson, Jacob Spotts.

IN 1888.

Peter Fasolt, Robert Barges, Mrs. John Kirkley, Jeremiah Hummel, Mrs. Sarah J. Schlaseman, Samuel E. Moore, Mrs. Henry Herwig, Miss Charlotte F. Adcock, Mrs. A. N. Wetzel, Daniel Fessler, Mrs. Lydia Ashbaugh, Mrs. Benjamin Evert, Mrs. Kate Eisenhuth, Mrs. Michael Weaver, John S. Miller, Miss Katie Billman, Mrs. Hannah Dillinger, Mrs. Eliza Morrier, Miss Sophie Hoffman, Laura May Benedict, William Saylor, Carrie Pearl Leiser, Frank McLennan, Thomas Montgomery.

* Assisted others.

CHRISTMAS. 1887.

The morning discourse was appropiate to the day. In the evening the School rendered a service entitled "The Prince of David." The chancel had been handsomely decorated, and a large arch had been erected just in front of the pulpit platform. It was covered with evergreen, surmounted by a large gilt star, and bore the word "Welcome" in large gilt letters on its face. Below this, from the lower side of the arch, also in large gilt letters, were the words Babe of Bethlehem. These were put there during the service, one letter at a time, being brought up successively by fifteen of the little children, each of whom repeated an appropriate Scripture truth before the letter was placed in proper position. Those who took part in this were Carrie Warm, Lidie Schock, Carrie Nagle, Mamie Miles, Virgie Jungkurth, Hattie Hill, Minnie Hill, Nettie Heffner, Harry Freeman, Isaac Bensinger, Jessie Heller, Tessie Hill, Lucy Hoepstine, Lizzie Wilde, Emily Hadesty. Those who were selected to give recitations were Callie Smith, Katie Cooper, Minnie Howell, Stella Deisher, Willie Forseman and Georgie Kirk. A fine large steel engraving of the Christ-Child in the manger, the gift of the Reading Circle to the Infant School, was then shown them for the first time and suspended during the closing exercises from the centre of the arch, just below the completed sentence Welcome, Babe of Bethlehem! A full house, as usual, greeted the speakers, and gave every evidence of gratification with the entire entertainment.

CHAPTER XI

ORGANIZATIONS.

COUNCIL.

The first in order of time, this body originally contained but four members—two Elders and two Deacons. But in 1871, under the Amended Charter, its number was increased to ten—five Elders and five Deacons. The resident pastor was in each instance, ex-officio Chairman. The Treasurer, it will be noticed, was sometimes within, and sometimes outside of, the limits of Council.

ELDERS.	DEACONS.
PASTOR, REV. DANIEL STECK.	
In 1852.	
W. L. Heisler, Sec.,	George Beyerle,
John Junk,	Peter Haas.
In 1853.	
W. L. Heisler, Sec.,	George Beyerle,
Jared Daniel,	Benjamin Evert.
In 1854.	
George Beyerle,	W. L. Heisler, Sec.,
Jared Daniel,	Benjamin Evert.
In 1855.	
George Beyerle,	W. L. Heisler, Sec.,
Jared Daniel,	Daniel Heil.
In 1856.	
George Beyerle, Tr.,	J. D. Rice, Sec.,
Jared Daniel,	Daniel Heil.
PASTOR, REV. W. H. LUCKENBACH.	
In 1857.	
George Beyerle, Tr.,	D. S. Kline, Sec.,
Jared Daniel,	From Nov. 26, Jas.
	Matter.
	Daniel Heil.
In 1858.	
George Beyerle, Tr.,	James Matter, Sec.,
Jared Daniel,	Daniel Heil,
From May 27,	From May 27,
—— Gallagher,	J. D. Rice.

ELDERS.	DEACONS.
PASTOR, REV. S. A. HOLMAN.	
In 1859.	
George Beyerle, Tr.,	C. A. Gundaker,
	From July 20,
From May 9.	William Zern.
J. D. Rice, Sec.,	To May 9.
	James Matter, Sec.,
	From May 9, A. K.
	Whitner.
In 1860.	
George Beyerle, Tr.,	William Zern,
J. D. Rice, Sec.,	C. H. Dengler.
In 1861.	
George Beyerle, Tr.,	Geo. Hofferkamp,
William Zern,	C. H. Dengler.
In 1862.	
James Matter, Sec.,	Geo. Hofferkamp,
William Zern,	Benj. Evert, Treas.
PASTOR, REV. L. M. KOONS.	
In 1863.	
James Matter, Sec.,	J. D. Rice,
William Zern,	Benj. Evert.
In 1864.	
James Matter, Sec.,	Geo. Hofferkamp,
William Zern,	From Sept. 14,
	D. Whitman,
	J. D. Rice, Treas.

ELDERS.   DEACONS.

PASTOR, REV. URIEL GRAVES.

In 1865.

David N. Heisler,	Edward Westley,
James Matter. Sec.,	Dan'l Whitman Tr.

In 1866.

J. H. Kurtz, Sec.,	D. Kershner, Tr.,
D. Heisler,	Edward Westley.
From July 2	
J. Matter,	

In 1867.

J. H. Kurtz, Sec.,	D. Kershner, Tr.,
C. H. Dengler,	William Auman,
	After Jan. 9, E.
\	Westley.

PASTOR, REV. DANIEL STECK.

In 1868.

Peter Fasolt, Tr.,	B. Wagner,
C. H. Dengler,Sec.,	Edwd. Westley.

In 1869.

Peter Fasolt,	N. Brownmiller,
C. H. Dengler, Sec.,	B. Wagner.
G. W. Mortimer, Treas.	

In 1870.

Peter Fasolt,	N. Brownmiller,
C. H. Dengler, Sec.,	John Rath.
G. W. Mortimer, Treas.	

PASTOR, REV. J. Q. McATEE.

In 1871.—AMENDED CHARTER.

Peter Fasolt,	N. Brownmiller,
George Beyerle,	John Rath,
C. H. Dengler,	J. D. Rice,
J. Huntzinger,	B. Evert,
Wm. B. Kurtz, Sec.,	C. Lord.
G. W. Mortimer, Treas.	

In 1872.

Peter Fasolt,	N. Brownmiller,
George Beyerle,	John Rath,
J. Huntzinger,	Charles Lord,
C. H. Dengler,	E. S. Nagle, Sec.,
Wm. B. Kurtz,	B. Evert.
G. W. Mortimer, Treas.	

In 1873.

P. Fasolt, Treas.	N. Brownmiller,
Geo. Beyerle,	Charles Lord,
J. Huntzinger,	Daniel DeFrehn,
C. H. Dengler,	Wm. Fasolt,
J. D. Rice,	E. S. Nagle, Sec.

ELDERS.   DEACONS.

In 1874.

Peter Fasolt, Treas.,	E. S. Nagle, Sec.,
George Beyerle,	D. R. Super,
J. Huntzinger,	Wm. Fasolt,
J. D. Rice,	Charles Lord,
C. H. Dengler,	Daniel DeFrehn.

In 1875.

Peter Fasolt, Treas.,	E. S. Nagle, Sec.,
George Beyerle,	D. R. Super,
J. Huntzinger,	Wm. Fasolt,
J. D. Rice,	Charles Lord,
John Rath,	J. W. Nagle,
Trustees, Charles Lord and W. Fasolt.	

In 1876.

N. Brownmiller,	E. S. Nagle, Sec.,
Daniel DeFrehn,	D. R. Super,
J. D. Rice,	Wm. Fasolt,
J. Huntzinger,	J. W. Nagle,
Wm. Haring,	Charles Lord.
Peter Fasolt, Treas.	
Trustees, Wm. Fasolt and J. W. Nagle.	

In 1877.

N. Brownmiller,	G. M. Rishel,
Wm. Haring,	Wm. Fasolt,
Geo. Rishel,	J. W. Nagle,
Charles Lord,	D. W. Nagle, Sec.
Daniel DeFrehn,	D. R. Super, Asst. Sec.,
	From Sept. 13,
	W. R. Williams.
Peter Fasolt, Treas.	
Trustees, D. DeFrehn and Wm. Fasolt.	

PASTOR, REV. JOHN McCRON.

In 1878.

J. D. Rice,	W. R. Williams, to
Wm. Haring,	May 2nd.
From May 23, W.	From May 16, H.
R. Williams,	M. Oberholtzer,
Daniel DeFrehn,	Geo. M. Rishel,
Charles Lord,	Wm. Fasolt,
George Rishel,	D. W. Nagle, Sec.,
	J. W. Nagle,
Peter Fasolt, Treas.	

In 1879.

J. D. Rice,	D. Nagle,
Daniel DeFrehn,	J. H. Helwig,
Wm. R. Williams,	H. M. Oberholtzer,
George Rishel,	From July 13,
N. Brownmiller,	Charles Lord.

ELDERS.	DEACONS.	ELDERS.	DEACONS.
	D. W. Nagle, Sec.,	H. W. Kriner, Tr.,	J. H. Helwig, Sec.,
	From July 6,	George Rishel,	J. H. Hart,
	Wm. Fertig,	W. R. Williams,	G. M. Rishel,
	George M. Rishel.		Asst. Sec.

Treas., Peter Fasolt.
Trustees, D. DeFrehn, N. Brownmiller.
PASTOR, REV. E. G. HAY.

Trustees, W. R. Williams and D. De-Frehn.

In 1880.

N. Brownmiller,	J. H. Hart,
J. D. Rice,	G. M. Rishel,
W. R. Williams,	J. H. Helwig, Sec.,
Daniel DeFrehn,	From April 25.
George Rishel,	E. L. Orwig,
	Wm. Fertig.

Treas., P. Fasolt.

In 1885

H. W. Kriner, Tr.,	John Teter,
W. R. Williams,	J. H. Helwig, Sec.,
George Rishel,	H. S. Sterner,
D. DeFrehn,	G. M. Rishel,
N. Brownmiller,	J. C. Adcock.

Trustees, W. R. Williams, George Rishel and J. C. Adcock.

In 1881.

W. R. Williams,	G. M. Rishel,
H. W. Kriner,	J. H. Helwig, Sec.,
George Rishel,	J. H. Hart,
D. DeFrehn,	C. Lord,
J. D. Rice,	C. Wagner.

Treas., P. Fasolt.

In 1886.

N. Brownmiller,	G. M. Rishel, Sec.,
W. R. Williams,	A. S. Paul, A. Sec.,
H. W. Kriner, Tr.,	J. C. Adcock,
G. Rishel,	H. S. Sterner,
F. E. Deisher,	J. H. Helwig.

Trustees, W. R. Williams, H. W. Kriner, F. E. Deisher.

In 1882.

George Rishel,	J. H. Helwig, Sec.,
H. W. Kriner,	G. M. Rishel,
W. R. Williams,	J. C. Adcock,
G. W. Mortimer,	Charles Lord,
N. Brownmiller,	Calvin Wagner.

Treas., P. Fasolt.

In 1887.

G. Rishel,	A. S. Paul,
W. R. Williams,	G. M. Rishel, Sec.,
H. W. Kriner, Tr.,	J. H. Helwig,
N. Brownmiller,	H. S. Sterner,
F. E. Deisher,	J. C. Adcock, A. Sec.

Trustees, W. R. Williams, F. E. Deisher, H. W. Kriner.

In 1883.

H. W. Kriner, Tr.,	J. C. Adcock,
G. W. Mortimer,	J. H. Hart,
N. Brownmiller,	H. S. Sterner,
W. R. Williams,	J. H. Helwig, Sec.,
George Rishel,	G. M. Rishel,

Trustees, W. R. Williams, H. W. Kriner.

In 1888.

F. E. Deisher,	H. S. Sterner,
H. W. Kriner, Tr.,	J. H. Helwig,
N. Brownmiller,	J. C. Adcock, A. Sec.,
G. Rishel,	G. M. Rishel, Sec.,
W. R. Williams,	S. S. Newcomer.

Trustees, W. R. Williams, J. H. Helwig, J. C. Adcock.

In 1884.

| D. DeFrehn, | H. S. Sterner, |
| N. Brownmiller, | John Teter, |

THE CHURCH CHOIR.

While the origin of this body can not now be definitely discovered, we have no doubt that a Choir in some form existed from the first, nor that its services were then, as now, second in importance to those of no other organization in the Church. Among its members have been William Zern, J. H. Kurtz, Daniel Heil, William Kurtz, Sarah Kurtz, Barbara Heisler, Mrs. Washington Heisler, William A. Bock, S. F. Penfield, Mrs. S. F. Penfield, Amelia Auman, Nettie Strauch, Edward Haas, Mrs. Edward Haas, Kate Ohnmacht, Lot K. Beyerle, Ellie R. Derr, Amelia Eiler, John Alexander, J. I. Alexander, C. H. Dengler, Lewis Reeser, Benjamin Erdman, Levi Huber, Clara Reeser, Ella Krebs, Sallie Beyerle, Fannie Hazen, Matilda Simmons, A. K. Whitner, William Auman, J. B. Meyers, Hannah Dawson, Edward Boheme, J. E. Small, Lucetta Harlan, J. H. Skeen, Martha Hadesty, Amanda Hadesty, Lizzie Bodefield, Mary Glover, Martha Kirkley, Sallie Kirkley, Annie Fasolt, Elora Evert, Annie Alexander, Sallie Reeser, Edward Nagle, James W. Nagle, George Snyder, Daniel W. Nagle, Thomas Erdman, J. W. Bock, Dr. P. K. Filbert, Mrs. Dr. P. K. Filbert, Emma DeFrehn, Clara Stichter, William G. Wells, W. W. Wells, Kate Steck, Vallie Steck, Daniel Super, George Thomas, Annie Simmons, Frank S. Bock, Ambrose Teter, J. C. Adcock, Charles Dentzer, Joseph Derr, Lilla V. Loose, Ella Loose, Charles T. Brown, George DeFrehn, Laura Stoffregen, Dollie Kirkley, Callie Roehrig, Laura Kershner, Mrs. H. S. Sterner, Mark Nagle, Aurelia Loose, Clara Fertig, Elsie Geier, Emma Adcock, Charles Wright, Allen Paul, Harvey Severn, Tillie Fredericks, Allen W. Sterner.

The Leaders and Organists of the Choir have been as follows:

LEADERS.—J. Henry Kurtz, S. F. Penfield, Benjamin Erdman, William Bock, John Alexander, Lot K. Beyerle, William W. Wells, Dr. P. K. Filbert.

ORGANISTS.—Nettie Strauch, Clara Reeser, Amelia Eiler, James I. Alexander, Martha Hadesty, George Thomas, Alva Kirkpatrick, John Cheetham, Lilla V. Loose, Aurelia Loose.

PRESENT ORGANIZATION.

Dr. P. K. Filbert, Leader; Mrs. George M. Rishel, Organist; Emma Adcock, Lot K. Beyerle, James W. Bock, Charles T. Brown, Emma DeFrehn, George H. DeFrehn, Elsie Geier, Mrs. H. H. Hill, Mary S. Miller, Mrs. Frank Roehrig, Mrs. H. S. Sterner, Clara Stichter, Charles Wright, Mrs. Charles T. Brown.

It is hard to describe the comfort and enjoyment we have had with our Choir. Under the able leadership of Dr. Filbert, they have not hesitated to attempt, nor failed to render, music of a high order in their Anthems, nor have they chosen unsuitable hymn tunes to the detriment of congregational singing. These are features of excellence that strangers have not been slow to note, and of which visitors often speak. And in more than one instance we have witnessed has the echo of their voices lingered as the last memory of earth and prophecy of glory, in the hearts of the dying. Sing on, ye faithful ones, no ministry on earth is laden with more precious fruitage than yours!

THE SUNDAY-SCHOOL.

This has naturally been an important feature of our Church life from the beginning. The membership and contributions for each year, will be found by the reader on other pages in this volume, among other facts there given, in a copy of our Parochial Reports to Synod. The principal events in the history of the School have already been given, but we have yet to present a record of Officers and Teachers, which we give from the year 1857, as far back as we can discover any data.

The Teachers have of course had frequent meetings for consultation and the transaction of business, from the beginning. In recent years at least these have been held monthly. On the 11th of February, 1883, however, a weekly meeting was established by brother H. S. Sterner for the study of the Lesson. A large proportion of the Teachers have attended this steadily ever since, and it has resulted in untold good to the School. Brother Sterner who has had charge of it from the first, always comes before the teachers after a careful and thorough study of the lesson himself, and imparts to them not only a great deal of useful information, but also valuable suggestions as to the manner in which they shall proceed to teach the lesson to their classes. He has done a work already among us that will not be forgotten, and we trust may long be spared to labor in this post of usefulness.

A word in explanation of the following chart. Among the Officers whose names are given thereon, some had assistants. The name of the principal is given first in each instance.

	SUPERINTENDENT.	ASST. SUPERINTENDENT.	SECRETARY.	TREASURER.
1857............	Daniel Heil.		From April, James Matter.	
1858............	Rev. W. H. Luckenbach.	Jackson Graves.	E. L. Haas.	Daniel Heil.
1859............	Rev. W. H. Luckenbach. From July, William Zern.	C. A. Gundaker. From Oct., James Matter.	J. E. Small.	Amelia Auman.
1860............	William Zern.	George Hofferkamp.	C. H. Dengler.	James Matter.
1861............	William Zern.	George Hofferkamp.	C. H. Dengler. From July, H. H. Huntzinger.	James Matter.
1862............	William Zern.	George Hofferkamp.	James Matter.	George Hofferkamp.
1863............	William Zern.	George Hofferkamp.	George Hofferkamp.	James Matter.
1864............	William Zern.	J. W. Alexander.	George Hofferkamp.	N. Brownmiller.
1865............	Rev. L. M. Koons.	William Zern.	C. H Dengler.	Henry Kurtz.
1866............	William Zern. From Nov., Henry Kurtz.	Henry Kurtz. From Nov., C. H. Dengler.	Emma E. Rosengarten.	C. H. Dengler.
1867............	J. H. Kurtz.	C. H. Dengler.	Jennie Graves.	Edward Westley.
1868............	C. H. Dengler.	J. W. Nagle.	D. W. Nagle.	E. S. Nagle.
1869............	Rev. D. Steck.	C. H. Dengler.	D. W. Nagle.	E. S. Nagle.
1870............	C. H. Dengler.	J. W. Nagle.	D. W. Nagle.	E. S. Nagle.

1871	C. H. Dengler.	J. W. Nagle.	D. W. Nagle, M. H. Nagle.	E. S. Nagle.
1872	J. W. Nagle.	Rev. J. Q. McAtee.	D. W. Nagle, T. J. Kershner.	E. S. Nagle.
1873	C. H. Dengler.	J. W. Nagle.	D. W. Nagle, T. J. Kershner.	E. S. Nagle.
1874	C. H. Dengler.	J. W. Nagle.	D. W. Nagle, T. J. Kershner.	E. S. Nagle.
1875	C. H. Dengler.	J. W. Nagle.	D. W. Nagle, D. W. Kershner.	E. S. Nagle.
1876	J. W. Nagle.	E. S. Nagle.	D. W. Nagle, D. W. Kershner.	W. Fasolt.
1877	J. W. Nagle.	E. S. Nagle.	F. W. Sterner, F. L. Nagle.	W. Fasolt.
1878	Rev. John McCron.	Geo. M. Rishel.	G. E. Shoemaker, F. L. Nagle.	W. Fasolt.
1879	Rev. John McCron.	Howard Oberholtzer.	F. L. Nagle, Geo. DeFrehn.	W. Fasolt.

	SUPERINTENDENT.	ASST. SUPERINTENDENT.	SECRETARY.	TREASURER.
1880............	Rev. John McCron.	Howard Oberholtzer.	F. L. Nagle, Geo. DeFrehn.	W. Fasolt.
1881............	Rev. E. G. Hay.	Geo. M. Rishel.	Geo. DeFrehn, John H. Hart.	Dr. P. K. Filbert.
1882............	C. H. Dengler.	H. S. Sterner.	Geo. DeFrehn, John H. Hart.	Frank Bock.
1883............	C. H. Dengler.	H. S. Sterner.	Geo. DeFrehn, J. C. Adcock.	G. M. Rishel.
1884............	H. S. Sterner.	G. M. Rishel.	Geo. DeFrehn, J. C. Adcock.	G. M. Rishel, From Apr., C. T. Brown.
1885............	H. S. Sterner.	G. M. Rishel.	Geo. DeFrehn, Chas. T. Brown.	J. C. Adcock.
1886............	H. S. Sterner.	G. M. Rishel.	Geo. DeFrehn, Chas. T. Brown.	W. H. Brown.
1887............	H. S. Sterner.	G. M. Rishel.	Geo. DeFrehn, Chas. T. Brown.	W. H. Brown.
1888............	H. S. Sterner.	S. S. Newcomer. From Aug. 19, J. H. Helwig.	Geo. DeFrehn, Chas. T. Brown.	W. H. Brown.

	MISSIONARY TREASURER.	ORGANISTS.	CHORISTERS.	LIBRARIAN & ASSISTANTS.	SUPT. OF INFANT DEPARTMENT AND ASSISTANTS.
1857............	....			Edward Haas.	
1858............	Mrs. Hoffman.			Luther Haas, Wm. Osler.	
1859............	Mary Olewine.			L. K. Beyerle, Harriet Heaton.	Mrs. Born.
1860............	Mary Olewine.			L. K. Beyerle, Wm. Dillinger.	
1861............	Mary Olewine.			James Matter, J. Kirkpatrick, From Oct., Ralph Cake.	
1862............	Fannie Hazen.			James Matter, Wm. Dillinger.	
1863............	Kate Ohnmacht.			Edward Wesley, Ivanhoe Huber.	
1864............	Amelia Eiler.			Edward Wesley, James W. Nagle.	
1865............				Edward Wesley.	
1866............			Wm. G. Wells.	James W. Nagle, Albert Zern, From Nov., John Ward.	
1867............			Wm. G. Wells.	James W. Nagle, John Ward.	
1868............			Wm. G. Wells.	W. A. Miller, James W. Bock.	
1869............		Martha Hadesty.	Annie Alexander, Sallie Reeser.	J. W. Bock, W. A. Miller.	Mrs. C. H. Dengler, Miss Dinmick.
1870............		Martha Hadesty.	Annie Alexander, Sallie Reeser.	J. W. Bock, W. K. Schertle.	Mrs. James W. Nagle, Mrs. L. Nagle.

	ORGANISTS.	CHORISTERS.	LIBRARIAN & ASSISTANTS.	SUPT. OF INFANT DEPARTMENT AND ASSISTANTS.
1871...............	Martha Hadesty.	Nettie Strauch, Kate Ohnmacht, Annie Alexander.	J. W. Bock, W. K. Schertle.	Mrs. C. H. Dengler, Miss Dimmick, Miss Thomas.
1872...............	Martha Hadesty.	E. S. Nagle, Nettie Strauch, Kate Ohnmacht, Annie Alexander.	J. W. Bock, M. H. Nagle.	Mrs. C. H. Dengler, D. R. Super.
1873...............	Martha Hadesty.	E. S. Nagle, Kate Ohnmacht, Nettie Strauch.	J. W. Bock, J. W. Derr, M. H. Nagle.	D. R. Super.
1874...............	Martha Hadesty.	E. S. Nagle, Kate Ohnmacht, Nettie Strauch.	J. W. Bock, J. W. Derr, M. H. Nagle.	D. R. Super, Jennie Kriner.
1875...............	Martha Hadesty.	E. S. Nagle.	J. W. Bock, J. W. Derr, T. J. Kershner, M. H. Nagle.	D. R. Super, Jennie Kriner.
1876...............	Laura Nagle.	E. S. Nagle.	J. W. Bock, J. W. Derr, T. J. Kershner, M. H. Nagle.	D. R. Super, Jennie Kriner.
1877...............	Laura Nagle.	Dr. P. K. Filbert, D. W. Nagle, Aurelia Loose.	J. W. Bock, J. W. Derr, T. J. Kershner, M. H. Nagle.	D. R. Super, Lilla V. Loose.
1878...............	To Oct., Laura Nagle. From Oct., Aurelia Loose.	Dr. P. K. Filbert, D. W. Nagle, Aurelia Loose.	J. W. Bock, J. W. Derr, John H. Hart, M. H. Nagle.	Mrs. L. K. Beyerle, Lilla V. Loose, Clara Fertig, From Oct., Laura Nagle.

		CORNETISTS.		
1879	Aurelia Loose.	Dr. P. K. Filbert, D. W. Nagle.	J. W. Bock, J. W. Derr, M. H. Nagle.	Mrs. L. K. Beyerle, Laura Nagle.
1880	Aurelia Loose.	Dr. P. K. Filbert, L. K. Beyerle.	J. W. Bock, Frank Bock, M. H. Nagle.	Mrs. L. K. Beyerle, Laura Nagle.
1881	Aurelia Loose.		J. W. Bock, Frank Bock, George Arbogast, M. H. Nagle.	Mrs. L. K. Beyerle, Mrs. E. G. Hay.
1882	Aurelia Loose.		J. W. Bock, Frank Bock, George Arbogast, J. C. Adcock, M. H. Nagle.	Mrs. L. K. Beyerle.
1883	Aurelia Loose.	W. McDaniel.	J. W. Bock, George Arbogast, M. H. Nagle.	Mrs. L. K. Beyerle.
1884	Aurelia Loose.		J. W. Bock, J. W. Derr, M. H. Nagle.	Mrs. L. K. Beyerle.
1885	Mrs G. M. Rishel.	J. W. Cheetham.	J. W. Bock, J. W. Derr, M. H. Nagle.	Mrs. L. K. Beyerle, Lilla V. Loose.
1886	Mrs. G. M. Rishel.	J. W. Cheetham.	J. W. Bock, J. W. Derr, M. H. Nagle.	Mrs. L. K. Beyerle, Lilla V. Loose.
1887	Mrs. G. M. Rishel.	J. W. Cheetham.	J. W. Bock, J. C. Adcock, M. H. Nagle.	Mrs. L. K. Beyerle, Katie Nagle.
1888	Mrs. G. M. Rishel.	Z. Pugh.	J. W. Bock, J. C. Adcock, M. H. Nagle.	Mrs. L. K. Beyerle, Mrs. A. L. Phillips, From Mar. Callie Smith, From Mar. Emma C. Adcock.

A complete list of Teachers for each year cannot be given. An attempt to do so would result in needless repetitions. We therefore give the names of all elected in the order in which they were chosen. Any repetition here is the result of the re-election of Teachers after temporary absences from the community.

TEACHERS ELECTED.

In 1857—Isaac Trieze, Lewis Matter, Mrs. Gensler, Caroline Seitz, Mrs. Hoffman, Miss Simmons, Amelia Auman, Margaret Eiler, Mary Seitz, Catharine Auman, Miss Leihr, Lewis Eberle, John Dannehower, Mrs. Emma Saaber, Mary Olewine, Edward Haas, Sarah Heaton, Miss Wigaman, Leonard Sheishun, Jackson Graves, Mrs. M. J. Graves, Amelia Boehme, Emma Seitz, C. A. Gundaker.

In 1858—George Beyerle, Catharine Klineginny, Mrs. Born, John Klineginny, Mrs. Small, Mrs. Luckenbach, Mrs. A. K. Whitner, Miss Sarah Heaton, Miss Turner, Amelia Eiler, Mary Riland, Anna Henson, H. Barr, Miss C. Seitzinger, J. E. Small.

In 1859—Mrs. C. A. Gundaker, George Hofferkamp, Miss Dawson, Mary Rosengarten.

In 1860—Kate Ohnmacht, Fannie Hazen, Alice Shearer, Joseph F. Dengler, Miss Stillwell, Miss Wolfinger, Miss Palmer, Mrs. Chambers, Mr. Dubbs, E. Haas, Annie W. Larer, Mr. Whitman, Frank Snyder, Ellen Krebs.

In 1861—Mrs. A. K. Whitner, H. H. Huntzinger, Rebecca Christian, Ellen Derr, Edward Westley, Celestine Glassmire, Louisa Glassmire, Nicholas Brownmiller, E. H. Boehme, Franklin Buchner, Mrs. Sarah Hoffman.

In 1862—Mrs. Edward Haas, Sallie Beyerle, Harriet Brown, Margaret Minds, Anna Gallagher, Martha Hadesty, Mary Kline.

In 1864—J. W. Alexander, C. H. Dengler, Mrs. Kirkpatrick, Mrs. Severn, Louisa Garrett.

In 1865—Henry Kurtz, Ralph Cake, Mrs. Edward Westley.

In 1866—Mary Lindenmuth, Carrie Rosengarten, Sallie Beyerle, Rosanna Drill, Wm. Wells, Mrs. Heffner, Mrs. Seiler, Mrs. C. H. Dengler, Harrison Hill, John Boyer, James Matter, Miss Fulmer, Mrs. Bonawitz.

In 1867—Mrs. Dunkleberger, Mr. Shontz, Mr. Kershner, Edward S. Nagle, Laura Rosengarten, Jeremiah Snyder, George Dreher, Walter Wolff, Ellie Lindenmuth, Annie Fasolt, Mrs. H. Huntzinger.

In 1868—James W. Nagle, H. H. Huntzinger, J. H. Kurtz, Miss Kirkley, Wm. Rosengarten, C. N. Barclay, Edward W. James, Edward Fox, E. Drill, M. Dillinger, Miss Dimmick, Miss Drill, Miss Haas, John Ward, William Miller.

In 1869—Miss Daniel, Mr. Eisenbrown, Mrs. Schenk, Miss Helms, Miss DeFrehn, Mr. Hubbard, Mr. Esterly, Mr. Hoeffer, Mr. Dentzer.

In 1870—Charles Fasolt, Miss Morgan, Miss Gallagher, Mrs. Dengler, Mr. Mattis, Mrs. Cable, S. A. Garrett, Miss Shum, Mr. Kurtz.

In 1871—D. R. Super, Mrs. Keller.

In 1872—Libbie Lord, J. A. Huntzinger, Mrs. Anna Morrison, Miss Hetherington, Mary Parton, Wm. Fasolt.

In 1873—Mr. Weigle, Mr. Holtzman, Mr. Gottschall, Jennie Kriner, Dr. Koser, Dr. P. K. Filbert, Ellie Rosengarten, Mrs. Mortimer.

In 1874—Miss Hetherington, Miss Fox, Mary Steinbach.

In 1875—J. Ruth, J. Seltzer, G. Farrow, Emma DeFrehn, Mrs. Geo. Kline, Mrs. Hower, Harry C. Nagle.

In 1876—Amanda Smeltzer, Mrs. Dr. P. K. Filbert, Miss Lloyd, Laura Rosengarten, George M. Rishel, Anna McGlone, Howard Oberholtzer, Mr. Smith, Ella Loose, Miss Lord, Miss Wineland, Mr. Westley, J. H. Helwig.

In 1877—Charles Glenn, Enoch Neff, Aurelia Loose, Miss Finney, Lilla V. Loose, E. Smith, Clara Fertig.

In 1878—Alva Kirkpatrick, Mary Jolly, Miss Smith.

In 1879—Mrs. J. McCron, Lizzie Leffler, Miss Sterner, Miss Christian, Mrs. C. H. Dengler, Mrs. Frank Smith, Lilla V. Loose.

In 1880—E. L. Orwig, Mrs. Morrison.

In 1881—Mrs. E. G. Hay, Mrs. John Cake, Bella Christian, Mollie Sterner, Dollie Kirkley, H. S. Sterner, Mrs. H. S. Sterner, Mary Teter.

In 1882—Bessie Burnette, Katie Nagle, Mrs. Geier.

In 1884—Mrs. E. Fox, Mrs. Geier, Mrs. S. E. Garrett, Laura Pflueger, Charles E. Sterner, Mrs. Treichler, Mrs. James Bowen, C. T. Brown, Carrie Roehrig, Mrs. Joseph Holt.

In 1885—Sallie Laubenstine, Emma Reed, Celia Conrad, Ida Stoffregen, John C. Adcock, Allen Paul, Wm. H. Brown, Libbie Brown, Bessie Burnette, Lidie Crosland, Mary Miller, Mamie Moser.

In 1886—Mrs. Charles Snyder, Maggie Dimmick, Mrs. Byron Phillips, Harvey Severn, Geo. W. Dentzer, Minnie Heisler, Anna Pyle, Mrs. C. Wiederholt, H. C. Keener, F. E. Deisher.

In 1887—Carrie Laubenstine, Katie Schartel, Mrs. Geo. Dentzer, Robert S. Bashore.

In 1888—Lilla V. Bruce, S. S. Newcomer, Laura Pflueger, Mrs. S. J. Kirk, Katie Dentzer, Prof. G. A. Transue, E. J. Skelly, Mrs. Skelly, J. C. Welker, Ella Zimmerman.

PRESENT ORGANIZATION.

FIRST DEPARTMENT.

OFFICERS—H. S. Sterner, Superintendent; J. H. Helwig, Assistant Superintendent; George H. DeFrehn, Secretary; Charles T. Brown, Assistant Secretary; William Brown, Treasurer; James W. Bock, Librarian; Marcus H. Nagle and John C. Adcock, Assistant Librarians.

CHOIR—Mrs. George M. Rishel, Organist; Zac. Pugh, Cornetist; Mrs. H. S. Sterner, Mrs. H. H. Hill, Emma DeFrehn, Elsie Geier, James W. Bock, George H. DeFrehn, Charles T. Brown.

TEACHERS—Robert Bashore, Julia Bernet, Lot K. Beyerle, Wm. Brown, Nicholas Brownmiller, Celia Conrad, Lidie Crosland, Emma DeFrehn, Katie Dentzer, Mrs. E. G. Hay, J. H. Helwig, Mrs. H. H. Hill, Carrie Laubenstine, Mrs. S. J. Kirk, Mrs. Geo. Kline, Lizzie Lord, Mary S. Miller, Mamie Moser, Allen Paul, Laura Pflueger, Mrs. A. L. Phillips, Emma Reed, George M. Rishel, Mrs. Geo. M. Rishel, Clara Rosengarten, Charlotte Schrader, Louise Schrader, I. Harvey Severn, Mrs. E. J. Skelly, Mrs. Frank Smith, Mrs. Charles Snyder, Emily P. Snyder, H. S. Sterner, Mollie Sterner, Ida Stoffregen, George C. Welker, Ella Zimmerman.

SECOND DEPARTMENT.

E. J. Skelly, Teacher; Martha Hadesty, Organist; Robert H. Weston, Secretary.

CHOIR—William Rishel, John Brownmiller, Mrs. Theodore Heilner, Mrs. Byron Phillips, Mrs. G. F. Weaver, Mrs. D. C. Freeman, Mrs. Theodore Batdorff.

INFANT DEPARTMENT.

Mrs. L. K. Beyerle, Superintendent; Emma Adcock, Assistant Superintendent; Callie Smith, Organist.

The Ladies' Mite Society.

The origin of this organization, in its present form, we have been unable to discover. Constituted largely of the married ladies of the congregation, it is probably a lineal descendant of the Ladies' Sewing Society which existed under the very first pastorate. Its meetings are held on the First Wednesday evening of each month, and the dues are at present, ten cents a month. At the time the parsonage was built, many of the members gave twenty-five cents a month for quite a season. It met for many years at the houses of the members, but now convenes in the Church Parlor.

Present Membership.

Mrs. A. B. Cochran, President; Mrs. Edward Fox, Secretary and Treasurer; Mrs. L. K. Beyerle, Mrs. J. A. Bowen, Mrs. Wm. Bock, Mrs. N. Brownmiller, Mrs. J. Brownmiller, Mrs. Daniel Christian, Mrs. Daniel DeFrehn, Mrs. Joseph DeFrehn, Mrs. J. E. Fredericks, Mrs. E. Britton, Mrs. J. A. Gilger, Mrs. F. Geier, Mrs. H. Hart, Mrs. E. G. Hay, Miss Mary Hartman, Mrs. Hannah Heffner, Mrs J. Hoffman, Mrs. N. Kemp, Mrs. H. W. Kriner, Mrs. L. Laubenstine, Mrs. A. Lee, Mrs. Chas. Lord, Mrs. W. H. Miles, Mrs. G. W. Mortimer, Mrs. Dr. G. M. Miller, Mrs. Jas. Nagle, Mrs. M. Reed, Mrs. Geo. Rishel, Mrs. A. Risheill, Mrs. E. J. Skelly, Mrs. Val Stichter, Mrs. Joseph Summons, Mrs. J. Teter, Mrs. W. R. Williams, Mrs. David Williams, Mrs. Martha Wolfinger, Mrs. Mayberry B. Bell, Mrs. A. Cable, Mrs. John Ebert, Mrs. Cyrus Sheetz.

We have secured complete records of the contributions given, only from November, 1876. They have all been spent, directly or indirectly, for the benefit of the Church. From November 1876, to November 13th, 1877, they contributed $48.95; on October 11th, 1878, $47.50; in November 1880, they gave $14.89 for the making of a carpet for the Infant Room; on October 5th, 1881, $100, and on January 3rd, 1883, $50, to the Sinking Fund for the Church Debt; in April 1884, $47.65 toward the purchase of the Organ; September 2nd, 1885, $3 for flowers; October 7th, 1885, $31.25 for repairs in Parsonage vestibule and the doorway of the Church; February 3rd, 1886, $22 for the refitting of the Infant School Room; April 7th, 1887, $36.60 for an Othello Range for the Parsonage; September 7th, 1887, $9.50 for Missions; in 1888, $14.44, for local benevolence and $20 toward the new building for the Infant Department of the Sunday-School; a total contribution, since November 1876, of $445.78. May the life and harmony and usefulness of this Society be perpetual.

The Young People's Sociable.

This is not the true title of the organization we are about to describe, but that by which it was popularly known. Its full title is The Literary and Social Circle of the English Lutheran Church. It was organized December 13th, 1876, in the Lecture Room of the Church. with brothers J. H. Helwig and Harry C. Nagle as temporary President and Secretary. An election resulted in the choice of Dr. P. K. Filbert as President, J. H. Helwig as Vice President, James W. Nagle as Treasurer, and Howard Oberholtzer as Secretary. Other charter members are

Sallie Laubenstine, Dollie Mortimer, Emma DeFrehn, Mollie Sterner, Maggie Leonard, Alva Kirkpatrick, Carrie Hildebrandt, Clara Fertig, Clara Stichter, Dollie Heffner, Kate Rishel, Mary Miese, Ella Rosengarten, Laura Rosengarten, Annie Simmons, Bessie Sauppee, Kate Bender, E. Kate Sterner, Clara Shum, Ellie Wildermuth, James W. Bock, Daniel W. Nagle, W. Fasolt, John Wolfinger, H. C. Nagle, Marcus H. Nagle, John C. Adcock, Eli Davis, Enoch Neff, Howard Fertig, Jas. W. Nagle, Daniel R. Super, Frank L. Nagle.

Those received in the course of the years that have followed are John Hart, Alice Hart, Mary Paul, John Dengler, John Sauppee, Alice Heffner, George M. Rishel, Bessie Burnette, Mary Teter, Christian Shum, John R. Mortimer, Joseph Derr, Daniel Keller, Carrie Thompson, M. Whittig, Mrs. P. K. Filbert, Mrs. D. R. Super, Mrs. J. W. Nagle, Frank Cochran, Frank Sterner, Libbie Brown, Annie Cruikshanks, Lillie Stantier, D. Glenn, H. Baumgarten, H. W. Bonawitz, Amanda Miller, Bella Christian, Mamie Mortimer, D. F. Yost, Laura Nagle, Clara Ebert, Frank Bock, Benjamin Cake, John C. F. Christian, Lilla Mortimer, Mary Miller, Ella Oberholtzer, Lizzie Bocam, Sallie Helms, Mary Stichter, Frank Shay, Ambrose Teter, George H. DeFrehn, Carrie Christian, Lizzie Wernert, Mary Sell, Calvin Bonawitz, Strange Wilson, Ella Trough, Fannie Moore, Annie Fegley, Hannah Seiler, George J. Thomas, Mrs. Lillie Thomas, Oscar Hoffman, Charlotte Schrader, Ida Bates, Savilla Heilner, Mary C. Walbridge, Bertha Huntzinger, Charles Thompson, George Arbogast, Dollie Kirkley, W. D. Hill, F. W. Matthews, Robert Hamilton, Valentine Sauppee, George Dentzer, Clara Brownmiller, Ella Bonawitz, Bert Ebert, Mary Aikman, Joseph Bocam, Louis Weston, Agnes Galbraith, Emma Auman, Hallie Evert, Kate Faust, Kate Eckenrode, Emma Skeen, Mame Hoffman, Mrs. E. G. Hay, Mrs. H. H. Hill, Katie A. Nagle, Laura Kershner, Louisa Gross, Lou. Detrick, Alice Jolley, Lizzie Lord, Ella Bonawitz, Mary Stichter, Dollie Heffner, Dollie McAdams, Savilla Heilner, J. C. Adcock, J. W. Bock, Lizzie Leffler, Emma Focht, W. Buchanan, W. H. Baker, Callie Roehrig, Lilla V. Loose, Aurelia Loose, George Arbogast, Mrs Roehrig, William Margnarth, George Dentzer.

The meetings of this society have been held upon the First Wednesday evening of each month, and the regular dues received, 10 cents a month. From its second assembly, January 3rd, 1877, to the 7th of October in the same year, it convened in Bright's Hall; afterwards at the houses of the members, with exception of an interval from November 6th, 1881, to January 10th, 1883, when it met in the Grand Army Hall. This organization has accomplished much good. It presented the Church, on July 1st. 1879. with our present silver Communion Service and Table, and also our Collection Plates. Besides this it conducted the following Festivities with the following Financial Results :

On February 25th, 1880, an Oyster Supper in the Lecture Room of the Church, $167.15; June 2nd and 3rd, 1880, a Fruit Festival in the same place, $38.47; Thanksgiving Day 1881, an Oyster-Supper in Centennial Hall, $101.17; January 24th and 25th, 1883, the same, $226; November 1883, the same, $337.14; March 5th and 6th, 1884, the same, $280.02; November 12th and .13th, 1884, the same, in City Armory Hall, $164.47. Out of these and other funds secured, the Society paid into the Church Treasury, March 20th, 1880, $125, used for current expenses; February 5th, 1883 ,$408.73, used in payment of the debt; April 29th, 1884, $717.31, used in purchase of the Organ; and July 7th, 1885, $179.22, used in refurnishing of the audience chamber—a total of $1430.26. Who shall say that they have not done well, and who does not regret that after such abundant activity the Society now slumbers so heavily that its inactivity is taken by many for absolute death. Its last regular meeting was held in May, 1885. But no doubt it shall soon arise and shine, a thing of beauty and a joy forever.

THE CHILDREN'S FOREIGN MISSIONARY SOCIETY.

Tradition says that Rev. A. D. Rowe himself visited our School and established a Society here, before going out as the first Children's Missionary to India. Beyond the statement of this fact we were unable to discover anything further in relation to this Society. It appeared to have disappeared. An organization, better described as an aggregation, was effected on the 13th of November, 1881, One Hundred and Ten of our Sabbath-School Scholars contributing Twenty Five cents each for this cause, with the pledge to continue a similar payment annually. Amid the multiplicity of financial efforts already described in these pages, the pastor hardly fostered this Society as he should, though lifting the collection and distributing the certificates annually. The list diminished gradually by removals and otherwise, and a quite imperfect one is all we now can furnish. It is as follows:

Jennie Bock, Laura Bell, Mrs. J. W. Bock, John Brobst, Wm. H. Brown, Katie Cochran, Jennie Conrad, George DeFrehn, Emma DeFrehn, Ella Deisher, George H. Dentzer, John Dillinger, Jerome Duey, Clara Ebert, Mrs. F. Emhardt, Irvin Esterly, Joe Esterly, Blanche Fernsler, Jacob Fox, Mrs. J. W. Fleet, Tillie Fredericks, Elsie Geier, Mrs. Katie Green, John H. Hart, Alice Hart, E. G. Hay, Mrs. E. G. Hay, Eddie B. Hay, Hannah Heffner, Harry Heller, J. H. Helwig, Mrs. H. H. Hill, James Hoepstine, Emily Hollenbach, Sallie Holt, Minnie Howell, Dellie Huntzinger, Hiram Keener, Josie Keer, Mrs. Geo. Kline, Carrie Laubenstine, Carrie Lord, S. E. Moore, Heber Moore, Mamie Moser, George Montgomery, John Montgomery, Howard Nagle, Allen Paul, Mamie Pflueger, Emma Reber, Charles Reed, Minnie Rishel, Geo. M. Rishel, Mrs. F. W. Roehrig, William Rosengarten, Carrie Rosengarten, Ella Rosengarten, Arthur Rosengarten, Clara Rosengarten, Charlotte Schrader, I. H. Severn, J. M. Shellhammer, Amanda Smeltzer, Mrs. F. Smith, Callie L. Smith, Emily

P. Snyder, Edward Spaecht, Fred. Spaecht, H. S. Sterner, Allen Sterner, Mollie Sterner, Pearl Weston, Mrs. A. Wetzel, Mrs. C. Wetzel, Mrs. C. Wiederhold, Emma Wiederhold, John Wollinger, Thomas Wright, Charles Wright.

By the reports of the General Synod it appears, however, that we are not sinners here above all Galileans, many other Societies having diminishing contributions also. By order of the same worthy body, a collection will be lifted annually henceforth in all Sunday-Schools, all contributors to which, whatever the amount of their gifts, will be considered members of the Society. Surely we should grow now!

THE YOUNG PEOPLE'S SOCIAL, AND LITERARY SOCIETY

Was organized on the 28th of April, 1886, at the residence of brother H. S. Sterner, 916 West Norwegian Street. Brother A. S. Paul was elected President ; Tillie Fredericks Vice President ; Emma Reed, Treasurer and Wm. H. Rosengarten, Secretary. Other charter members were

Mary E. Aregood, Ellie L. Brown, Wm. H. Brown, Celia Conrad, Grant Ebert, Harry Hill, Mary Miller, Mamie Moser, Katie Schartel, I. H. Severn, Ida M. Sterner, and Allen W. Sterner.

The following members have been since received :

Elsie Geier, Cora Walbridge, Minnie Heller, Robert Sterner, Howard Nagle, Tillie Silliman, Lidle Crosland, Tenie Toussaint, Bertha Work, Sallie Parker, Walter Engle, R. S. Bashore, Katie Kaiser, Carrie Staehle, Annie Detzner, Annie Gerhard, C. D. Miller, Frank Keiser, James A. Rinck.

Regular meetings have been held the Third Monday evening of each month from May to October, and the First and Third Monday evenings of each month from October to May. No members are eligible to *office* unless members of our Church or Sunday-School. All funds, except those needed for the current expenses of the Society, are devoted to such improvements as may be made to our Church property. The regular dues are ten cents a month. On the 17th and 18th of November, 1886, a Festival and Oyster Supper was held by this Society in Centennial Hall, for the benefit of Church and Sunday-School. The General Executive Committee was Allen W. Sterner, A. S. Paul, and William H. Rosengarten. The proceeds were $201.85, of which $100.75 was given to the Church Treasury, and the balance to that of the Sunday-School.

On the Twenty-Eighth of April, 1887, at the residence of Bro. H. S. Sterner, the Society met to celebrate their first Anniversary. The membership had increased from Sixteen to Twenty-Nine.

The social element had flourished with tropical luxuriance and the literary feature had been sustained with a faithfulness and to a degree hardly anticipated at the beginning.

After the singing of a patriotic song by the Society, the pastor congratulated them upon their organization and development, and expressed an earnest hope for their future prosperity and usefulness. Then followed a heartrending description, by R. J. Calm, of the Dutchman's missing canine, and the mingled joy and grief at his discovery.

A violin solo by Howard Walbridge, a prophecy by Howard P. Nagle, and a select reading by Miss Crosland are other features of the evening which memory now recalls, nor do we forget the games that followed, nor the groaning table, beautiful in its agony, around which after grace had been said. we sat in busy silence, for "mum" was then the word, and alas for the pocket book of him who forgot it! On the Twenty-Ninth we returned to our homes well pleased with Our First Anniversary.

After a comparatively uneventful, but a very pleasant year, the Society met on the evening of April 30th, 1888, at Centennial Hall. and celebrated in a very suitable and enjoyable manner, their Second Anniversary. The Pastor and wife were among the fortunate few who were honored with invitations, and since there was another feast on hand besides the literary one, it was not strange that the invitations given were not multitudinous. We will do the best we can for those less fortunate than ourselves, and while unable to give them a taste of the delightful and abundant refreshments provided, will at least afford them a vague idea of the Programme of Exercises.

There was first of all an Anniversary Ode, sung by the whole Society.

ANNIVERSARY ODE.

We are happy and rejoice, giving thanks with heart and voice ;
And we'll join the swelling chorus, singing loud and clear ;
Ringing out a merry strain, as this day returns again,
Bringing gladness and rejoicing while we're gathered here.

CHORUS :—

Sing, Sing, we're happy while we sing, chant the chorus loud and clear ;
Happy hearts are gathered round, and our songs of joy resound,
While we chant a merry chorus to the closing year.

Gentle friends we turn to you, with a welcome fond and true ;
Happy hearts and smiling faces greet our natal day ;
Listen to the joyful song, how its notes are borne along,
Flinging rays of golden sunshine on our earthly way.—CHORUS.

Let our hearts be tuned to love while the angels from above
Scatter blessings on our pathway as we onward go ;
And when years have rolled away may the coming of this day
Bring us all a sweet remembrance of the long ago.—CHORUS.

This was followed by a few words of congratulation by the pastor, with the repetition of an original poem entitled "The Elm Tree of Gettysburg," Instrumental music—A March by Wallarhaupt—by Tina Toussaint, Reading—"The Grand Army,"—by Bertha Work,

Duett—"See the pale Moon,"— by C. Elsie Geier and Mary S. Miller, Declamation—"A Sociable "—by William H. Rosengarten, Essay—"Education "—by Mary S. Miller, Instrumental music—"Song of the Wind," by Katie Kaiser, Prophecy, by Dr. C. D. Miller, Solo—"Maid of The Mill,"— by C. Elsie Geier, Oration, by J. A. Rink, Esq., and a closing song as follows :

> All together, all together, once, once again ;
> Hearts and voices light as ever, gladly join the welcome strain.
> Friendship's link is still unbroken, bright is its chain ;
> Where the parting word was spoken, now in smiles we meet again.

CHORUS:—
> O could we ever dwell in social pleasures here,
> No more to sever from the friends we love so dear !

> While the absent we are greeting, let us forget,
> In this hour of social meeting, every thought of past regret :
> Since the present full of gladness, bids us be gay,
> Banish every cloud of sadness, and be happy while we may.—CHORUS.

> When the warning " we must sever," comes once again,
> Yet in feeling true as ever, shall our faithful hearts remain.
> Oft shall memory breathing o'er us sweet friendship's strain,
> Bring this happy time before us, till we all shall meet again.—CHORUS.

Under the head of Games, various activities were indulged in, which prepared us to more highly appreciate the festivities which followed, when seated at a table so lengthy that he who was at the foot appeared small to the one seated at the head. The Committee on Entertainment, R. S. Bashore, Esq., H. P. Nagle, Lidie Crosland and Mary S. Miller, were deserving of the vote of thanks tendered them, and which came from our hearts and everywhere.

On the 13th of August, 1888, the Society voted $40, the amount then in its treasury, toward the erection of the New Building for the Infant School.

PRESENT OFFICERS.

Allen S. Paul, President ; Tillie Fredericks, Vice President ; William H. Brown, Secretary ; William H. Rosengarten, Assistant Secretary ; Mary S. Miller, Treasurer.

THE WOMEN'S MISSIONARY SOCIETY

Was organized in the Church Parlor, December 1st, 1886. The original officers were Mrs. E. G. Hay, President ; Mrs. Thomas Geier, Vice President ; Mrs. Edward Fox, Secretary ; Mrs. H. H. Hill, Treasurer ; Mrs. A. E. Lee, Corresponding Secretary.

The other charter members were

Mrs. John Bell, Mrs. J. A. Bowen, Mrs. E. Britton, Emma DeFrehn, Mrs. Susan Dentzer, Katie Dentzer, Kate Faus, Mrs. John Gilger, Mrs. W. R. Williams, Mrs. H. W. Kriner, Mrs. Byron Phillips, Mrs. J. A. Rath, Emma Reed, Sallie Reed, Mrs. George Rishel, Mrs. Charles Snyder, Mrs. H. S. Sterner, Mollie Sterner.

There have been since received into this Society :

Mrs. C. Wiederholt, Mrs. M. Wolfinger, Mrs. Geo. Foltz, Laura Foltz, Mrs. A. B. Cochran, Mrs. Mary Schum, Mrs. Samuel Moore, Tillie Sillyman, Mrs. D. C. Freeman, Mary Faus, Mrs. J. E. Fredericks, Mrs. A. E. Lee, Mrs. L. F. Heller, Mrs. Frank Smith, Mrs. Eliza Miller, Ellen Nagle, Mrs. John Ebert, Callie Smith, Mrs. Mary Neff, Libbie Bindley, Mrs. G. H. Dentzer, Agnes Johnston, Sallie Reber, Mrs. John Conrad, and as Honorary Members, E. J. Skelly and E. G. Hay.

The time of meeting is the Last Wednesday Evening of each Month. No regular dues were at first received, but a collection was lifted at every meeting. The first Nine Dollars collected were given to meet the obligations of the Congregation toward the Lutheran Church at Port Carbon, that being, at the time, a Home Mission station within the bounds of the Lebanon Conference. September, 1887, the Society became a regular Auxilliary of the Synodical Organization, since which time its contributions have been given toward the congregations sustained thereby. At their meeting of November 30th, 1887, it was agreed that the members pledge themselves to the payment of a specified amount monthly, according to their several ability. They have thus far contributed $64.25, $42.25 of which has been given during the present year, and $11.00 of which was received from the Mission Band.

PRESENT OFFICERS.

Mrs. E. G. Hay, President; Mrs. T. Geier, Vice President; Mrs. Edward Fox, Recording Secretary; Mrs. A. E. Lee, Corresponding Secretary; Mrs. H. H. Hill, Treasurer.

THE YOUNG LADIES' SEWING CIRCLE

Was organized on the 15th of December, 1886, at the residence of Mr. Edward Green, 1300 Mahantongo Street, by the election of Mrs. Edward Green as President and Charlotte Schrader as Treasurer. Other charter members were Emma DeFrehn, Mrs. F. Emhardt, Mrs. E. G. Hay, Mrs. A. Lee, Katie Nagle, Sallie Reed, Emma Reed and Louise Schrader. The meetings have been held at differing intervals according to the seasons, but have usually been held on Wednesday Evenings, They are at present upon the Second and Third Wednesdays of each month. Dues are ten cents a month.

This Society has been very helpful. It has prepared many articles for sale at our recent festivals; it purchased for the congregation that excellent cut of our Church and Parsonage which is presented in this volume, and appears also regularly on the title page of The English Lutheran, and it has met monthly at the parsonage since the origin of this Church Paper, in December, 1886, to fold and sew the pages as they come from the hands of the printer. They also purchased a beautiful floral cross as a contribution to our Easter Decorations this year.

In addition to charter members, there have been received,

Mrs. F. Ebert, Mrs. H. H. Hill, Mollie Sterner, Dollie McAdams, Mrs. A. N. Wetzel, Clara Hill, Lizzie Lord, Mrs. S. Moore, Laura Pflueger, Katie Schartel, Tillie Sillyman, Mrs. H. Sterner, Mrs. S. A. Garrett, Mrs. A. B. Cochran, Sallie Dailey, Mrs. T. Geier, Mrs. A. A. Greenawalt, Mrs. L. F. Heller, Nellie Hill, Mrs. J. B. Hoffman, Mrs. William Johnston, Mrs. George F. Moore, Mrs. S. Morgan, Mrs. Charles Parker, Mrs. Mary Severn, Miss Emily P. Snyder, Carrie Burnette, Clara Stichter, Mrs. Edward Fox, Mrs. J. E. Fredericks, Tillie Fredericks, Mrs. John Bell, Mrs. D. Christian, Mrs. G. M. Rishel, Mrs. Charles Snyder, Mrs. L. K. Beyerle, Mrs. George Hamilton, Sallie R. Moore, Mrs. Samuel Moyer, Ida Stoffregen, Mrs. G. A. Transue, Mrs. F. C. Currier.

PRESENT OFFICERS.

Mrs. E. G. Hay, President; Dollie McAdams, Secretary; Charlotte Schrader, Treasurer.

OUR YOUNG MEN'S CHRISTIAN ASSOCIATION

Was organized in the Church Parlor on the 9th of February, 1887. Brothers J. H. Helwig and R. J. Calm were elected temporary President and Secretary. Others present at this meeting were H. S. Sterner, George M. Rishel, George W. Nagle, George H. Dentzer and O. P. Whitman. It was decided to hold future business and devotional meetings in that place; the former on the Second Wednesday Evening of each month, the latter every Sunday Evening at 6.30.

Members afterwards received are

Elmer F. Schlaseman, John H. Wolfinger, Howard P. Nagle, Charles J. Wright, William Schroyer, George F. Egolf, A. L. Warm, S. S. Newcomer, E. G. Hay, E. J. Skelly, Heber T. Moore, J. F. Spaecht, William K. Parker, R. S. Bashore, George A. Welker, Clinton D. Rishel.

The following standing committees were appointed.

On Music, J. H. Helwig, Howard P. Nagle, Charles J. Wright; on Devotional Exercises, J. H. Helwig, H. S. Sterner, E. J. Skelly; on Visitation of the Sick, Elmer Schlaseman, George M. Rishel, Charles J. Wright; on Membership, J. Wolfinger, S. S. Newcomer, R. S. Bashore.

As early as the 20th of March they determined, with the help of the Lord, to attempt still greater things: to sustain a Young People's Meeting for both sexes in the Lecture Room of the Church every Sunday Evening an hour before regular Service. This has been conducted regularly to the present time, and the attendance and influences have been excellent. The Lord prosper the work!

Topics, *chosen by the young men themselves*, are selected three months in advance of their presentation, and neatly printed upon cards. These are distributed among strangers who are invited to attend. They are also printed in The English Lutheran, our Church Paper. These topics, and the respective leaders who have presented them, have been, as nearly as can now be learned, as follows:

YOUNG PEOPLE'S MEETINGS, 1887.

DATES.	SUBJECTS.	LEADERS.
Mar. 20	What shall I do?.................Luke 16: 3.	Geo. F. Egolf.
" 27.	Where no wood is, there the fire goeth out...Prov. 26: 20.	H. S. Sterner.
April 3.	Temptation is no excuse for sinning...Gen 3: 12; Matt. 4: 1–11, Heb. 2: 18.	E. F. Schlaseman.
" 10.	How two young Disciples enjoyed the first Easter.... Luke 24; 13–36.	R. J. Calm.
" 17.	Arise therefore, and be doing............1 Chron. 22: 16.	O. P. Whitman.
" 24.	The first Psalm.	Daniel Downey.
May ..1.	Silver and gold.................Eccl. 2: 8.	Geo. M. Rishel.
" ..8.	A young man financially embarrassed....Luke 15: 2–24.	Geo. H. Dentzer.
" 15.	What is man.................Job 7: 17. Psalm 8: 4.	H. S. Sterner.
" 29.	No other way.................Acts 4: 12; John 14: 6.	J. H. Helwig.
June ..5.	Three things young men need more than money......... Prov. 3: 19–26.	Howard P. Nagle.
July ..3.	An Invitation to Praise.................Psalm 147.	H. S. Sterner.
" 10.	The work of one young man.................Mark 1: 40–45.	R. J. Calm.
" 17.	Two are Better than One.................Eccles. 4: 8–12.	Geo. F. Egolf.
" 24.	Faith.................Heb. 11.	Geo. M. Rishel.
" 31.	Be not afraid.................Deut. 20: 1; Prov. 3: 25.	E. F. Schlaseman.
Aug. ..7.	The Judgment.................Rev. 20: 12.	R. S. Bashore.
" 14.	A great Tumult.................Acts 19: 23–41.	H. P. Nagle.
" 21.	The Ten Virgins.................Matt. 25: 1–13.	O. P. Whitman.
" 28	Hope.................Rom. 8: 24.	E. G. Hay.
Sept ..4.	The most flattering prospects blasted by sin............. 1 King 3: 5; 9: 11; 14: 11.	J. H. Helwig.
" 11.	Early Piety.................2 Chron. 34: 1–8; 2: 40–52.	Daniel Downey.
" 18.	A service of song.	Wm. Schroyer.
Oct. ..9.	Master over ones self.................1 Cor. 9: 25.	R. J. Calm.
" 16.	Christian Paitence.................Job.	Geo. M. Rishel.
" 23.	The Victory of Faith.................John 5: 4.	E. G. Hay.
" 30.	Repentance.................Luke 13: 3–5.	S. S. Newcomer.
Nov. 6.	The new birth.................2 Cor. 5: 17; John 3: 3.	J. H. Helwig.
" 13.	All may be saved.................Heb. 7: 25; John 3; 16.	E. F. Schlaseman.
" 20.	Found.................Luke 19: 1–10.	H. S. Sterner.
" 27.	Service of Song.	Howard P. Nagle.
Dec. 4.	Danger ahead.................Prov. 4: 14–15.	R. S. Bashore.
" 11.	Saying is not doing.................Matt. 7: 21–27.	Geo. F. Egolf.
" 18.	The good Samaritan.................Luke 10: 30–37.	O. P. Whitman.
" 25.	Christmas.................Luke 2: 1–20.	Daniel Downey.

YOUNG PEOPLE'S MEETINGS, 1888.

DATES.	SUBJECTS.	LEADERS.
Jan. ..8	The Friend of Sinners, who will accept him?............. Matt. 11: 10; Rom. 5: 8; John 3: 16.	J. H. Helwig.
" 15.	Bible Reading.	E. J. Skelly.
" 22.	The only time to be saved.	S. S. Newcomer.
" 29.	A great light.................Act. 25: 13; John 8: 12.	H. S. Sterner.
Feb. ..5.	Consecration.................1 Cor. 6: 19, 20.	E. G. Hay.
" 12.	The talents.................Matt. 25: 14–30.	O. P. Whitman.
" 19.	Song Service.	H. P. Nagle.
" 26.	What may be bought without money......Isa 45: 1, 2.	Geo. M. Rishel.
Mar. ..4.	What shall I do with Jesus?.................Matt. 27: 22.	S. S. Newcomer.
" 11.	Plans for life.................Luke 12: 18.	E. F. Schlaseman.
" 18.	What think ye of Christ?.................Matt. 22: 42.	Geo. F. Egolf.
" 25.	Friend how camest thou in hither?....Matt. 22: 11–14.	R. S. Bashore.
Apr. ..1.	No meeting—Easter Service with School.................	
" ..8.	Delaying Repentance............Eccl. 12: 1; 2 Cor. 6: 2.	E. G. Hay.

Apr. 15. Terms of peace.............................Luke 15: 11–24. E. J. SKELLY.
 " 22. The Eleventh Hour.............................Josh. 24: 15. GEO. M. RISHEL.
 " 29. Punishment of Hypocrites.................Acts 5: 5–10. J. H. HELWIG.
May ..6. Ashamed of Christ.............................Mark 8: 38. S. S. NEWCOMER.
 " 13. It can't be done...............................Matt. 6: 24. GEO. C. WELKER.
 " 20. Everlasting Punishment...2 Thess. 1: 7–9. Matt. 25: 46. E. F. SCHLASEMAN.
 " 27. Fault finding...............................Luke 11: 37, 38. H. S. STERNER.
June ..3. Almost—but lost.............................Acts 26: 28 H. P. NAGLE.
 " 10. Life here and hereafter............Mark 8: 35–37. J. H. HELWIG.
 " 17..Doth the way of the wicked prosper?... ....
           Jer. 12: 1; Ps. 37: 20; Rom. 6: 23.   R. S. BASHORE.
 " 24.|No meeting—Children's Day Service with School.......
July ..1. Seeking the lost.............................Luke 15: 1–10. O. P. WHITMAN.
 " ..8. A Bible Reading. Rescue the Perishing .... E. J. SKELLY.
 " 15. A Sure Foundation..........................1 Cor. 3: 4–15.|J. H. HELWIG.
 " 22. Love, the motive power for service..............1 Cor. 13.|GEO. M. RISHEL.
 " 29. Sowing and Reaping.......................Gal. 5: 3–10. O. P. WHITMAN.
Aug ..5. Faith Rewarded, or the Bible by faith. A Bible
           Reading.   E. F. SCHLASEMAN.
 " 12. Telling and Hearing news ....Acts 17: 13–31. H. S. STERNER.
 " 19. Enthusiasm..............................Acts 5: 25–42. E. J. SKELLY.
 " 26.|Obedience and Courage...................Jer. 35: 1–6, 8.|G. C. WELKER.
Sept ..2.|The Riches of Men, or the great lesson to learn. A|
        | Bible Reading.   J. H. HELWIG.

PRESENT OFFICERS.

J. H. Helwig, President ; Elmer F. Schlaseman, Vice President; S. S. Newcomer, Secretary ; Howard P. Nagle, Treasurer.

THE CHRISTIAN WORKERS

Organized November 27th, 1887. They hold their meetings every Saturday Afternoon at Three O'clock in the Church Parlor. It is a class of the Sunday-School, of which Miss Mollie E. Sterner is teacher. Organized with no definite object in view, save helpfulness in any good work of the Church which might demand their activities, they associated themselves soon afterwards, on the 29th of February, as a Mission Band, with the Women's Missionary Society. On this occasion and on the month following they gave the members of the Society and the visitors an opportunity at the close of the meeting to purchase beautiful and edible things they had provided. The proceeds of the sales amounted to $11, which was given at once into the treasury of the larger Society.

PRESENT ORGANIZATION.

Miss Mollie E. Sterner, President; Miss Alberta Cable, Vice President ; Miss Minnie Gottschall, Secretary ; Miss Nellie Mortimer, Treasurer ; Annie Bock, Coolie Bohn, Nellie Brey, Clara Candy, Minnie Clarkson, Florence Clarkson, Katie Cooper, Jennie Conrad, Stella Deisher, Bessie Dieffenderfer, Ella Deisher, Lena Deisher, Katie Ferryman, Maggie Gordon, Esther Gordon, Mamie Heller, Sadie Heller, Minnie Howell, Katie Hutchinson, Mamie Pfleuger, Emma Reber, Jennie Shaw, Callie Smith, Bertha Staehle, Carrie Stoffregen.

CHAPTER XII.

RELATIONS OF OUR CHURCH TO OUR SYNOD.

THE CONVENTIONS OF SYNOD IN POTTSVILLE.

The East Pennsylvania Synod, with which our Church is connected, has been four times entertained by our congregation.

Its *first* sitting here was as early as September 30th, 1852, under the pastorate of Rev. Dr. Steck, but little more than five years from the date of our organization. Thirty-One ministers were embraced within its limits at this time. The President was Rev. T. Stork, D. D.; the Secretary, Rev. J. J. Riemensnyder. Revs. Victor L. Conrad, Matthias Sheeleigh and Samuel Yuengling were Licensed, and Rev. S. Henry Ordained.

The *second* presence of Synod here was on the 25th of September, 1867, under the pastorate of Rev. U. Graves. It had then attained a clerical membership of Seventy-Two, and received Twelve more during its sessions. The President was Rev. S. Sentman; the Secretary, Rev. H. C. Shindle. At their own request, Thirteen of the clerical members were honorably dismissed in order to constitute the "Susquehannah Synod." Revs. H. C. Grossman, T. C. Billheimer, T. H. Griffith and Joseph Hillpot were Licensed.

It was on this occasion, as already stated, that Synod convened in the Second Presbyterian Church of this place, our own being then in process of enlargement.

The *third* convention of our Synod in Pottsville occured on the 9th of September, 1874, under the pastorate of Rev. J. Q. McAtee. It then contained Fifty-Seven clerical members. The President was Rev. B. C. Suesserot; the Secretary, Rev. S. Henry. Revs. J. Croll Baum and J. H. Leeser, were Licensed, and Rev. W. H. Dunbar was Ordained.

The *fourth* and last convention of Synod here was upon the 20th of September, 1882, under the present pastorate. Sixty-Seven clerical members were at that time on its roll. The President was Rev. W. M. Baum, D. D.; the Secretary, Rev. George C. Henry. Revs. M. P. Hocker and Isaac P. Zimmerman were Licensed; and Revs. E. H. Delk and H. M. Oberholtzer were Ordained.

OUR REPORTS TO SYNOD.

The most of our readers are familiar with the fact that one of the duties of each pastor is to give an Annual Report, to the Synod, of the State of his Congregation. These reports relate both to the Spiritual and Financial condition of the people, and are always, in substance, printed in the Minutes of Synod.

It has seemed good to us to attempt to gather together, out of the Minutes of successive years, the reports of our congregation, and to present them in one continuous statement, to our readers. We have done so, but with some omissions and some changes which we desire in part to explain.

The Synodical Reports embrace additions to membership, and also losses. It was thought needless to include these in our report, inasmuch as all recorded receptions for each year have already been given herein, and the total increase or loss can be discovered in our column on Communicants.

But, in even that which we have reported, we have found difficulties which render the result of our efforts here only an approximation of the truth. The practice of the Synod has varied in these years, as to the number of items concerning which she has requested her pastors to report. Columns have thus been added to her tabulation, and again removed—and the totals when given have varied accordingly.

With exception of what has been given by it each year for Missions, the contributions of the Sunday-School should be added to the totals named, to render them absolutely correct.

From the year 1878, the totals include the amount of the pastor's salary, an item not previously reported.

And now reader, with the presentation of the following report, we must bring this volume to a close. It has been prepared amid difficulties that few can properly appreciate, and which should modify severity of judgment upon its many manifest defects.

God bless and prosper our beloved English Lutheran Church of Pottsville!

The Annual Reports of our Church to Synod.

	Communicants.	SUNDAY-SCHOOL.			CONTRIBUTIONS.			
		Teachers and Officers.	Scholars.	Contributions.	Missions.	Local Objects.	External Objects.	Total for all Objects.
Under pastorate of Dr. Steck.								
1848	--	--	--		$ 8.00	$	$	8.00
1849	80				28.00			28.00
1850								
1851	100				31.00			31.00
1852	125	38	200		77.50	2000.00		2077.50
1853	143	30	350		144.00	2000.00	70.00	2214.00
1854	111	28	204		117.65	363.73		481.38
1855	120	30	250		30.00	690.00	100.00	820.00
1856	100	30	240		140.00	40.00	40.00	220.00
Under pastorate of Rev. Luckenbach.								
1857	140	50	300	850.00	98.75	220.00	50 00	368.75
1858	130	28	200	45.00	80.00	200.00		280 00
Under pastorate of Dr. Holman.								
1859	124	20	200	20.00	5.00			5.00
1860	125	27	239	92.00	30.00	479.00	15.00	524.00
1861	109	28	240		5.00	712.00		717.00
1862	93	40	175		25.00	5.00		31.00
Under pastorate of Rev. Koons.								
1863	90	20	160		18.62	260.00	14.00	292.62
1864	92	24	175		18.00	1357.00	92.00	1467.00
Under pastorate of Rev. Graves.								
1865	124	21	200	100.00		1400.00	34.00	1434.00
1866		23	230	200.00	60.00	160.00	150.00	370.00
1867	130	50	300	350 00	266.25		400.00	666.25
Under second pastorate of Dr. Steck.								
1868	165	43	415	443.00	318.00	6084.19		6402.19
1869	220	35	500	516.56	105.00	800.00		905.00
1870	235	30	337	338.96	89.00			89.00
Under pastorate of Rev. McAtee.								
1871	175	35	416			5000.00		5000.00
1872	220	28	483	300.00	55.00	2900.00	160.00	3115.00
1873	297	28	452	700.00	94.00	590.00	154.00	838.00
1874	329	30	436	550.00	194.32	600.00		794.32
1875	314	31	496	380.00	169.89	780.00		949.89
1876	301	30	400	480.00	74.79	625.00		699.79
1877	284	31	413	257.00	35.00		210.00	245.00
Under pastorate of Dr. McCron.								
1878	280	30	400	200.00	32.00	1000.00	660.00	1692.20
1879	140	35	280	200.00		1300.00		1300.00
1880	179	30	300	350.00	84.50	1300.00	5.00	1389.50

	Communicants.	Teachers and Officers.	Scholars.	SUNDAY-SCHOOL. Contributions.	Missions.	CONTRIBUTIONS. Local Objects.	External Objects.	Total for all Objects.
			Under present pastorate.					
1881	300	30	300	243.54	83 60	916.40		1000.00
1882	350	30	400	295.00	225.97	2970 58	200.00	3396.55
1883	340	35	400	311.99	257.82	2762.71		3020.53
1884	342	40	400	276.81	268 91	2881,37	78.11	3228.39
1885	362	40	400	264.69	237.63	2013.81		2251.44
1886	391	42	423	330.17	241.94	3253.94		3495.88
1887	430	44	556	414.38	306.60	2847.51		3154.11